ALSO BY ALEX MARLOW

Breaking Biden
Breaking the News

BREAKING THE LAW

EXPOSING THE WEAPONIZATION OF AMERICA'S
LEGAL SYSTEM AGAINST DONALD TRUMP

ALEX MARLOW

THRESHOLD EDITIONS
New York   Amsterdam/Antwerp   London
Toronto   Sydney/Melbourne   New Delhi

Threshold Editions
An Imprint of Simon & Schuster, LLC
1230 Avenue of the Americas
New York, NY 10020

First Threshold Editions hardcover edition June 2025

THRESHOLD EDITIONS and colophon are trademarks of Simon & Schuster, LLC

For information about special discounts for bulk purchases,
please contact Simon & Schuster Special Sales at 1-866-506-1949 or
business@simonandschuster.com.

The Simon & Schuster Speakers Bureau can bring authors to your live event.
For more information, or to book an event, contact the Simon & Schuster Speakers
Bureau at 1-866-248-3049 or visit our website at www.simonspeakers.com.

Interior design by Jaime Putorti

Manufactured in the United States of America

10   9   8   7   6   5   4   3   2   1

Library of Congress Cataloging-in-Publication Data has been applied for.

ISBN 978-1-6680-8878-4
ISBN 978-1-6680-8880-7 (ebook)

To Donald J. Trump

"At his best, man is the noblest of all animals;
separated from law and justice he is the worst."
–Aristotle

CONTENTS

BREAKING THE LAW

PREFACE

began working for new media pioneer and conservative web impresario Andrew Breitbart in 2008. Today I am the editor in chief of his namesake website, Breitbart.com. Andrew was a man of many talents; he was funny, fearless, fundamentally decent, open-minded, charismatic, and even handsome in a husky-male-model sort of way. But what drew me to him more than anything else was that he was a visionary. Not only did he have a knack for seeing the political and cultural landscape with clarity, but he was also able to spot trends coming over the horizon long before anyone else in media.

I hitched my wagon to his dark green Range Rover while I was still in college and have been enjoying the ride ever since, even after Andrew passed away in 2012.

Andrew and his band of merry pranksters (all of us would also report stories, and, as it turned out, we were pretty good at it) had several crucial objectives; first and foremost was fighting the political left's creep into core American institutions.

Andrew saw the politicization of critical elements of our society—namely the entertainment industry, the news media, and academia—as a grave threat to our country. Since Andrew first issued the warning cry, we have made significant progress on these three fronts. The news media has been thoroughly discredited. Jeff Bezos himself, Amazon founder and owner of the *Washington Post*, wrote in a 2024 op-ed that his own paper lacks credibility. He also noted in the same piece that journalism is the least-trusted profession.[1]

I declared the news media broken in my 2021 bestseller, *Breaking the*

News, so Bezos could have drawn this conclusion years earlier, but still, better late than never.

Score one for Andrew, for me, and for the *Breitbart News* crew.

Another key participant in the culture war, Big Hollywood, has never faced more opposition than it faces today. Celebrity endorsements are a liability for politicians who receive them. They instantly become meme fodder for conservative provocateurs online. Box-office returns are trending in a terrible direction (I explain this phenomenon as well as Joe Biden's fascinating and fundamental role in Hollywood's decline in my second bestselling book, *Breaking Biden*). In fact, independent social media influencers and content creators have arguably surpassed the entertainment media establishment's cultural clout.

This is another glorious development.

The third essential front in the culture war, academia, is still overwhelmingly dominated by leftists and remains openly hostile to conservatives. But a college degree seems to matter less each year. A 2024 Pew survey suggested that fewer than a quarter of Americans believe a four-year college degree is "worth it" if it's necessary to take out loans. Meanwhile, economic outcomes for young people without a college degree have improved.[2]

The college bubble appears poised to burst. At the same time, it has never been easier to get an online education from pro-America conservative groups such as PragerU. You might not get a piece of paper at the end of your experience, but you will actually learn something of value. Or you can keep paying $50,000+ a year to take classes like Taylor Swift and Her World at a traditional university.[3]

It's clear that in recent years, much of America has woken up to Andrew's message that these three key institutions were the problem. More Americans than ever, it seems, *get it*.

So, we should rejoice, right?

Not so fast, actually.

The left, ever vigilant and perpetually developing new tactics to gain a political edge, never intended to stop their quest for cultural dominance of these three areas of American life. Since Andrew shuffled off this mortal coil, they have opened up new fronts in the culture war, setting their sights on other elements of our social fabric. They have gained a strong foothold in the sports world. And, by initiating DEI (diversity, equity, and inclusion) in the workplace, the left has taken over whole swaths of corporate America, particularly the immensely powerful tech sector. These developments, also known as woke-ification, have been deeply divisive and socially disruptive.

Yet in my view, there is one core institution among all others that, should the left commandeer it, would mean the end of America as we know it.

That is our legal and judicial system.

I was raised to believe that America is an exceptional country with exceptional people and exceptional values. That's why I'm a conservative. I want to conserve those values, especially E Pluribus Unum (out of many, one), In God We Trust, liberty, the First Amendment of the U.S. Constitution, and the Second Amendment, among others.

These are, to my knowledge, the greatest set of foundational principles established by any country in history. Whether they endure depends on one crucial factor: We must remain a society of law and order.

Or, if you'd like to start from a more cynical place, we must return to being one. Fast.

Without law and order, everything that has defined America as we know it—from our cultural preeminence to our wealth to our entrepreneurial and pioneering spirit—is in jeopardy.

In a society that upholds law and order, justice must be blind and impartial, we must show reverence to our Constitution and founding documents, and we must enforce the laws that we have put on our books.

It's that simple, really.

Yet one side of the political aisle has turned against the basic idea that without law and order, we have nothing.

When they were in power, the Democrat Party jailed their political opponents and undermined the law enforcement officials tasked with keeping peace in our streets. They even compromised the U.S. Constitution itself, as I will explain later in this book.

Though the concept is not entirely new, Democrats have drastically increased the practice of "lawfare," a combination of the words *law* and *warfare*. As the media's influence over the electorate has waned, this has become the preferred tool of political combat in corners of the American left.

So, while Andrew Breitbart was correct to zero in on Hollywood, the media, and academia in his day, we are in a new phase of the battle for the soul of America.

In this moment, the American left's *political* strategy is to use the legal system to target their opponents.

The left's lawfare warriors have set their sights on one man more than any other: Donald J. Trump. Trump is at the very tip of the spear of the American culture war and is a perpetual threat to "the establishment" wherever it exists. Trump has been known to say things like "They want to take away my freedom because I will never let them take away your freedom. They want to silence me because I'll never let them silence you. In the end they're not after me, they're after you, and I just happen to be standing in the way."[4]

This statement is fundamentally true. President Trump is hardly their only target. He's just the most powerful.

If America is to endure, we must acknowledge that Trump's words aren't merely political rhetoric but a solemn warning: Defeat lawfare and those who have used it to accumulate power for the political left, or lose the country.

The stakes are that high.

Lawfare is the new normal. Now is the time to understand what is happening and prepare ourselves for legal battles yet to come.

It is time to fight back.

INTRODUCTION

What is lawfare?

My definition has two parts: (a) the use of the legal system against political and cultural adversaries; and (b) the weaponization of the legal system for partisan political purposes. Traditionally, lawfare has come from the left. Its close cousin, judicial activism, has been a reliable tactic for modern liberals since Franklin Delano Roosevelt, who called for adding justices to the Supreme Court to give the left generational control of the judiciary. He argued that the new Supreme Court built according to his design ought to treat the Constitution as "a system of living law." The "living law" or "living constitution" is a euphemism for activist liberal and "progressive" justices reinterpreting the plain meaning of the law to advance their political agenda.

Judicial activism, or "legislating from the bench," became commonplace during the Warren Court, the period from 1953 to 1969 when Earl Warren served as the chief justice of the Supreme Court. This is widely regarded as the most liberal court in history.

The Warren Court marked the beginning of the end of judicial restraint. During this time, the court aggressively pursued issues that were not previously considered under their authority. Progressive justices began to impose their vision on the country, against the wishes of the other branches of government.

Judicial activism shares DNA with modern lawfare. As you'll find in this book, this is the spirt of the lawfare targeting Trump: The law itself is subject to the prevailing liberal politics of the time.

Under the Warren Court, the left was ascendant. Liberals consistently got what they wanted. But as is typically the case, they only wanted more.

In 1973, the liberal court issued a landmark decision that would define a generation of American politics, *Roe v. Wade*. The decision reframed abortion as a privacy issue and legalized it across all fifty states. Abortion was suddenly a constitutional right.

Regardless of your opinion on the morality of abortion, this was an unprecedented decision. Never before in American history had the court taken a controversial debate out of the public square and imposed its collective view on all of American society. With this decision, in an instant, the liberal Supreme Court's new role was not merely to interpret and uphold the law but to reform society at large.

The court had to expand its scope to do this. Liberal justices concocted a wild legal theory that envisioned a right to privacy that exists in "penumbras" of the Constitution. *Penumbras* is a pretentious way of saying that a given right, in this case the right to privacy, isn't literally in the Constitution but is somehow implied by other enumerated rights. Why? Because enough justices say so.

And just like that, abortion became a part of our national culture. The hot-button issue of all hot-button issues—whether a woman had an unrestricted right to terminate a life inside her body—was taken out of the realm of political debate and was treated as a civil right. While people's personal opinions on abortion didn't dramatically change after *Roe*, the business of terminating nascent human beings in the womb boomed.

After *Roe*, conservatives began organizing to reassert influence over the judiciary. They took an approach that might seem novel in our hyperpartisan modern times: They would work slowly, gradually, and *not* challenge the legitimacy of the court.

Their approach worked, and by the Reagan Revolution of the 1980s, the right had rebalanced the Supreme Court.

But the left is always innovating. Today conservatives face a new form of judicial activism that threatens the fabric of our republic. It's called lawfare, and it's as dangerous as any other iteration of judicial activism the country has ever seen.

The only difference is that instead of legislating from the bench, liberal judges across the judiciary are taking the enforcement of the law and the implementation of policy into their own hands. Particularly, they have decided they have the right to bend the laws when it comes to one man, President Donald J. Trump, because they fear him and the movement he leads.

Stopping lawfare will require a vigilant, disciplined conservative movement as intelligent, influential, and far-seeing as the jurists who took back the Supreme Court and eventually overturned *Roe*. The challenge is enormous, but it has been met before.

We can end lawfare with our political will. But first we need to understand how exactly it works.

OBAMA AND HOLDER ACCELERATE LAWFARE

Lawfare radically accelerated during Barack Obama's presidency. In fact, my friend and colleague Peter Schweizer, the top investigative researcher in conservative media, argues that Obama and his attorney general, Eric Holder, used tactics born of the Global War on Terror against his political opponents, which ushered in the new lawfare age.

One such tactic was targeted sanctions, where the U.S. Treasury's Office of Foreign Assets Control would blacklist financiers of international terrorism. Obama and Holder had a clandestine project known as "Operation Choke Point," with the goal of choking off industries considered unfavorable to Democrats (such as gun dealers[1] and payday lenders[2]) from the banking sector.

Though the House of Representatives voted to end Choke Point in 2016, conservatives have claimed that debanking continued. Even Melania Trump wrote in her 2025 memoir, *Melania*, that she and her son Barron had been debanked.[3]

Another example of Obama-era lawfare was the Operation Fast and Furious gun-running scandal. Attorney General Eric Holder allowed roughly 2,000 guns to be sold or transferred into Mexico that were designed to be a part of a Bureau of Alcohol, Tobacco, Firearms and Explosives sting operation. The ATF lost track of the majority of these arms, primarily assault rifles, some of which were used to commit crimes both north and south of the border. One of the weapons was found at the scene of the murder of United States Border Patrol Agent Brian Terry. This example often is thought of as "lawfare" because Holder's DOJ used legal tactics to stonewall a Republican-led investigation. He should have resigned or been impeached, yet he was never held accountable at all.

Another instance of abuse of legal power by the Obama administration was the targeting of conservative groups' nonprofit tax status by the Internal Revenue Service. Obama's tax collection agency used political labels to screen tax-exempt applications for conservative groups for special scrutiny. A 2013 inspector general's report revealed the IRS had isolated terms like *patriot* and *tea party* (a term associated with conservative grassroots protests during the Obama presidency) to delay processing. In some cases, the groups were told the IRS would barter with the conservative groups, offering an expedited process in exchange for restrictions on their activities. While this example doesn't exactly fit my definition of "lawfare," it certainly marks a new era of the executive branch using legal means to target their political opponents for harassment.

HIGH CRIME, EXPLAINED

Lawfare explains why some people or groups are targeted while others are protected. It's a political strategy designed to weaponize the law against the opposition.

Hate-crime laws are a particularly pernicious example of lawfare, as they have been enforced selectively depending on the political zeitgeist. The federal government defines hate crimes as criminal offenses "against a person or property motivated in whole or in part by an offender's bias against race, religion, disability, sexual orientation, ethnicity, gender, or gender identity."[4] Christian groups have been targeted for daring to speak out against abortion, but since the media never considered this a national crisis, nobody has been convicted of a "hate crime" for attacking Christians.

Likewise, in the run-up to the 2024 election, Democrats hesitated to defend Jews who were targeted in "hate" attacks. Democrats considered anti-Zionist activists their friends and Zionist Jews their enemies. They had to use the law wherever possible to defend their friends. And if they ever criticized Zionism, they inserted boilerplate language to denounce "Islamophobia" as well.

Under Democrat rule, certain types of crime were not considered significant enough to warrant legal action. The most obvious example is illegal immigration. In American "sanctuary states" (all of which are run by Democrats), it is not treated as illegal to enter the country without our government's knowledge or permission. I hail from one, California, which has become an increasingly lawless place since I became politically cognizant over two decades ago. Throughout that time, the Golden State has sanctified illegal immigration.

It is California's original sin. It broadcasts to the world that we selectively enforce some laws but not others. Things have spiraled from there.

Take shoplifting, for example. "Why is shoplifting so rampant? Because state law holds that stealing merchandise worth $950 or less is just a misdemeanor, which means that law enforcement probably won't bother to investigate, and if they do, prosecutors will let it go," wrote one fellow at Stanford's Hoover Institution.[5] The state could make it easier to prosecute, but they choose not to. Why? The answer is all too obvious: That would lead to a drastic statistical uptick in crime, which would make the ruling class look bad.

And in California, the ruling class is synonymous with the Democrat Party establishment.

Thus, if you're a Democrat, it's politically safer to let crime fester than actually address it, which would necessarily start with an admission that it is rampant.

California is far from the only state that is destroying itself in this way. In New York, crime has skyrocketed, while the percentage of arrests that result in protections is down significantly. Crime in New York City was 33 percent higher in 2023 than in 2019.[6] Arrests resulting in a prosecution dropped steeply in 2020 and have barely returned to their pre-COVID numbers, despite the large increase in crime.[7] Much of this is due to a recent bail reform that quickly lets criminals back onto the streets, empowering unscrupulous offenders to wreak havoc.

Those who run New York intentionally allow taxpaying, law-abiding citizens to suffer as they coddle criminals. Why do this? New York is a single-party city, run by the Democrats, who are beholden to the far-left flank of their party. That includes radical activists who support "Black Lives Matter," the movement that normalized mass riots in 2020. Ironically, soft-on-crime policies are unpopular among nearly every meaningful constituency, including black voters, but the activists with the loudest voices, like BLM, are the ones who have called the shots in deep blue areas in recent years.

All of this demonstrates that politics is driving much of the American judicial system today.

There is no clearer recent example of that than what happened in the aftermath of the events at the U.S. Capitol on January 6, 2021.

Even more essential, in my view, is that the judicial system has become a political weapon to wield against Donald Trump and his supporters.

THE LAWFARE TIDAL WAVE

Trump supporters who protested at the Capitol on January 6th had the book thrown at them. Before January 6, 2021, Trump allies Michael Flynn, George Papadopoulos, and Paul Manafort had already served prison time at least in part due to their association with Trump, so targeting Trump wasn't exactly new. But the pro-Trump Capitol riots sent lawfare against ordinary Trump supporters into overdrive.

A man named Russell Alford was given a yearlong sentence for disorderly conduct. D.C. Circuit Court of Appeals Judge Karen LeCraft Henderson admitted that "he was neither violent nor destructive" during brief moments he spent in the Capitol, yet somehow was deemed to have "jeopardized public safety."[8]

If you're keeping score at home, burning buildings and looting stores on the street of Minneapolis or Kenosha or Los Angeles in 2020 did not count as "jeopardizing public safety" in most cases, but wandering around the Capitol for a few minutes on J6 did.

Even the most tenuous connection to Donald J. Trump—maybe you liked a pro-Trump post online one time—and suddenly, after J6, you ran the risk of losing your ability to do business or perhaps even your freedom itself.

If this tactic were to succeed, it would render Trump's network, and thus Trump himself, politically impotent.

"They're not after me, *they're after you.*"

In the three years since January 6, 2021, when pro-Trump demonstrators trespassed in the Capitol, causing momentary disarray, federal prosecutors charged over 1,200 defendants. Arrests continued into December 2024, when Donald Trump was transitioning back to the White House.[9]

Around half these defendants received criminal sentences; hundreds were jailed,[10] and hundreds of others received lesser penalties like probation or house arrest.

Proud Boys leader Enrique Tarrio received a twenty-two-year prison sentence for his role in the mayhem, even though he wasn't even present in Washington, D.C., that day (he had been arrested two days before for allegedly defacing a Black Lives Matter sign).[11]

But it wasn't just well-known activists who were caught up in the dragnet. My friends and neighbors in California were shocked when actor and vice chair of the Republican Party of Los Angeles County Siaka Massaquoi was arrested in November 2023. Siaka, a first-generation American whose mother emigrated from Liberia, was arrested for questioning by the FBI and pulled away from his pregnant wife after arriving at Bob Hope Airport in Burbank.[12]

Siaka is best known for appearing in sketches in conservative media like for the *Babylon Bee*. Meanwhile, his home was raided by "about 20 agents armed and outfitted in tactical gear shortly before 6 a.m."

By the end of 2024, we at *Breitbart News* estimated that 1,500 or so Americans had been charged for supposed J6-related crimes. The protest was mostly peaceful, if ill-advised, and Trump supporters didn't kill anyone, much less come anywhere close to "overthrowing an election."

The establishment media and Democratic Party reacted hysterically to the day's event and overcharged a lot of people. They thought it was their ticket to get Trump off the national stage forever. They were wrong. Most Americans didn't take the bait. A December 2024 Rasmussen Reports survey showed that 49 percent of the country wanted pardons for the J6 prisoners.[13]

Considering that the Democrat regime insisted for four years that there was a violent insurrection, that number is stunningly high, and you can bet the number only went higher as President Trump was reelected and pardoned everyone involved.

I'm certainly in the group that wanted mass pardons, especially considering the fact that the same people responsible for persecuting the J6 Trump supporters had encouraged or even fundraised for Summer of Love rioters. To say nothing of the fact that President Biden, who comes from a family of junkies and criminals, pardoned his crack-addicted adult son and five other family members for undefined crimes (more on this later).

The J6 charges and sentences were politically motivated. Full stop. That's why we needed pardons, and why Trump delivered them en masse.

Surveillance videos of the Capitol riot revealed that most of the people charged did nothing wrong and certainly stopped short of violence. Many did nothing more than peacefully enter the Capitol when the doors were opened for them. The punishment ought to fit the crime. But for the people who were there on January 6th, it often did not. And ordinary people knew it.

THE J6 OVERREACTION

The January 6 Select Committee was formed on July 1, 2021, through a House resolution. Initially the committee was supposed to include five Republicans, but then-Speaker Nancy Pelosi took the unprecedented and nakedly political position to ban House Minority Leader Kevin McCarthy nominees, Representatives Jim Jordan (R-OH) and Jim Banks (R-IN). McCarthy pulled his remaining nominees. Ultimately, anti-Trump Republicans Liz Cheney of Wyoming and Adam Kinzinger of Illinois were the only members of the GOP on the supposedly "bipartisan" committee. They both would go on to endorse Kamala Harris for president in 2024.

Representative Bennie Thompson (D-MS) chaired the committee, which prominently featured key anti-Trump fixtures Jamie Raskin (D-MD) and Adam Schiff (D-CA).

The committee would spend eighteen months investigating the causes and events of the incident at the Capitol on January 6th, conducting over 1,000 interviews and producing over 140,000 documents. The committee included teams of lawyers and spent millions. They scheduled public hearings for television "prime time" in order to maximize media attention[14] for their prized witnesses, but much of the investigation was done behind closed doors. Some witnesses complained that their testimony was selectively edited in order to distort its meaning.

After Republicans regained the House of Representatives in 2022, the J6 committee rushed out an 845-page report that concluded, in the least surprising reveal of all time, that everything that happened leading up to and on J6 was Trump's fault.

Raskin announced he would refer former President Trump for criminal investigation to the Department of Justice for four charges. These were for show—as was the entire committee—as there was nothing in the committee's enabling resolution granting it that authority.[15]

McCarthy ordered the committee to preserve all documents associated with the investigation. "It is imperative that all information collected be preserved not just for institutional prerogatives but for transparency to the American people," he wrote. This would enable Republicans to investigate the investigation itself. Thompson initially indicated he would comply with the request, but later admitted that records and videos had been destroyed before the rest was handed over to Republicans.[16]

The committee was largely ceremonial in nature. It had the power to subpoena and hold hearings, but it could not issue binding resolutions or impose penalties.

Some Trump allies refused to grant it any legitimacy. Senior Advisor to President Trump Steve Bannon and Trade Czar Peter Navarro refused to comply with congressional subpoenas, which landed them in prison.

Though the J6 committee could never jail Trump, the Democrats were able to use it to further their goal of keeping J6 in people's consciousness for as long as possible. If their plan worked, it would have damaged him with the voters and he would have lost the 2024 presidential election.

Still, there was an ever-present dubiousness to the proceedings. First of all, the insistence of using the term *insurrection* was conspicuously political. Literally speaking, an insurrection is the violent overthrow of the government. Most of the protesters were peaceful, and few were even armed at all. There was only a single gunshot that day, by Police Lieutenant Michael Byrd, which killed Trump supporter Ashli Babbitt, a military veteran who was apparently attempting to climb through a broken window into the Speaker's Lobby of the Capitol.

The alleged "insurrectionists" didn't kill anyone that day.

To illustrate how little gun violence occurred at the Capitol, the anti-Trump media were relegated to amplifying a claim from Cassidy Hutchinson, a former Trump White House aide who became a star witness for the J6 committee, that she had overheard some attendees talk about guns.

That's a rather lame attack on the protesters.

Hutchinson also testified that she had heard Trump tried to hijack[17] a presidential limousine and drive it to the Capitol. Naturally, there was no evidence of anything of the sort, with Trump himself noting that that is physically impossible given the layout of the interior of such vehicles.[18]

As dramatic as things felt that day, Congress reconvened mere hours later.

If this is classified as an insurrection, it was certainly the lamest insurrection in world history.

What's more, Trump emphatically claims he offered Pelosi at least 10,000 soldiers and/or National Guardsmen to be on hand but the then-Speaker turned him down.[19] Long after the J6 committee had been brought to a close, video surfaced of Pelosi stating "I take responsibility" for the lack of preparedness.[20]

The Justice Department eventually revealed that twenty-six FBI informants attended the J6 protests. "This report confirms what we suspected," House Judiciary Committee Chairman Jim Jordan told Fox News. "The FBI had encouraged and tasked confidential human sources to be at the Capitol that day. There were 26 total present. Four entered the Capitol and weren't charged, which is not the same treatment that other Americans received." "This has been our concern all along—agencies being weaponized against the American people," he continued.[21]

Christopher Wray, the FBI director at the time, was originally appointed by Trump during his first administration but built a reputation for allowing investigations into conservative and religious groups. For example, his FBI had infiltrated Catholic congregations supposedly to rid the country of the scourge of violent "radical-traditionalist Catholics" (RTCs),[22] who may or may not exist, as far as I can tell. He also famously deployed antiterrorism tools to target parents who objected to coronavirus pandemic protocols in schools.[23]

So it was hardly a surprise when FBI malfeasance came to light. Nor was it surprising to learn that they had put five thousand agents on the cases that sought to investigate and lock up the J6 protesters.[24]

Americans saw through the political charade. Polling data from

Quinnipiac University suggested that the opinion of Donald Trump stayed stable throughout the committee's tenure.[25] By April 2022, the polling analysts at fivethirtyeight.com suggested the American people were already writing off the committee with the headline "Americans Are Moving On from Jan. 6—Even If Congress Hasn't."[26]

Navarro spoke to *Breitbart News* during his prison sentence and summed it up as follows: "[T]his was not equal justice under law but unrestrained lawfare designed to interfere with the 2024 election."[27]

I wholeheartedly agree with this assessment. Not only was all of this political, it was designed to keep Americans focused on ethereal ills supposedly done by Donald Trump and his supporters and not on Joe Biden's fledgling presidency, which was marked by ballooning inflation, a flood of illegal migration, and escalating foreign tensions.

THE ULTIMATE GOAL

The (over)reaction to January 6th was illustrative of the left's ultimate goal: stopping Trump and his movement.

Donald J. Trump is the focal point of the left's lawfare attacks. His political opponents have brought the heat of a thousand suns upon him. He has been charged with trying to overturn an election, accused of retaining documents he could have declassified at any point while he was president, as well as bank fraud, sexual assault, defamation, and on and on.

It's the spaghetti method: Throw everything against the wall and see what sticks.

No former president has ever been treated this way in our country's history.

The left attempted to use the courts to vanquish Donald Trump as a political threat. From Robert Mueller's special counsel to the two impeachments that occurred during his first administration, to cases both criminal and civil in his postpresidency, there seems to be no end to the left's bloodlust. I expand on all of this in this book.

I go into great detail on Jack Smith's special counsel, which charged Trump with trying to overturn an election and subvert the U.S. government. Smith also pursued brazenly partisan classified-documents charges against Trump, whereby the former president was unreasonably held to a law that Barack Obama, Joe Biden, George W. Bush, Mike Pence, and CIA directors were not.

Once the election was over, so were these cases, proving they were political in nature.

I will also cover a civil case where Trump was accused of sexually assaulting and then defaming columnist E. Jean Carroll. Trump told me personally he doesn't even know who she is. There is a list of problems with this case—it gets more absurd with each new detail—but the most glaring is that the suit was funded by Democrat megadonor Reid Hoffman (a recurring villain in the Marlow Universe of investigative research) and orchestrated by anti-Trump TV pundit and lawyer George Conway. This deep corruption wasn't merely tolerated, it was an invention of the Democrat establishment.

Trump shared with me his opinion of Hoffman in a 2025 interview: "He's a big, fat sleazebag, and a criminal."

I'll cover New York State Attorney General Letitia "Tish" James's New York City bank fraud case that saw Trump fined nearly half a billion dollars despite the fact that his supposed crime was entirely victimless.

I'll cover the Alvin Bragg and Juan Merchan business records case in New York City that led to dozens of convictions. Out of all the cases I cover in this book, it was the weakest of them all, yet it was the only one that yielded a conviction. I'll explain why.

Then there's the Georgia election interference case, led by partisan lawfare-ista Fani Willis. This case also has glaring flaws, but what is most relevant to the broader thrust of this book is that Willis, like Tish James in New York, had actually planned the Trump prosecution before she even took office.

Many of the lawfare practitioners profiled herein promised to target Trump and did so out loud.

All of this is brand new in this nation. It is also a Rorschach test for committed partisans. If you are a supporter of Donald Trump, you will find one outrage after the next within this book. It might even cause your faith in our country (at least our legal system) to waver. If you're a full-fledged Trump hater, you probably see each one of these cases as legitimate.

Yes, we are that divided.

Scary stuff.

With the establishment media on board, the Democrats' main strategy for the 2024 election cycle was to frame Donald Trump as a singular threat to democracy. According to exit poll data, this did drive a strong percentage of their voters to polls. But is it really Trump who is the major threat?

Is it truly democratic to try to sue (that is, jail) the front-runner of a major political party?

It does not show confidence in our democracy if one of the major political parties fearmongers by falsely claiming that fascists and Nazis will take over the country if their candidate doesn't win. Ironically, the claim that democracy dies if you lose is patently undemocratic. That's emotional blackmail, and it's what the Democratic establishment does on a routine basis.

So, what comes next for America? I offer a grave warning, but also some optimism. The political left hopes to turn the judiciary into a tool of executive power. This would leave their megadonors, party elite, and activist classes as the stewards of our politics.

If they prevail, the political prosecutions will intensify. There will be more harassment, more intimidation, more deplatforming, and even more incarceration for anyone who is a threat to their power.

In other words, it will be the end of democracy as we know it.

Yes, locking up their political opponents is on their agenda, but that's not all. They will attempt to pack the court, expand voting rights to residents as opposed to citizens, and curtail free speech, among other agenda items that will convert the legal system from a roadblock against the usurpation of power into a tool to sanctify the "progressive" agenda.

But it doesn't have to be this way.

After Trump's resounding victory in the 2024 election, I can confidently say there is still time. Conservatives and originalists can claw back crucial elements of our legal system. We have done this, to one degree or another, in each of those three core American institutions Andrew Breitbart identified. We can do it again now—and we must.

Toward the end of the 2024 campaign, Joe Biden said of Donald Trump, "We gotta lock him up." This candor surprised me to a degree. I studied Biden, the patron saint of lawfare (more on this later), for well over a year for *Breaking Biden*, and I chronicled his presidency every day at *Breitbart News*. He doesn't speak this directly often. The leader of the

Democratic Party came clean: If they can't stop Trump and his movement at the ballot box, they will stop him in the courtroom.

That's not democracy. That's not America.

The *law*, as in the court system that exists to uphold and interpret our customs and rules, is broken.

It was broken by Joe Biden and the Democrats to target Donald Trump and his supporters.

We must recognize this fact and its perilous nature, and then do the hard work to fix it.

President Trump sees exactly what is happening. He summed it up to me in a 2025 interview: "The left is using this, their final weapon, to take down America."

We cannot let them.

CHAPTER 1

BROKEN SCALES

In his final minutes as president, Joe Biden gave blanket pardons to five of his family members. The list included three siblings and their respective spouses: James "Jim" Biden and his wife, Sara Biden; Valerie Biden Owens and her husband, John T. Owens; and Francis "Frank" Biden. All three siblings have been suspected of potential crimes.

For years reports have indicated that Joe's brothers Jim and Frank Biden used the family name to bag foreign cash and engage in questionable business dealings. Valerie, Joe's sister, leveraged her last name to nab lucrative consulting gigs stateside. Sara Biden, Jim's wife, was accused of laundering money for her husband and brother-in-law when Jim admitted to lending Joe $200,000 without a repayment plan.[1]

Controversial as the Biden family pardons were, the uproar was a fraction of what had come before. These were not the first Biden family pardons. Just a few weeks earlier, Joe had granted his son Hunter a full and unconditional pardon dating back more than ten years for any crimes of which he might be accused in the future. America had largely grown numb to Biden family antics, but this news was jarring, especially since Hunter had been investigated for several crimes during Joe's presidency.

In June 2024, Hunter was convicted of three felony charges related to a gun offense. Reports of Hunter's criminal misdoings had circulated for years, amplified by a leak of the contents of his laptop in the run-up to the 2020 election. The fact that he was convicted on a gun charge and only a gun charge was notable, as it was Hunter's only alleged crime (to my knowledge) that did not implicate Joe. Hunter got away with any impropriety in his extensive business ties to oligarchs around the world, especially in China and Ukraine. He never registered as a foreign agent even though he clearly took money from influential people and businesses with close connections to foreign governments.

The pardons extended all the way back to 2014, right before Hunter's career as an international businessman took off. Anyone who thinks this is a coincidence isn't paying attention.

Pardon recipients extended beyond the Biden family. Biden made wide use of preemptive pardons that granted high-profile political allies amnesty from future prosecution. Recipients included Dr. Anthony Fauci (who had overseen the mismanagement of funds that were used for gain-of-function research at the Wuhan Institute of Virology and then lied about it in a Senate hearing), Congresswoman Liz Cheney (who appeared to tamper with at least one witness on the January 6th Committee), and General Mark Milley (who had told the Chinese Communist Party that he would warn them if President Trump had planned to attack). Most if not all of Biden's high-profile pardons extended back to January 1, 2014, a period spanning ten years.

The stunning breadth of these pardons all but guarantees that many crimes will go uncovered and uninvestigated. We will probably never learn the full truth of Hunter's influence-peddling, since he was pardoned of all potential wrongdoing before anyone investigated his actions.

It was the most far-reaching use of the pardon power in American history, a gross act of hypocrisy—even for an administration that traded in doublespeak and propaganda. But there are only two creatures that never forget a thing: elephants and the Internet. And the internet soon took Joe Biden to task for his about-face regarding the rule of law.

Clips quickly flooded social media of Biden and his media allies criticizing Trump for even contemplating granting preemptive pardons on his way out in 2020. Biden and his surrogates repeatedly stated that he would not pardon his son. This, like so many of Biden's utterances over the years, was bullshit.

"You sit there and go, if you haven't done anything wrong, then what do you need a preemptive pardon for?" asked lawfare poohbah and Mueller Report henchman Andrew Weissmann on MSNBC.

At that time, Biden responded with emphatic bullshit: "It concerns me in terms of what kind of precedent it sets and how the rest of the

world looks at us as a nation of laws and justice. You're not going to see in our administration that approach to pardons."[2]

In his first administration, President Trump never issued the pre-emptive pardons liberals had fixated on, not even one. Joe Biden, on the other hand, dished them out like dollar bills at an erotic club.

It was ironic, infuriating, and darkly hilarious—the perfect way for Joe Biden to end his failed presidency. His last act confirmed what we already knew: The man who standardized the modern practice of lawfare (more on this momentarily), proved once and for all that two systems of justice exist in the country.

I saw it coming, of course. We weren't being entirely tongue-in-cheek at *Breitbart News* when we began calling them "The Biden Crime Family." I knew from my extensive research into the Bidens that Joe would never let his family members go to jail, so long as he could help it, nor would he let protracted legal entanglements bankrupt them.

Unending lawsuits, expensive legal bills, and judicial harassment from your political opponents? That was for the Trump family! For those MAGAts who stormed the U.S. Capitol on January 6th! No Biden was ever going to rot in a cell.

Throughout the Biden administration, Democrats tried to bankrupt Trump by filing civil cases against him in liberal districts. Judges and juries who hated Trump awarded absurd penalties to accusers in flimsy cases. And when that failed to alienate Trump from the American public, Biden's DOJ, together with some suspiciously recent DOJ alumni, tried to throw him in jail.

Yet, luckily, they all failed. In the end, Trump fought off his most malicious detractors and proved they were powerless against him. At least for the time being.

Despite Trump's victory, however, it's still important to consider the damage the left has done to our legal system. Lawfare is a multifaceted tool. The left deploys it at the court to enact change and tarnish their adversaries. They use it at the White House to circumvent constitutional roadblocks. They use it at the ballot box so they don't leave a single close election to chance.

Joe Biden, a famously lousy law student (as thoroughly documented in *Breaking Biden*), had introduced modern lawfare decades earlier with the "borking" of Supreme Court nominee Robert Bork and the unsuc-

cessful high-tech lynching of nominee Clarence Thomas. In the intervening years, the Democrats built a lawfare superstructure that remains one of their most potent political weapons.

The Democrats always had long odds for the 2024 election. They had a weak candidate at the top of the ticket, then swapped him out for a candidate who was even worse. Republicans had both political and cultural tailwinds and a candidate so strong it looked at times like God himself willed Trump to take back the presidency.

The Democrats should have known they were in a losing battle. They should have stood down and lain low. But they are fighters, and they fought to the bitter end. This was a fateful choice because it meant they didn't just lose in November, they exposed their playbook in the process. Now it's on us to identify its elements, dismantle what we can, and prepare for the battles ahead.

If we fail, the machine will only get stronger. The left plans to use lawfare to expand voter eligibility to include illegal aliens, eliminate voter ID requirements, and widen the time window in which people can vote. They want to rig the deck so they can't lose. They will game campaign finance laws so that they always have a fundraising advantage. They will pack courts to limit the power of conservative and originalist judges. They will add new left-leaning states, grant mass amnesty to illegal aliens, and more. Scariest of all, they will try to declare the conservative movement an existential threat to "democracy" itself with no legitimate right to exist.

If they had their way, 2024 would have been the last real election. Under a second Biden or Kamala Harris administration, the political left would have used their power to cement their gains and guarantee that no sane Republican would ever test the lawfare machine again.

Anyone who challenged them would have been subjected to the Trump treatment.

It would have been the end of democracy as we know it.

In November 2024, we got a stay of execution, but we still have much to fear.

The left believes that America is not an exceptional place and that our core institutions are not worthy of respect. Once you understand this fundamental outlook, you can begin to understand how easily they are willing to bend the system to their will. They don't believe in precedent, tradition, and principle: their only pursuit is power.

THE LEFT HATES LAW AND ORDER

The left has never regarded the rule of law as essential. They consider it a means to an end, and when it doesn't work in their favor, it's viewed as an obstacle on the way to their progressive utopia that can be swept aside. That attitude made the prosecutions of Trump possible.

My first conscious experience with the left's anti–law and order culture concerned immigration, and illegal immigration specifically. Our open border was a national disgrace, and I dedicated much of my career to bringing attention to that fact. The left has waged war on immigration enforcement to boost their long-term electoral prospects. They want as many illegal immigrants to come as possible, even though that means violating the law.

Growing up in California, I didn't have to be particularly observant to notice the disastrous effects of illegal immigration on our quality of life. The influx of people hurt everything from schools and hospitals to crime and everyday safety.

When I got older, I realized that our illegal immigration crisis is fundamentally an issue of lawfare. It reveals the left's contempt for the firm standards that law and order demand.

People from around the world sought to enter America by any means necessary to seek work and gain access to the American economy. And Democrats let them. The illegal immigrant population doubled from 1995 to 2005.[3] From 2005 to 2015, for example, chain migration, the process where family and community members follow another immigrant to settle in a new country, added as many new people to the USA as any two years of American births during that decade.[4]

Our southern border was abandoned for decades. Until Donald Trump came down that escalator on June 16, 2015, to announce his campaign for president, both political parties seemed comfortable with massive demographic change, mostly for political reasons. Democrats thought they benefited from a new influx of families that would eventually support Democrats once they gained the right to vote, and Republicans feared being branded "racist" if they dared to speak out against lawlessness.

Migrants crossed our border without even offering the courtesy of signing the proverbial guest book. One party considered it, in essence, not *not* legal. The other political party was too afraid to address the problem because they feared political fallout.

For the elite on both sides, the flow of migrants lowered the cost of their gardeners, nannies, and an assortment of other laborers.

The Democrats saw their path to a permanent majority, and they moved to try to secure it by manipulating the language to end any debate on the issue. "Illegal aliens" were rebranded "undocumented workers." Illegal alien children became "Dreamers," named after the Development, Relief, and Education for Alien Minors (DREAM) Act of 1991. When I was a student at the University of California, Berkeley, from 2005 to 2008, it was popular to say that "no human being is illegal," because the literal and accurate term *illegal alien* was deemed dehumanizing.

These euphemisms were designed to mask the reality of the situation. The term *illegal alien* refers to their immigration status, not their humanity. Duh. Illegal immigrants were "undocumented" because they had broken the law to get here. It was that simple. And as to the term "Dreamer," President Trump said it best in his 2020 State of the Union speech: "Americans are dreamers too."

America had the most idiotic immigration policy in the world. We left our border open for years. And until Trump, not a single mainstream political figure with the power to change things was willing to address the issue. It was madness.

From the day he took office in 2016, Donald Trump's administration provided a brief moment of sanity in an otherwise insane sixty-year period, implementing policies such as "Remain in Mexico," Title 42, and building new sections of border wall. However, Joe Biden undid all that the moment he got into power. Biden's decision to deliberately undo Trump's efforts to secure our border made clear to the rest of the world what most of them already knew: America's southern border was a lawless place.

The whole border mess started when Senator Ted Kennedy shepherded the Immigration and Nationality Act of 1965 through congress. The bill prioritized chain-migrants and capped legal immigrants from our hemisphere, thus leading to widespread illegal immigration. This proved to be a political benefit for Demorats. Half a century later, Democrats Barack Obama and Joe Biden refused to enforce our laws, again to benefit Democrats. Changing the law and refusing to enforce it were both considered viable options so long as it helped Democrats win.

But Democrats weren't the only ones who benefited. The Mexican cartels that smuggle drugs and human beings into our country benefited too, while American communities suffered as crime and fentanyl flooded our streets.

The debasing of our immigration system is perhaps lawfare's greatest triumph to date. One major political party, the Democrats, has gone to great lengths to not enforce a set of laws because they believed that would help them electorally. And until recently, establishment and globalist Republicans were comfortable with this lawlessness because the influx in people lowered the cost of blue-collar labor, which could potentially save them money. (Plus, the left has successfully framed the debate so that for many years, if you raised the issue of illegal immigration, you were likely to be called a racist and a xenophobe in the press. Republicans have not traditionally had a strong enough stomach to handle bogus charges of racism.)

The scope of the immigration laws that the left openly violated is immense. As I wrote in *Breaking Biden*, our refusal to enforce a border "sends a message to foreigners that if you violate our rules, you might get prioritized ahead of those who abide by them."

Not only does an open border broadcast to the rest of the world that we don't even have respect for our own laws, but it also leads to humanitarian crises downstream. It created a black market for fentanyl, which has been trafficked over our border in quantities large enough to kill every American, devastating countless American communities. What's more, the conditions for the migrants themselves are often dangerous and always filthy and degrading. Families are separated. Females are raped and assaulted. And when they arrive, they often work for wages that are below our minimum wage, some of which must be sent to their cartel traffickers.

It's all horrific and a stain on our country. Yet the Democrats will go to terrific lengths to keep things exactly as they are. In President Trump's first term, Democrats harped on the "kids in cages," referring to unaccompanied alien minors who were sometimes housed in fenced-off warehouses while they were processed. They paid no mind to the fact that these facilities were often built during the Obama-Biden administration, a story we broke at *Breitbart News* in 2014.[5] Yet once the Democrats saw an opportunity to weaponize the use of the "cages" against Trump and his supporters, they took it, framing it as white nationalism.[6]

It's all dishonest. A disgrace, frankly. But as a practical matter, these lies are pernicious because they lead to more lawlessness, which is exactly what the institutional left wants.

Our lack of a wall and inadequate border enforcement are the beginning of the lawlessness. Our asylum system is routinely abused with the "catch and release" policy that was in place both before and after Trump's first term. In essence, if a border crosser encounters law enforcement, all they need to do is claim that they are seeking asylum and they are welcomed to stay until they are given a hearing, which is likely years off. What's more, the asylum claimant almost certainly had passed through another country that has similar asylum rules as the USA, so they don't need to be here; they simply want to be here.

Joe Biden expanded the Temporary Protected Status (TPS) programs during his presidency, which allowed foreign nationals from countries like Nicaragua and Venezuela to be paroled into the country with little or no vetting. He even had a smartphone app, CBP One, that made the process go smoother *for the illegal alien.*

Donald Trump had cut aid to the "Northern Triangle" countries (El Salvador, Guatemala, and Honduras) for allowing migrant caravans to head toward the U.S. unabated. He also put Title 42 in place, which allowed for the swift removal of any alien who had recently been in a country with a contagious disease (which in the post-COVID era was all of them). Joe Biden canceled all of those upon taking office.

These basic details are probably familiar to anyone reading this book, but it is nonetheless important to identify what it represents: The mainstream viewpoint among Democrat policy makers is that padding their voter rolls is more important than living in a society that respects its own laws. They believed an open border was their path to a permanent majority, and that is reason enough for the lawlessness.

They had the choice between the rule of law and chaos, and they chose chaos.

Upon taking office a second time, Donald Trump immediately began restoring rationality to the process. Illegal immigration was a fixable problem—it's just that nobody wanted to fix it. Trump proved that the border could be closed within weeks, thus also proving that it was left open by design.

THE SHOPLIFTER VOTE

Crime is political for the left. Joe Biden and former Vice President Kamala Harris both had moments in their career when they were tough on crime when it served them politically, and at other moments they sided with the criminals over the citizens.

The challenge for modern Democrats is that while a commitment to keeping crime to a minimum is a de facto priority for all politicians, the left flank of their movement has insisted on engaging in sociological experiments that have caused rising crime and deeper safety concerns in our streets.

Many Democrats, particularly among the base, regard crime as a symptom of racial and economic injustice and think that criminals ought to be treated with leniency. Society, not the perpetrator, really caused the crime, so any punishment is inherently unjust. The laws on the books are inherently problematic, they say, and ought to be subverted when possible.

This poses a political conundrum for them: Crack down on crime and lose the left, or indulge the woke and watch cities fall apart. In blue areas, laissez-faire approaches to crime are politically beneficial. In the single-party, Democrat-run state of California, for example, some shoplifting is de facto legal. This is because state law says that stealing $950 or less of merchandise is merely a misdemeanor, which disincentivizes law enforcement and prosecutors from investigating these petty crimes and enforcing the law.[7]

Mundane items such as candy, shampoo, and shaving supplies are often kept behind lock and key at stores to reduce the pilfering, but that accomplishes only so much. Video footage of mobs clearing out stores routinely go viral online, eliciting outraged and embarrassed responses. Only recently has there been any broad interest in changing these laws.

Since moving back to the Los Angeles area four years ago, I have witnessed petty theft on multiple occasions, including in wealthy enclaves. I've seen clerks pathetically plead with thieves to stop, knowing that a call to law enforcement is a time-consuming dead end.

There is only one conclusion to draw from this set of facts: The shoplifter vote is a very influential part of the Democrat coalition.

Democrats, Kamala Harris in particular, are famously associated with the movement to "defund the police." They have also championed bail reform. States like New York ended cash bail for nonviolent crime, including felonies. The left sees the concept of cash bail as racist. They contend that "communities of color" are overpoliced and that bail is set at higher levels for them (these arguments are typically offered without noting the nature of the crimes committed and whether the defendant is a repeat offender, both of which will factor into how high the bail is set).

Efforts to end cash bail,[8] led by far-left activists such as the Kamala Harris–backed Minnesota Freedom Fund,[9] have led to a national crime wave. Meanwhile, the media covered for Democrats, pretending that the rise in crime was an illusion conjured up by conservative media. They insisted that the violent crime rate dropped in 2022,[10] for example. But the FBI quietly revised the stats to show a 4.5 percent increase for the year.[11] The data ultimately matched what we had been reporting via anecdote after anecdote at *Breitbart News*: There was a big jump in violence under Joe Biden and Kamala Harris.

This blatant disregard for law and order and public safety created an endless font content for conservative media. At *Breitbart News*, for example, we highlighted a 2023 study from the John Jay College of Criminal Justice that found that 72 percent of violent crime suspects in New York City who were freed without bail went on to commit more crime.[12]

Other recent headlines we've published:

- New York Bail Law Freed Illegal Alien Wanted by Feds, Now Accused of Rape[13]

- Watch: Migrants Brutally Attack NYC Cops, Get Freed from Jail Without Bail[14]

- "Sanctuary Church" Helps Free from Jail Illegal Alien Charged with Migrant Mob Attack on NYPD Officers[15]

- New York: Five Illegal Migrants Escape After Being Released on Bail Following Jewelry Store Theft[16]

"No cash bail" is one of the tenets of the "criminal justice reform" movement, which aspires to reduce perceived structural issues in the way the law is enforced in the country. Proponents of "criminal justice reform" see overcriminalization as the problem, not lax law enforcement. They believe that the law is applied unfairly against minority groups. In other words, law and order is racist.

Thus, by merely entertaining the idea that society ought to enforce the law, you run the risk of being branded as a racist or worse.

Foisting this belief on the public is its own form of lawfare.

As time has gone on, the Democrats have gotten increasingly tolerant of criminals, so long as you don't defraud people of *too much* money. California State Senator Lola Smallwood-Cuevas (D) introduced a bill in early 2025 that would decriminalize welfare fraud under $25,000.[17] "This bill is about keeping families out of the criminal justice system from making administrative errors on raising the threshold for welfare fraud prosecutions," she wrote on social media.

You see, in the warped minds of at least one blue-state Democratic lawmaker, stealing $25,001 from the government is fraud, but $24,999 is an "administrative error."[18]

This isn't merely disrespecting the principles of law and order to pander to the criminal class, it shows outright contempt for taxpaying citizens.

SOROS-FUNDED DAS

The primary culprit for the legal revolution in our cities is what we in conservative media have labeled "Soros-funded DAs" and "Soros-funded prosecutors." This group of district attorneys and prosecutors received financial support from the famed leftist billionaire philanthropist and chaos agent George Soros.

"The Soros empire spent at least $40 million to elect its prosecutors. It then invested an additional $77,663,316 to twenty leftist nonprofits to coordinate and control the prosecutors, bringing the total Soros spending to at least $117,663,316," according to a report called "Law & Disorder" from the conservative Media Research Center (MRC). "At least 30 percent of the U.S. population currently lives under the boot of the Soros prosecutors who were pressured to sign pledges vowing to adhere to various Soros priorities. The Soros machine orchestrated 33 of these 'joint statements' and pledges, which were signed by 123 of the 126 Soros prosecutors," the MRC continued.

More than any other man, the leftist billionaire, currency manipulator, and philanthropist George Soros is responsible for the ruinous effect crime has had on our metropolises in recent years. He spent lavishly on approximately seventy-five radical left-wing prosecutors in 2022, but that number might be much higher, according to a report by the Law Enforcement Legal Defense Fund (LELDF). The report notes that more than 72 million people, including half of America's fifty most populous cities and counties, live in one of the affected areas.[19]

How does he do it? "Soros uses a series of shell organizations, affiliates, and pass-through committees to steer contributions to both candidates and his robust support network for progressive prosecutors, which provide gravitas and perks to preferred prosecutors," the LELDF wrote.[20]

Soros consistently ranks among the top funders of leftist political activity in America. Though George Soros is in his mid-nineties, his thirty-nine-year-old son Alexander, who chairs his father's far-left Open Society Foundations, is poised to continue the family business for decades to come. In 2024, Alexander Soros became engaged to Hillary Clinton's longtime aide and confidante Huma Abedin, instantly making them one of the most powerful couples in all of polictics.

Among George Soros's stable of radicals was San Francisco District Attorney Chesa Boudin. Boudin was so unpopular that he was recalled by the voters of the far-left California city in 2022. Boudin has far-left activism coursing through his veins. His parents were both convicted Weather Underground terrorists who took part in one of the most famous violent robberies in our nation's history: a botched heist of an armored Brinks truck in 1981 that left a guard and two police officers dead.[21] The purpose of the heist was to abscond with millions of dollars that would fill the organization's coffers so they could fund more radical activism.[22]

Boudin's father, David Gilbert, and mother, Kathy Boudin, were convicted on felony murder charges and given lengthy sentences. Gilbert was granted clemency by then–New York Governor Andrew Cuomo in 2021.[23]

Boudin used his misfortune of having incarcerated parents as justification for his soft-on-crime policies. Yet, while he may have been a victim of unfortunate circumstances, his parents were not. Yet, the fact that they were imprisoned became an excuse for him to engage in a form of lawfare.

Call it "refusal to enforce the law . . . fare."

Boudin, like many of Soros's minions, wanted to end cash bail and shift law enforcement resources away from nonviolent crime.[24] He declined to press charges for the majority of assault arrests.[25]

He claimed a decline in reported crime on his watch, but the voters saw through that charade. The declining numbers didn't convey a decline in crime but rather the absence of all hope. Law enforcement had gotten so weak that residents decided not to bother to report certain crimes, knowing that nobody would show up to help.

Boudin proved too radical for even leftist San Francisco, which recalled him by a double-digit electoral margin.

Soros also funded District Attorney Pamela Price of Alameda County, which is in the East Bay region of Northern California and includes crime-riddled Oakland. She embraced the "defund the police" strategy and paid the price for it, first in her personal life (her own laptop was stolen from her car),[26] and then at the ballot box.

The LELDF estimated that Soros spent $2 million on electing Chicago's Kim Foxx, $1.1 million on New York City's Alvin Bragg, $1.3 million on Philadelphia's Larry Krasner, and $4.7 million on Los Angeles's former DA George Gascón, among others.[27]

Of America's criminal coddlers, George Gascón is perhaps the most infamous. He served as the DA of San Francisco from 2011 to 2019, succeeding Kamala Harris, with disastrous results. He prosecuted only 40 percent of misdemeanor cases during his two terms, which led to a wave of low-level crimes and a surge in car break-ins. Nonetheless, Gascón portrayed his refusal to prosecute misdemeanors as an accomplishment, according to the *Los Angeles Times*,[28] and it helped him get elected in L.A.

Gascón has a bleeding heart for people who break the law. "By putting people even for short terms, in jail, when they are poor, they lose their jobs, the safety net is not there and then they lose their homes," he said.

Yes, he takes pride in letting criminals run wild.

This sentiment is not only delusional, it's cruel to the law-abiding amongst the citizenry.

Reports such as this from Fox News's Los Angeles–based Bill Melugin quickly became the norm: "LAPD arrested a man for stabbing the neck of a construction worker, nearly killing him. Despite a prison recommendation from Probation Dept., L.A. D.A. George Gascón's admin agreed to give him diversion instead. He is now charged with murdering his neighbor last week."[29]

L.A., the city of angels, quickly became a paradise for criminals. Murder rates spiked as they declined nationally, nearly doubling from 2019 to 2021.[30] Car thefts increased by 65 percent over the same period.[31]

"It's been an absolute disaster for the community," Los Angeles County Sheriff Alex Villanueva said of Gascón's time in office. "It's been a disaster for public safety. It's been a disaster for law enforcement."[32]

Gascón arrived in Los Angeles in 2020, at the height of the Black Lives Matter antipolicing movement. He was quickly endorsed by the Democrat Party establishment and then-Mayor Eric Garcetti, who withdrew his prior endorsement of the more moderate DA Jackie Lacey, Los Angeles's first black DA. After he won, Gascón seemed to get even more radical. Right away he issued a special directive that prevented his office from seeking the death penalty, sentencing enhancements, and cash bail for nonviolent criminals.[33] His policies put criminals back on the street, ready to offend again.

In L.A., criminals call it a "Gascón Special." It's when you commit a crime—typically theft—knowing that even if you're arrested, you're likely back on the street the next day.

In May 2023, the New York Post reported that Gascón, who built a reputation for operating as an "authoritarian," had accumulated a 10,000-case backlog. The environment in his office was described by prosecutors as toxic.

"In my career as a prosecutor, I've never had victims' families actually hate us until I came into this office," one former deputy district attorney told the Post.[34]

Things got so bad that there was an open rebellion among rank-and-file prosecutors. Gascón survived two recall attempts. The second one probably would have succeeded if not for a technicality that allowed county officials to disqualify it from the ballot.

The voters finished Gascón off in 2024, when he was whupped at the polls by challenger Nathan Hochman by a staggering 61.5–38.5 percent spread.[35]

Despite his shocking track record, Gascón is probably only the second most well-known "Soros-funded prosecutor" behind Alvin Bragg. Bragg figures prominently later in this book for his prosecutions of Donald Trump.

"New York City District Attorney Alvin Bragg (D), the prosecutor behind charges against former President Donald Trump, has built a record of dropping felony charges, decreasing felony convictions, downgrading felonies to mere misdemeanors, and not bothering to request bail for suspects accused of felonies," John Binder wrote for us at *Breitbart News*.

Bragg's DA office has specifically shunned the "broken windows policing" strategy associated with much safer times in the Big Apple, where officers were tasked with focusing on low-level crimes like vandalism and loitering. Bragg specifically permitted drug misdemeanors, turnstile jumping, trespassing, prostitution, driving with a suspended license, obstructing officers, and more, Binder notes.[36]

According to one report, he downgraded most—about 52 percent—of felony cases to misdemeanors in 2022, a drastic increase compared to his predecessor. He also got a far lower percentage of convictions in felony and misdemeanor cases while declining to prosecute far more cases.[37]

So, what was Bragg doing while he wasn't enforcing the law? He was targeting Donald Trump. And as a rule, Bragg prioritized harassing normal citizens over maintaining public order. He released a man who assaulted NYPD officers without bail.[38] He pursued charges against a bodega owner who killed an assailant in what was clearly self-defense.[39] He pressed manslaughter charges against Daniel Penny, a Marine veteran who put a fatal chokehold on a psychotic homeless man threatening passengers. Witnesses said the deceased, Jordan Neely, who had been hospitalized more than a dozen times, was screaming at passengers that someone was "going to die."[40]

But in Alvin Bragg and George Soros's world, Jordan Neely did nothing wrong. Daniel Penny is the bad guy for standing up for his fellow passengers.

Law and order is not one of their values. But, apparently, chaos is.

Chicago's Kim Foxx is another Soros-funded operative. Her list of misdeeds seems endless. As Cook County state's attorney for Illinois, she dismissed more than 25,000 felony cases.[41] She refused to charge gang members in a Chicago veteran's murder,[42] leading federal prosecutors to take on the case. She sided with Jussie Smollett during his 2019 hate-crime hoax, most notably by dropping the initial sixteen charges against the *Empire* actor without offering any explanation.[43] When the Illinois Supreme Court reversed Smollett's conviction, Foxx gloated even though she acknowledged he was guilty.[44]

There are other Soros-backed prosecutors who practiced lawfare but didn't receive notoriety, such as St. Louis Circuit Attorney Kim Gardner, who admitted to misusing public funds. She also was reprimanded by the Missouri Supreme Court for ethics violations when she tried to prosecute Missouri Governor Eric Greitens (a Republican, of course) and oust him from office. She also appeared to engage in another brazenly political prosecution when she prosecuted Mark and Patricia McCloskey, a prominent Republican couple, who pointed firearms at Black Lives Matter protesters who smashed their way into their gated community.[45] She was kicked off of that case after using it in fundraising emails.[46] (The McCloskeys would plead guilty to misdemeanors and were eventually pardoned by Republican Governor Mike Parson.)[47] The "controversies" section of Gardner's Wikipedia page was over three thousand words long as of the time this book was written, which is exceedingly rare for left-wing public figures. In other words, even the bad guys know she's a bad guy.

LOWER THE CRIME RATE WITH ONE EASY TRICK

The Soros DAs represent a broader attitude on the American left that holds that law and order is racist and must be undermined at all turns. This attitude took over the establishment media, which portrayed police officers as racially bigoted murderers.[48] The *Washington Post*'s Pulitzer Prize–winning Fatal Force database, launched in 2015, presupposes that police officers are driven primarily by racism. Others in the media say the same thing. Routine policing procedures are products of "systemic racism." In other words, the entire system needs to collapse for racism to end in America.

These conclusions are wildly dishonest. Racism is not the primary driver of police behavior, and studies prove it. Evidence suggests that compliance, not skin tone, is by far the most common determining factor in whether a police encounter escalates. Suspects who comply with police officers don't face escalatory action; those who don't risk death.

Selective media coverage intent on pushing a narrative has costs. The claim that all cops are racist, for example, caused a severe decrease in proactive policing across the country. This is known as the Ferguson Effect, named for the increase in violent crime in many U.S. cities after the shooting of Michael Brown in Ferguson, Missouri, in 2014.[49] Following several high-profile incidents of supposed police brutality, police reduced proactive enforcement; increased crime rates followed. A 2017 Pew Research study showed a large uptick in violence against police officers in the intervening years, including a dramatic rise in officers shot and killed.[50] Obama's Department of Justice enacted enhanced federal oversight over local police forces, entering into what is known as consent decrees with law enforcement agencies across the country. He did this fifteen times (in comparison, George W. Bush did this three times during his eight years as president). This meant that Obama was leveraging federal authority to ensure that law enforcement agencies reformed.[51]

Apparently, his definition of "reform" was to enforce the law less strenuously.

The left's war on law enforcement hit its peak after George Floyd was killed in 2020. That summer will always be remembered for riots that broke out nationwide. But the hostility against cops also caused officers to quit and retire in droves. Retirements nationwide rose 45 percent. Resignations jumped 18 percent from April 2020 to April 2021, according to the *New York Times*.[52] NYPD's head count was at record lows in 2024,[53] though it finally began to recover in other parts of the nation.[54]

Democrats have also counted high-profile criminals among their most prolific donors. Disgraced FTX CEO Sam Bankman-Fried, for example, sought to outpace even George Soros among Democrat donors.[55] Jeffrey Epstein, Sean "Diddy" Combs, and Harvey Weinstein are household names who all gave heavily to the party that opposed law and order. Volumes have been written on their wrongdoings, and I can guarantee more are yet to come.

To be fair, the Republicans are imperfect on this issue as well. Plenty on the right hobnobbed with Epstein. Donald Trump himself tried to pursue criminal justice reform via his son-in-law Jared Kushner, whose father is a convicted felon. Yet this was a relatively minor part of Trump's agenda and was met with skepticism from his base.

There are valid criticisms to be made about America's prosecutorial complex. America has the most incarcerations and one of the highest incarceration rates in the world among countries from where we can get reasonable data.[56] It's not wrong to want to lower those numbers. But the policies carried out in recent years in Democrat-run cities decreased the incarceration rate by increasing crime. A robust police force acting as a deterrent is better than what Democrats want: to keep law enforcement to an absolute minimum.

A HISTORIC OPPORTUNITY

The Democrats' leniency toward criminals in our streets, insistence on keeping our southern border open, and inconsistent application of hate-crime laws have ceded the issue of equality before the law to Republicans.

There is some evidence, however, that big swaths of rank-and-file Democrat voters are fed up with at least some of their party leadership's leftist instincts on the subject. Californians, for example, overwhelmingly voted to stiffen penalties for criminals by passing Proposition 36 in 2024. The ballot initiative, which increased penalties for repeat offenders, introduced tougher punishments for offenses involving fentanyl, and cracked down on aggravated theft and "smash-and-grab" looting. It passed by a margin above two-to-one despite vigorous opposition from top Democrats, including Governor Gavin Newsom.[57] Kamala Harris notably abstained from taking a stance in favor or against.[58]

Of twenty-five Soros-backed district attorneys who were on the ballot in 2024, twelve were recalled or lost their elections.[59]

Still, the party brass is no longer in touch with voters on the issue of crime. Despite losing a statewide ballot initiative, liberals doubled down on undermining law enforcement after the 2024 election. Within days the Los Angeles City Council moved to become a sanctuary city, prohibiting "any City resources, including property or personnel, from being utilized for any immigration enforcement."[60] Yet there is a budding awareness that voter sentiment has shifted. Democrats are now in an electoral conundrum where a tough stance on illegal immigration could risk alienating base voters, but the opposite will certainly cost them votes from political centrists.[61]

This troubling reaction presents a historic opportunity to Republicans. There is nothing more fundamental to the quality of life for Americans than the reassurance that you and your loved ones won't get mugged in your own neighborhood, and that if you are, the perpetrator will be brought to justice. Yet, this viewpoint is seemingly unspeakable at high levels of Democrat politics.

The shoplifter vote must be a larger bloc than I had imagined.

Republicans can take command of this conversation, expose the Democrats for who they are, and show the country what left-wing policies have wrought on our cities. If they do that, Republicans will earn the trust of new voters across demographics.

It doesn't matter what you look like or what else you believe: All decent Americans in their heads and in their hearts want the law-abiding protected and the long arm of the law to come down hard on the crooked.

That is, of course, unless you're a part of the Democrat Party.

CHAPTER 2

THE TRIAL THAT NEVER SHOULD HAVE HAPPENED

While crime is certainly not a priority for the Democrats, getting Donald J. Trump is.

The left has tried to use lawfare to destroy Trump before he even assumed office.

Congressional Democrats claim that Trump has been violating the Constitution since January 20, 2017, the day he was sworn in as commander in chief of the United States of America. They claimed on day one that he was earning money from foreign business which put him in violation of the Constitution's "Emoluments Clause." Emoluments are a salary, fee, or profit from employment or office. The leftist Citizens for Responsibility and Ethics in Washington (CREW) and some hospitality-industry plaintiffs joined in, arguing that the fact that Trump was president meant that he had an unfair competitive advantage in the marketplace. His name made his properties too big of a draw. Thus he needed to completely sever all connections to his business interests, which they suggested that he could not effectively do due to his notoriety, making Trump ineligible to serve as president.

Norm Eisen, who founded the Soros-funded CREW and worked for Barack Obama as the White House "ethics czar," architected a strategy to conceal records of who visited the White House for meetings,[1] earning public castigation led by none other than Andrew Breitbart himself.[2] Eisen has gone on to become one of the top lawfare coordinators throughout the continued legal harassment of Donald Trump.

The emoluments lawsuit was so absurd that it was eventually shut down by a Clinton-appointed federal judge.[3]

Yet the efforts to use lawfare to destroy Trump had officially begun.

The Democrats would try to impeach Trump obsessively throughout his first administration, for pretty much everything. Representative Al Green (D-TX) tried to impeach Trump for obstructing justice. They tried to impeach him for the Charlottesville, Virginia, "Unite the Right" rally and "fine people on both sides" hoax. (Trump specifically said that neo-Nazis and the white nationalists "should be condemned totally."[4] A full accounting of this hoax appears in *Breaking the News*.)

Democrat megadonor and Joe Biden ally Tom Steyer launched a petition to impeach Trump because he "brought us to the brink of nuclear war" with North Korea, apparently. They would try to impeach him for firing FBI director James Comey (again, something Trump as president had every right to do).

The Democrats were obsessed.

Here is a partial list of items for which Democrats attempted to impeach Donald Trump:

- Violations of the Domestic Emoluments Clause

- Violations of the Foreign Emoluments Clause

- Obstruction of justice

- Inappropriately disclosing classified information

- Destruction of public records

- Payment of ransom with federal funds in violation of international law

- Authorizing security clearances for people who are known security risks

- Failure to protect U.S. elections from foreign interference

- Campaign finance law violations

- Condoning white nationalism

- Using law enforcement to punish political enemies

- Attacking the press as "enemies of the people"

- Mismanagement by failing to fill vacancies

- Separation of immigrant children from their families

All these efforts were building up to Special Counsel Robert S. Mueller III's long-anticipated report on Russian collusion. Former FBI Director Mueller had been appointed in May 2017 and spent nearly two years investigating Moscow's alleged efforts to sabotage the 2016 presidential election. In March 2019, Mueller sent a memo to Attorney General William P. Barr that summarized the findings, completely exonerating Donald Trump, concluding "the Special Counsel did not find that the Trump campaign, or anyone associated with it, conspired or coordinated with the Russian government in these efforts, despite multiple offers from Russian-affiliated individuals to assist the Trump campaign."

Despite spending countless thousands of hours and conducting interviews with five hundred witnesses (a list of witnesses released to CNN and *BuzzFeed* was thirty-five pages long)[5], Mueller came up with literally nothing connecting Trump to the Kremlin.

Two days after Mueller effectually dashed the dreams of the impeachment crowd, Trump had a phone call with Volodymyr Zelenskyy in which he encouraged the Ukrainian president to look into strange circumstances surrounding the Bidens and the Ukrainian energy company Burisma. Hunter Biden had landed a board seat that paid about a million dollars per year despite not having any professional background in energy or Ukraine; this raised suspicions and led to an investigation in that country. Then–Vice President Biden told the Ukrainians to drop the investigation into his corrupt son's corrupt company or else they would not receive a billion dollars of funds appropriated by Congress. Trump told Zelenskyy that "a lot of people want to find out about that" and encouraged him to reopen the investigation.

A low-level CIA analyst (widely believed to be Eric Ciaramella), who had heard *about* the call—he wasn't even on the call himself—wrote a memo to Senate Intelligence Committee Chairman Richard Burr and House Intelligence Chairman Adam Schiff about what he had heard about the call, suggesting that Trump was soliciting a foreign government to interfere in a U.S. election by having him dig up dirt on a political rival.

This led to two articles of impeachment: one for abuse of power, and another for obstructing Congress's efforts to carry out their impeachment inquiry. They were passed mostly along party lines.

(*Breaking the News* has a thorough and entertaining account of the impeachment and its inevitable death in the Senate.)

Years later, Biden would pardon his son for crimes unknown committed during this time, vindicating Trump's interest in Burisma once and for all.

As I stated in my first book, the impeachment was ultimately meaningless, but it did ramp up the lawfare machine and introduce much of the country to some of its field generals like Adam Schiff, Andrew Weissmann, and Daniel Goldman, all of whom played key roles in the impeachment and are recurring characters throughout this book.

What it also did is normalize the use of the legal system to attack and attempt to destroy Donald Trump.

Those efforts would intensify after his first administration.

SIX CASES THAT BROKE THE LAW

There were five major efforts to destroy Donald Trump by bankrupting him, destroying his reputation, or jailing him. These cases dogged him throughout the four years between his two administrations. There are six cases in all. Each gets its own chapter in this book aside from the two brought by Special Counsel Jack Smith; I take those on together.

I believe this series of cases fundamentally *broke the law* in this country. If Trump had lost in 2024, it would have meant that lawfare had won. Either the Democrats had broken Trump's will with this relentless onslaught, had him deemed ineligible to be president, or they had convinced the voters that Trump really was unfit for office, or a combination thereof.

In the end, Trump bested them all, but if he had less resilience, less willpower, less heart, and frankly, less money, they would have succeeded.

The institutional left and their lawfare superstructure may have failed this time, but they will try again, either against Trump or another target that threatens what they hold dear. That's why we must understand the breadth and depth of their immoral and often illegal actions. We have to be prepared.

I have elected to address each major case one at a time (two at a time in the case of Smith's cases) because I think it makes for a far smoother reading experience than trying to weave them together all at once. However, living through these cases was never a "smooth" experience for Donald Trump. He had to deal with all these cases concurrently, with major moments in separate cases occasionally occurring at precisely the same time. (I do interrupt my linear case-by-case narrative structure to note when those moments come up.)

There absolutely was coordination among the instigators of each case, but the extent of their collusion largely remains a mystery. These are the instances that ought to be investigated by Republican legislators, and I highlight those throughout.

It is important to emphasize that while each of these cases represent a lawfare front unto itself, Donald Trump had to fight all of them at the same time, all while gearing up to run for president and then campaigning.

Taking the cases collectively, it is an absolute marvel that Donald Trump survived it all and won the presidency again.

Yet when you take the cases on their own, the arguments against Trump range from legally questionable to outright absurd. There isn't one strong case in the group.

Yet they each posed their own slate of problems for President Trump, his allies, and his movement.

We begin with what is arguably the weakest case of them all—a trial that should never have happened.

Yet this is the only one that resulted in a criminal conviction.

STRANGER THAN FICTION: THE "FACTS" OF THE CASE

The alleged "hush money" case against Donald Trump dates all the way back to 2006, when Trump met porn star Stephanie Clifford, aka "Stormy Daniels," at a celebrity golf tournament in Lake Tahoe. She claims they had a sexual encounter at that event, which Trump has denied.

(I note at the outset that the case was not actually about "hush money," which is not illegal. It was about falsifying documents. The anti-Trump media preferred "hush money" branding because it sounds sinister, and it stuck.)

Daniels, who started stripping in high school, had starred in, written, or directed well over 150 X-rated movies and received a number of porn industry awards.[6]

We begin from an unlikely premise: The germophobic Trump allegedly risked it all to engage in a tryst with a professional nasty person. Trump had a new wife who was somehow even more beautiful than his first two beautiful wilves: Melania Knauss. The Slovenian model who speaks six languages would give birth to their son, Barron, later that year. *The Apprentice* was also on the air, and Trump was on track to take over yet another quintessential American industry: network television. Yet he found Daniels so enticing that he just couldn't control himself.

Or that's at least what we're supposed to believe.

Daniels said she was twenty-seven and thought Trump was about sixty at the time. She said she accepted a dinner invitation from Trump because "it'll make a great story."[7] That claim certainly tracks.

The night supposedly started in Trump's penthouse hotel suite, which Daniels described as "three times the size of my apartment." Trump donned "silk or satin" pajamas, which inspired Daniels to fire off a zinger: "Does Hugh Hefner know you stole his pajamas?" She then asked him to change, she says.

Trump supposedly obliged.

He allegedly grilled her on the business aspects of the pornography industry, which she appreciated, before he asked her if she ever had a sexually transmitted disease.

At one point, she said, Trump pulled out a magazine with himself on the cover and said, "Someone should spank you with that." She said she then rolled it up and hit him with it.

Apparently, Trump got politer at this point and soft-pitched her coming on his TV show. At this point, according to Daniels, he told her, "You remind me of my daughter."

Daniels claims that they talked for two hours.

She also claimed she was surprised when she returned from the restroom to find Trump disrobed, on the bed in just boxer shorts and a T-shirt. They ended up having sex without a condom, she claimed, saying it was brief but that he enjoyed it.[8]

"He always called me Honey Bunch," she said.

So far, the entire premise of this case relies on a hard-core porn star's word that Trump raw-dogged her. I'm not saying I know the story isn't true, but none of this so far makes sense based on what we know about Trump.

Their next encounter was supposedly in January 2007 at a launch event for Trump vodka. It was there that he introduced her to Karen Mc-Dougal, a *Playboy* "Playmate" with whom Donald Trump was allegedly having an affair at that time. (Trump has denied the claim.) The porn-stress says they saw each other again a few months later, at which time Daniels shot down a sexual advance from Trump.

Trump hadn't booked her on *The Apprentice*, and he never did.

"WHAT KIND OF A LAWYER WOULD TAPE A CLIENT?"

Nothing of note happened on this score for five years, when, in 2011, Daniels shared her claim with the *In Touch* gossip magazine. Trump fixer and attorney Michael Cohen said that they would take legal action if the full story was printed. It was shelved and did not see the light of day until 2018.

When Trump began his presidential run in 2015, it soon became clear that lots of stories attacking Trump's character would be sold to the highest media bidders. In August of that year, Trump solicited David Pecker, then CEO of *National Enquirer* publisher American Media Inc., also known as AMI, to act as his "eyes and ears." Pecker would tip Cohen off to any allegations against Trump so that one of them could purchase the story (thus quashing it) before it hit the public, a practice known as "catch and kill."

Stories like this came up from time to time. For example, a former Trump Tower doorman, Dino Sajudin, tried to sell a story that Trump had fathered a bastard child with an employee. The *National Enquirer* bought it for a measly $30,000 and later said that they did not believe it to be true. The importance of this incident is hard to understate, as it establishes the precedent that Trump and Pecker were willing to pay to kill false stories. Just because money changed hands, that does not make the story in question true.

Playboy model Karen McDougal's allegation of an affair with Trump had been purchased by AMI. AMI said that they had actually bought two years' worth of fitness columns from the 1998 Playmate of the Year as well as exclusive life rights to the story of the alleged affair. "AMI has not paid people to kill damaging stories about Mr. Trump," AMI told the *Wall Street Journal* in a statement. Trump has maintained that stories of the affair are fabrications.[9]

On October 7, 2016, the 2005 *Access Hollywood* tape came out, and Stormy saw the opportunity to make her move. The next day, a representative for Daniels told the *National Enquirer* she wanted to tell her story of sex with Trump. A few days later, Cohen had negotiated a $130,000 deal to acquire her story, effectively silencing her.

Cohen wired payment via a shell corporation, Essential Consultants LLC. According to her lawyer, Daniels signed a confidential settlement and nondisclosure agreement using the pseudonym Peggy Peterson; Trump went by David Dennison on the NDA.

The deal was signed; Trump evaded scandal. And two weeks later, he won the election.

In early 2017, Cohen sought reimbursement from the Trump Organization for his $130,000 payment to Daniels plus assorted other fees and bonuses.

In January 2018, Daniels denied having a sexual and/or romantic affair with Trump on two occasions (though she would later say it was under legal duress). Trump maintained he wasn't even aware of the payment to her. Cohen even told the *New York Times* that he had paid the porn star out of his own pocket.[10] Thus far, there are no signs of potential lawfare anywhere.

Things intensified on April 9, 2018, when federal agents raided Cohen's office and seized records including the payment to Stormy. Cohen's lawyer said that the U.S. attorney's office in New York obtained protected attorney–client communications.

"I just heard that they broke into the office of one of my personal attorneys," Trump said at the time, declaring it "a disgraceful situation" and "a total witch hunt."[11] The investigators seized financial records and other documents hoping to find campaign finance violations, bank fraud, or other crimes that Cohen and/or Trump had committed.

By this point, Trump was certainly accustomed to witch hunts. He was neck-deep in the Russian-collusion hoax. But a major new lawfare front was about to open up.

This is where personal lawfare involving Trump and Stormy Daniels and the federal investigation into Russian collusion would collide. Cohen was a key subject of the Russia-gate investigation. He had been monitored by federal investigators looking to prove he coordinated with Moscow to rig the election.[12]

Here is the big lawfare moment: The FBI first got a warrant to surveil Cohen's Gmail account via the Justice Department and Special Counsel Robert Mueller's investigation. Mueller's office was also investigating Cohen for possibly acting as an unregistered foreign agent. Around three weeks later, the U.S. attorney's office for the Southern District of New York got warrants to access Cohen's emails as well.

The extent of the coordination is not known, but it seems as though the basis for the Stormy Daniels lawsuit was the Russian-collusion probe, which never should have existed.

That's not very fair!

Cohen was also probed over more than $20 million in loans to taxi companies he and his family owned; he was facing charges for bank fraud.

Things were not going well for Cohen, which made things much worse for Donald Trump. Trump and Cohen were having a dramatic falling-out that was unfolding on the front pages.

Cohen quickly pleaded guilty to campaign-finance violations, among other charges, likely to take some of the heat off. He claimed Trump had directed him to pay out hush money to Daniels and McDougal. The media portrayed it as Cohen implicating Trump in a crime, but it is not at all clear what law Trump had supposedly broken. Cohen made statements that intentionally made it seem as though Trump was complicit in a crime, telling a federal judge that he made the payment "in coordination and at the direction of a candidate for federal office," and "under direction of the same candidate," but it was far from clear whether any of this was criminal.[13]

Cohen pleaded guilty to eight counts, including tax evasion, and was sentenced to three years in prison.

The long arm of the law wasn't done with Cohen yet. Deputy U.S. Attorney Robert Khuzami said that Cohen failed to report more than $4 million in income between 2012 and 2016 and lied to a financial institution in order to obtain a $500,000 home equity line of credit. Cohen allegedly used that credit line to fund the Daniels payment.

It also came out that Cohen had taped conversations with Trump discussing the payments in 2016 and had handed them over to investigators. "What kind of a lawyer would tape a client? So sad! Is this a first, never heard of it before?" Trump tweeted.[14]

"If those payments were a crime for Michael Cohen, then why wouldn't they be a crime for Donald Trump?" Cohen's lawyer, Lanny Davis, tweeted.

A narrative was forming.

Trump was the sitting president at the time, so he could not be indicted while in office, but he could be charged after he left office. It was only a matter of time.

Meanwhile, the porn actress was milking the moment. She hired Michael Avenatti as her attorney. The flamboyant lawyer instantly became a fixture on CNN because of his candid attacks on President Trump. At one point, he announced he was considering running for president himself against Trump, telling CNN, "I have three things the president lacks: brains, heart, and courage."

He was immediately taken seriously by lawfare architect Laurence Tribe, who tweeted a resounding endorsement of Avenatti's rapid rise: "Avenatti's contribution to the political dialogue deserves a hearing. He's smart, clear & committed to facts and evidence. A powerful fighter, he seems to be a good listener, knows how to use the media, knows what he doesn't know, & seems practical as well as progressive."[15]

Avenatti also represented Julie Swetnick, who leveled wild and baseless accusations against Brett Kavanaugh during his tumultuous Supreme Court confirmation, as detailed in *Breaking the News*.

Avenatti's star burned hot for a brief moment, but he would soon get his comeuppance.

NOTHING TO BRAGG ABOUT

Alvin Bragg, a Democrat, was elected Manhattan district attorney in November 2021, succeeding Cyrus "Cy" Vance Jr. Vance was no fan of Trump, but nothing could have prepared us for what we were about to witness with the new DA, Bragg. As the *New York Times Magazine* put it, Bragg is "a man of unmistakable ambition who has hitched his aspirations to the pursuit of Donald J. Trump."

Alarming.

Bragg was featured earlier in this book because he took a strong stance against charging New York's worst criminals. He has supported the typical left-wing criminal-justice-reform stances like keeping offenders on the street instead of in prison. He had other priorities.

Namely, Donald Trump.

Bragg also was backed by George Soros, who supported his candidacy with a seven-figure donation to the Color of Change PAC, which supported Bragg.[16] This cash may have been the difference in Bragg winning his primary. Not that Democrats care about such things, but it is contra the spirit of democracy when one wealthy donor buys an election, and the winner of said election immediately charges the donor's primary political opponent with crimes.

With Soros's money, Bragg won the race on the promise of prosecuting Trump and touting his past lawsuits against the now-former president. "It is a fact that I have sued Trump over 100 times," Bragg told the *New York Times* while on the campaign trail in April 2021. The "100 times" figure is exagerated, but that didn't stop him from making the same claim "everywhere," including to CNN and the BBC. (Bragg sued Trump about thirty times and joined around a dozen other suits that he did not lead.[17])

The *New York Times Magazine* glorified Bragg, who has two degrees from Harvard, as the "nerdy prosecutor" who would become the first to try Trump. Actually, he was the first to criminally charge a former president. The lede sentence of the piece gave away the whole lawfare game: "Alvin Bragg, the Manhattan D.A., campaigned as the best candidate to go after the former president. Now he finds himself leading Trump's first prosecution."

The *Times* and Bragg confessed that the goal was to find a crime, any crime, and convict Trump of it. It appeared as though they considered Trump's mere existence a criminal act and were determined to find charges they might press. Even the dependably anti-Trump Gray Lady saw Bragg's inherent bias, noting that he broke lawyerly protocol by publicly fantasizing about taking down Trump.

"The case is not—the core of it's not—money for sex," Bragg said in a radio interview. "We would say it's about conspiring to corrupt a presidential election and then lying in New York business records to cover it up."

Yet Bragg was initially reluctant to prosecute Trump. The case would inevitably rely on testimony from Michael Cohen, who had been convicted of perjury and fraud and would rely on untested legal theories. For these reasons, Cyrus Vance struggled to find a legal strategy to charge Trump. It had been revived and dropped so many times that prosecutors allegedly began to refer to it the "zombie case."[18] Even some Trump critics acknowledged the case had significant weaknesses.[19]

Yet political pressure was mounting for Bragg to prosecute. Though Bragg struck an "apolitical tone," according to *Politico*, throughout the prosecution, Trump came to believe that the D.A. was swayed into prosecuting him because of that pressure.

Mark Pomerantz, for example, who had led the criminal division in the U.S. attorney's office in Manhattan, had left his partnership at the white-shoe law firm Paul Weiss specifically to pursue Trump. He insisted the case was not only solid, but easy to explain to a jury. Bragg moved slowly, frustrating Pomerantz to the point where he resigned in dramatic fashion, calling Bragg's reluctance to quickly bring charges "a grave failure of justice." His resignation letter became public in March 2022,[20] shaming Bragg. Pomerantz, who wanted Trump prosecuted for a variety of other alleged crimes as well, would go on to write a book called *People vs. Donald Trump*, which included scathing attacks on Bragg.[21]

Bragg's strategy began to take shape that summer, focusing on the payment to Daniels. A conviction for falsifying documents would be misdemeanors, but Bragg bumped it up to felonies by arguing that Trump did so to further another crime. How could he do that? Bragg would frame Trump's payments to Stormy Daniels as a campaign finance violation.

Bragg impaneled a new grand jury in January 2023. An indictment came down on March 30 against Trump "for falsifying New York business records in order to conceal damaging information and unlawful activity from American voters before and after the 2016 election." There were thirty-four counts in all. Mainstream legal scholars immediately voiced skepticism of Bragg's maneuver.

Liberal Harvard Law School Professor Emeritus Alan Dershowitz,

and Edwards had a much weaker case than Trump. Edwards's case was federal, he actually acknowledged the affair, and the statute of limitations was still intact.

Still, Edwards got off.

But for all the similarities between the two cases, there were two important differences, and they were the only ones that mattered: Only one case was brought in New York and involved Donald J. Trump.

That's why Dershowitz said the conviction of Trump was all but a guarantee: "As Chief Judge [of the New York Court of Appeal Sol] Wachtler once said, 'You can get a grand jury to indict a ham sandwich.' In New York, you can get them to convict a ham sandwich; a petit jury if the ham sandwich's name is Trump. So [Bragg] may have an easy job getting an indictment and even getting a conviction."

Bragg had been elected to bag Trump. Now public pressure demanded that he do so by any means necessary.

The man who had made a career downgrading felonies to misdemeanors was now trying to supercharge a misdemeanor into a felony to bring down a former president and current presidential candidate. And the truth of the matter is that in New York City, he needed only the thinnest of pretenses to win a case against the Bad Orange Man.

A politically motivated DA, jury pool, and media could overwhelm the truth.

That is the definition of lawfare.

Trump was arraigned on April 4, 2023. He pleaded not guilty.

STORMY WEATHER

On the same day Trump was arraigned in New York, he won a legal victory against Daniels in the U.S. Court of Appeals, Ninth Circuit, ordering her to cover legal fees incurred by Trump during a failed defamation lawsuit she brought against him in 2018 for accusing her of a "con job." Trump obtained over $600,000 in the litigation.

Trump was understandably pleased.

"The lawsuit was a purely political stunt that never should have been started, or allowed to happen, and I am pleased that my lawyers were able to bring it to a successful conclusion after the court fully rejected her appeal," he said in a statement. "Now all I have to do is wait for all of the money she owes me."[24]

During the years this was playing out, Avenatti fell out of favor with Daniels, the media, and the legal establishment.

He was arrested under suspicions of domestic violence in November 2018, though he was never charged.

In 2019, he was indicted in California and New York for extortion, tax evasion, fraud, and embezzlement. He was indicted for embezzling money from a client and defrauding a Mississippi bank. He was alleged to have not filed tax returns for years. He was charged for embezzling funds from an NBA client to buy a private jet. The U.S. attorney for the Central District of California charged him with dozens of financial crimes, suggesting that Avenatti had stolen millions from clients to further other crimes.

Avenatti also admitted that he "corruptly obstructed and impeded the IRS's efforts to collect unpaid payroll taxes." The federal government estimated at the time that he owed about $5 million.[25]

He was charged with wire fraud and aggravated identity theft in a case brought by Stormy Daniels herself. He was convicted and sentenced to four years in prison for defrauding her of nearly $300,000 in book advance money.

His ability to practice law has been suspended as of May 2020 due to his criminal conduct. That same year, he was convicted of extorting Nike during an overly aggressive settlement negotiation and sentenced to thirty months in prison. In December 2022 he was sentenced to another fourteen.[26]

Considering that he was for a brief moment in time a potential president and was given the key to the city of West Hollywood in 2018, it was a precipitous fall from grace.

But his role in the Stormy Daniels saga is not done yet.

MERCHAN THE MENACE

Trump's trial began on April 15, 2024, in Manhattan with Judge Juan Merchan presiding. Merchan, an immigrant who was born in Bogotá, Colombia, was tasked with being a neutral arbiter who ensured "equal justice under the law" for the former president. He was out of central casting for the job: He is handsome, bespectacled, well tailored, and has connections to Democrat power structures. He is a small-dollar Joe Biden donor.

This last detail alone is grounds for an ethics investigation. Under Section 100.5 of the New York Code of Judicial Conduct, sitting judges cannot "directly or indirectly engage in any political activity." Prohibited political activity includes "soliciting funds for, paying an assessment to, or making a contribution to a political organization or candidate." The New York State Advisory Committee on Judicial Ethics is unequivocal: "A sitting judge may not make political contributions at any time, even to a U.S. presidential candidate."

He literally gave to a group called "Stop Republicans." It wasn't much money, ten dollars, but that's ten too much according to the law.[27]

Merchan had also urged the Trump Organization's former chief financial officer Allen Weisselberg to cooperate against Trump in another fraud and tax evasion case. Trump lawyers repeatedly claimed that the case was politically motivated. He ultimately fined Trump's businesses $1.6 million plus taxes and penalties (the maximum allowed under New York State law) and sentenced Weisselberg to five months in prison; he would serve about one hundred days.[28]

Merchan's daughter, Loren Merchan, is an activist Democrat with ties to the prosecution. She is president of a Chicago-based leftist consulting firm, Authentic Campaigns, which counts the Senate Majority PAC, a major fundraiser for Democrats, and then-Congressman Adam Schiff as clients. Schiff was the lead manager prosecuting Trump in his first impeachment trial and would go on to become a senator from California.[29]

The *New York Post* reported in March 2024 that Loren Merchan's consultancy had raised at least $93 million in campaign donations for the election cycle. That number no doubt ballooned from there.[30]

Authentic Campaigns bagged a staggering $36,414,889 during the 2024 election cycle, according to Open Secrets.[31] This would make Loren Merchan one of the Democrats' biggest fundraisers. For her father to preside over a trial where Trump is the defendant in an election is, as Trump put it to me, "the greatest conflict of interest of all time."

She was also tied to Dan Goldman, another impeachment attorney who prepared Michael Cohen to testify against Trump.[32] Goldman had paid Merchan's daughter's firm over $407,562, according to disbursement filings.[33]

She had previously worked for Vice President Kamala Harris's failed 2020 presidential campaign as "Director of Digital Persuasion" for "Kamala Harris for the People."

While actions of adult children aren't necessarily disqualifying for a judge, given the nature of this particular case, that is, that it involves the standard-bearer of the other major political party, would it have been so much to ask to ensure that the judge's immediate family didn't have a vested interest in seeing the defendant go down in flames?

Merchan should never have been involved in this case, and his partisanship became apparent almost instantly. Trump's team asked for a recusal (naturally), and didn't get one (naturally).

He gagged Trump, ordering him to not make public comments about witnesses, Manhattan District Attorney Alvin Bragg, connected family members (did he have his Democrat consultant daughter in mind?), and others. He threatened Trump with fines or up to thirty days in jail.

I asked President Trump in March 2025 if the gag order remained in place. "Nobody knows," he said. "The case is over and nobody knows if it still applies. He never took it off. You know why? Because he knows how crooked it was."

Trump was forced to sit in what he described as a "very freezing-cold courtroom" for weeks instead of campaigning. Now his First Amendment rights had been truncated by a partisan team of witch hunters while his political schedule was curtailed.[34]

It was only a matter of time before Trump violated the order. It appeared as though he was already preparing himself to go to jail. "If this Partisan Hack wants to put me in the 'clink' for speaking the open and obvious TRUTH, I will gladly become a Modern Day Nelson Mandela— It will be my GREAT HONOR," he posted to Truth Social shortly after the trial was underway.[35]

He quickly violated it ten times and was assessed fines of $1,000 for each violation[36] but avoided jail.

"I should be out campaigning now instead of sitting in a very cold courthouse all day long," Trump told reporters outside the courtroom. "This is a Biden prosecution. It's election interference at a level that nobody in this country has ever seen before." "This all comes from in the White House," he said.[37]

He was 100 percent correct. If Joe Biden had suggested this was an unfair targeted prosecution at any point, the charges certainly would have been dropped and America could have resumed our tradition of free and fair elections. But it was not to be. Bragg, Merchan, and Biden were going to see this through to the bitter end, which they no doubt believed saw Trump in an orange jumpsuit.

Meanwhile, what was happening inside the courtroom was getting out of control. Merchan allowed the porn star and professional provocateur Stormy Daniels to take the stand, and her testimony was exactly what you would have expected. It got off to an embarrassing start when prosecutors stated that her testimony would not "involve any details of genitalia."

That's quite the standard for a "business records case" that could shift the entire balance of power in the country.[38]

Daniels's testimony was panned, even by anti-Trump legal analysts. She shared graphic details of the alleged encounters that left jurors cringing. She reportedly made jokes that fell flat.

Even Judge Merchan showed a little buyer's remorse after he allowed the stripper the biggest stage of her life, telling the prosecution that she was giving "unnecessary" details.

Judge, she's a porn star! What did you expect?!

"I agree that it would have been better if some of these things had been left unsaid," Merchan said.

No kidding.

Stormy's credibility was further damaged (don't laugh) when she elected to portray herself as a #MeToo victim. She delivered lines like "He was bigger and blocking the way," "my hands were shaking so hard," and "I felt ashamed that I didn't stop it and that I didn't say 'No.'" She also claimed she "blacked out" during the encounter.

This approach was directly contradictory to her past statements. She had been clear that this was "not a Me Too case" and "I wasn't assaulted. I wasn't attacked, or raped, or coerced or blackmailed."[39]

Now that she had the media spotlight, she was singing a different tune.

Her attitude toward the encounter with Trump seemed incongruous with a person who has sex on camera for a living.

CNN chief legal analyst Paula Reid said the defense's cross-examination of Daniels was "devastating for Stormy Daniels' credibility." This was not simply because of the graphic attention-seeking storytelling, it was because the Trump team was able to draw out of her that she hates Trump and wants him in jail.[40] She had previously written that "I won't walk, I'll dance down the street when he is 'selected' to go to jail,"[41] yet seeing her cop to a personal animosity against Trump was, in Reid's words, "eviscerating."

Yet the money shot for the defense was when Daniels finally admitted her motivations for all this effort: "I had a chance to get the story out and make some money, yes."

In other words, she was an X-rated part of the anti-Trump lawfare superstructure, and she tried to get rich off of helping it destroy him.

(She also acknowledged that she owed Trump more than $600,000 from failed civil cases against him, which she had elected not to pay.[42])

Trump attorney Todd Blanche argued that her "testimony was overly prejudicial, and that the government was asking questions 'to inflame this jury.'"

It was another reminder that the prosecution had built their case on the testimony of a porn star and Michael Cohen, a turncoat with suspect moral character, who had claimed for months that Trump did not know about payments to Stormy Daniels—until he suddenly began alleging the exact opposite.

Yet given the nature of Juan Merchan's Manhattan courtroom, Trump's team would have to make an overwhelming case to eke out a victory.

CHOOSE YOUR OWN CRIME

Almost all the facts of this case and the characters involved were absurd—yet somehow the prosecutorial approach was even more ridiculous. Bragg needed to get creative, and Merchan would have to go along with it if they were going to get a conviction. Recall that Bragg needed to prove that Trump had committed the business-records crime while knowingly committing a second crime. Trump's team raised the Sixth Amendment in objection:

In all criminal prosecutions, the accused shall enjoy the right to a speedy and public trial, by an impartial jury of the state and district wherein the crime shall have been committed, which district shall have been previously ascertained by law, and to be informed of the nature and cause of the accusation; to be confronted with the witnesses against him; to have compulsory process for obtaining witnesses in his favor, and to have the assistance of counsel for his defense.

Jury impartiality was always going to be in question in a New York courtroom. But arguably the bigger constitutional issue was whether Trump was "informed of the nature and cause of the accusation" against him. The other crime or crimes elevating the case to a felony was not specified in the indictment. Trump's team was not given adequate notice of the nature of the secondary crime. In fact, the Trump team would not learn what Trump was accused of until jury instructions were doled out at the end of the trial. This is clearly a violation of the Constitution. And we can all see why. It's totally unreasonable for the defense to make a case that their client didn't commit a crime before they know what that crime actually is.

Trump's attorneys raised this with Merchan, but he didn't act. This egregious infringement on Trump's civil rights didn't concern the judge.

The second crime finally came to light during the jury instructions. According to the court, Donald Trump attempted to influence an election by "unlawful means." What were the unlawful means? Well, nobody ever specified. Instead of solving the unnamed crime issue, this only made it worse. The charge introduced a third (!) mystery crime piggybacking off the second one.

If this is sounding ridiculous, just wait until you hear that the third crime was not specified, ever!

Merchan told the jury that the third crime could be multiple choice. It was a choose-your-own-adventure trial. He informed the jury that if they agreed that Trump falsified business records to influence an election, they no longer had to agree unanimously.

At a constitutional level, the jury verdict needed to be unanimous. But in Merchan's courtroom, it did not need to be unanimous on the third crime. The jury merely needed to agree that there was a third crime, any crime.

The reason this approach seems unfamiliar is that as far as my research goes, it has never been tried before. No judge in history has ever given such a jury instruction.

Clearly this was a move to box in jurors who might not hate Trump as much as Bragg and Merchan themselves. They just had to believe he was guilty of any crime ever, and they had the green light to convict.

In addition to Trump's being denied his Sixth Amendment rights to being informed of the nature and cause of the accusation, Merchan was now denying Trump due process rights afforded to him by the Fifth Amendment.

So what was the menu of third crimes? There seemed to be three categories from which the jurors could choose: 1) a Federal Election Campaign Act (FECA) violation, 2) falsification of other business records, or 3) violation of tax laws.

Merchan did not explain to the jury what constitutes a FECA violation, so the Trump team wanted to bring law professor and former member of the Federal Election Commission Bradley A. Smith to explain it to the jury. He's one of a few people in the country who certainly know this area of law well. Smith would have made the point that NDAs are not campaign expenditures and do not need to be reported, which would have been devastating to the prosecution. It would have wiped out the FECA violation and tax law violation arguments.

He could have prevented any jury confusion on the matter, but Merchan blocked his testimony. The most likely explanation for this decision: the judge was determined to get Trump.

THE SUPREMACY CLAUSE

The defense had another powerful angle: the Supremacy Clause of the U.S. Constitution, which establishes that federal law takes precedence over state law. Congress creates federal law and designates what federal agency is responsible for enforcing it. When it comes to FECA, the FEC enforces civil violations and the DOJ prosecutes criminal violations. As previously noted, the FEC does not consider these NDA payments FECA violations, and even Biden's DOJ chose not to prosecute this case against Trump despite years of opportunity to do so.

The federal government does not consider NDAs as campaign expenditures, so it was not necessary for Trump to report it that way. Yet Bragg made the case that calling these business records a legal expenditure instead of a campaign expenditure was falsifying business records and thus committing a federal crime.

It other words, he claimed it was against federal law to not list the payout to the porn star as a campaign expense, even though the federal government has a different interpretation of the same federal statute. Thus Bragg employed a legal dirty trick that he could have attempted only in the courtroom of a partisan judge such as Merchan. He asserted an interpretation of federal law that is different from the federal government's own interpretation of it. He's the Manhattan DA, yet he's claiming authority on a matter that is clearly in the federal sphere.

From what I've been able to surmise while researching this book, this was literally unprecedented. A state official can't overrule federal officials. Constitutionally, Bragg and Merchan's position appeared to be untenable.

Yet that's the stance they took.

Their whole cases hinged on NDAs being FECA violations. They had to have known that is not so, yet they proceeded anyway and made sure the jury was unaware of this fact.

How they got away with this ought to be investigated.

In summary, the only way to get a felony conviction from the initial business records crime was if it was committed in concealment of another crime he had already committed. Each crime would need to be proven beyond a reasonable doubt for a criminal conviction. Yet the indictment did not specify the additional crime that had been committed, much less the specific elements of the crime.

Eventually we learned the second crime was a New York elections law violation that itself was a two-step crime, meaning that he was trying to interfere in an election by way of another crime, which was unspecified.

Merchan unilaterally deemed that the jury did not need to be unanimous about the third crime that Trump had supposedly committed while violating New York election laws.

We do know that the jury did not need to be unanimous on that third crime, which means it was essentially a grab bag, and to this day we don't know what exactly the jury chose or if they were all in agreement.

Trump was never made aware of the second crime he had committed until jury instructions and even to this day he cannot be entirely sure of the nature of the supposed third crime they say he committed because the jury was given the aforementioned multiple-choice menu. How can you mount a defense when you don't know the crimes of which you're being accused? This is fundamentally unfair.

Nonetheless, the Manhattan jury found him guilty of thirty-four felonies because he spread the payments out over about a year, each of which generated multiple business records, and each record was another felony. It is not clear that the jury was unanimous on any one charge for a guilty verdict for the third supposed crime.

The truth of the matter is, as Dershowitz predicted, the trial was decided when the judge and jury had been selected.

The former commander in chief had become a convicted felon.

We don't know how many votes the stain of the bogus trial cost the former president in his third presidential election. Maybe it was millions, but maybe it was none. As the trial wore on, Americans began to take it less seriously. "After all the testimony in Trump's hush money case, the effect on the public has been zero. Voters simply just don't care that much," CNN's Harry Enten posted the night before the verdict was rendered. "They are far more tuned into news about inflation, immigration, etc. than Trump's trials."[43]

A plurality of Americans had thought for weeks that Trump would get convicted of something, yet his lead over then-candidate Joe Biden was holding in the polls.[44] The word had gotten out that this was just the latest chapter in the longest witch hunt in American history.

Meanwhile, the media and the left debased themselves in national media. Speaking of Judge Merchan, former Assistant U.S. Attorney Andrew Weissmann said, "I have a man crush on him."[45] Cohen drooled over the judge to MSNBC's Rachel Maddow: "Judge Juan Merchan, who is an absolute gentleman, to see him on that stand is to see poetry. It's to see a masterful judge who was quick with decision-making. He was absolutely judicial perfection," he said on television right after the verdict came down.[46]

Pathetic.

Meanwhile, Trump was riding his victim status to the bank. His campaign raised nearly $53 million in the twenty-four hours after the conviction.[47]

The sentencing would get delayed until after the election, which Trump would go on to win. Merchan set it for January 10, 2025, but indicated Trump would not get sentenced to prison.

This raised yet another issue regarding the Constitution's Supremacy Clause and presidential immunity.

It is well known that the president is immune during the months he's in office, but whether a president-elect is covered here is a gray area of the law. If Trump is not immune, then he will have to appeal his conviction, presumably during his presidency. That means that he will have that distraction looming over him as he takes on the most important job on earth: President of the United States of America.

Logically, all criminal proceedings ought to end at the latest January 20, the day the new president is sworn in. Any appeals process that pushes beyond that should simply be dismissed. Merchan took the approach that so long as he enters final judgment before that date, then it's out of his hands and it's now solely Donald Trump's concern whether he chooses to appeal or not. Thus Trump was given the option of living with a felony conviction, perhaps for the rest of history, or taking on the burden of an appeal.

All of this is, again, unprecedented.

The Constitution is clear here: All legal burdens that a president must face ought to be removed before he takes office.

The only way to remove the burden is to dismiss the case. That's what Merchan should have done. But he was never going to see it that way. After all, he wanted Trump to lose. In the courtroom, at the ballot box, everywhere. He allowed for the Stormy Daniels X-rated testimony while blocking the FECA expert selected by the Trump defense team. He allowed for the secondary crime to remain a mystery until the very end of the trial. He allowed the jury to convict without unanimity on the secondary (or was it the tertiary?) crime.

He made a mockery of our judicial system to execute the left's political goals.

Politics aside, this is not what is in the best interest of our nation, nor is it what the American people want, as evidenced by the fact that Trump won the popular vote in the November 2024 election while all this was playing out. The court of public opinion weighed in on behalf of Trump.

As my colleague Joel Pollak put it at *Breitbart News*, "The craziest thing about Donald Trump's trial in Manhattan is that it happened at all."[48]

This was clearly a case of the ruling party, led by Joe Biden, trying to imprison their political opponent on Trumped-up charges.

A few private partisans had conferred upon themselves power they did not have in order to try to stop the man the people wanted as their president.

It's that bad. And they weren't even subtle about it.

The lowest point of the entire trial had to have been on the morning of Tuesday, May 27. That day, the Biden-Harris campaign held a press conference with "special guests" outside the Manhattan Criminal Courthouse, where Trump's trial was taking place. At the event, actor Robert De Niro was revealed as one of the special guests. The Oscar winner and Biden surrogate showed up outside Judge Merchan's courtroom to reveal what this case was truly about: destroying Trump.

"If [Trump] gets in, I can tell you right now, he will never leave! He will never leave! You know that. He will never leave," De Niro said, claiming that Trump would be "dictator for life."

He added that Trump is "a danger" to our lives. "This is not a threat," the actor said, threateningly, before calling Trump supporters clowns.

Next he yelled at Trump supporters, unironically, that Democrats are "trying to be gentlemen in this world," before repeatedly saying "fuck you" to angered Trump supporters. (To be fair, he was getting heckled pretty hard by the crowd.)

Though Biden himself had stayed quiet about the trial to this point, this gave away the game to anyone who was not yet convinced that this case was lawfare, straight up.

It worked, short term. The Democrats got their chance to brand Trump a "convicted felon," and the media dutifully repeated that phraseology on a loop through the election and beyond. But we'll never know for certain if Stormy, Cohen, Bragg, De Niro, Biden, and Merchan pushed the electorate away from Trump, or closer to him.

In retrospect, the lawfare superstructure won the battle, but Trump won the war.

There's a word for that: justice.

THE CONVICTED FELON PRESIDENT

Judge Merchan set sentencing for President Trump during the transition of power from Biden to Trump, on January 10, 2025. The establishment media acted shocked—the Associated Press called it "an extraordinary turn"—but it was, like much of this case, entirely predictable. Merchan wanted to make sure he could brand Trump with the "convicted felon" tag before he became president, when it would be impossible (or at least overly complicated) to take the case any further.

Trump's lawyers tried their best to block the sentencing, filing an emergency petition to the Supreme Court to try to delay it, citing that the president had constitutional responsibilities and an inevitable appeal process would weigh down on him after he assumed office. "This court should enter an immediate stay of further proceedings in the New York trial court to prevent grave injustice and harm to the institution of the presidency and the operations of the federal government," Trump's attorneys argued. Trump's team put forward the view that they were entitled to an appeal to a higher court before the jury verdict was made official due to presidential immunity.

They elaborated in the petition that they are confident the appeal will eventually result in a dismissal anyway due to the violation of due process and the nature of what was clearly a politically motivated prosecution. They also raised presidential immunity, which states that the president cannot be prosecuted for official acts. (The payments to Daniels were made while President Trump held office, which sparked a debate over the extent to which presidential immunity applies and what constitutes an official act.)

In other words, the Supreme Court was put to a decision: Either they would regard Trump's case as exceptional enough that they would relieve him from the onerous and time-consuming appeals process while he leads the country, or they would allow for the process to proceed as if Trump were a normal citizen.

Unfortunately for Trump and the MAGA faithful, Merchan had accurately predicted the Supreme Court's response. They sided with him, allowing him to officially approve the jury verdict and proceed with sentencing. Justice Amy Coney Barrett, who had been appointed by Trump, and Chief Justice John Roberts joined the three liberals on the court

(Ketanji Brown Jackson, Sonia Sotomayor, and Elena Kagan), siding with the lawfare-istas.

In New York State law, a judge has discretion to dismiss a prosecution in the interest of justice or the public benefit. Merchan had a chance to do that, and in doing so he would have defended the presidency as an institution. Instead, he did the opposite. He sentenced Trump to an unconditional discharge, meaning he would serve no prison time or incur any other penalties, but he would bear the "convicted felon" scarlet label so long as the conviction was not overturned upon appeal.

That was what this was all about from the start: a political talking point for Democrats to tarnish their political foe while they wasted his precious time.

Merchan signed off the hearing with an epic troll: "Sir, I wish you god speed as you assume your second term in office," he said to the past and future president, knowing full well he signed Trump on for years of additional nuisances.

President Trump probably will pursue appeals. And he still has three chances to achieve total victory: first at the New York State Appellate Division (in their intermediate court), then the Court of Appeals (the state's highest), and eventually the case would head to the United States Supreme Court. I'm optimistic that it will get overturned somewhere along the way. Still, the left will get to attack Trump over this conviction as if it were legitimate until it does.

The good news is that while Trump did not win over Merchan's jury, he did win over the American people, and there is no additional harm that Stormy Daniels, Juan Merchan, or Alvin Bragg can do to him for now. But if he wants to clear his name—and he certainly does—it will take years of effort. And as in many lawfare cases, the process itself is the punishment.

You have Alvin Bragg, Juan Merchan, and now Amy Coney Barrett to thank for that.

On January 29, 2025, Trump's lawyers filed a notice of appeal to overturn this conviction, arguing the law was applied for a "political witch hunt."

The appeal process is ongoing as of spring 2025.

THE COLANGELO CONUNDRUM

There is a hidden villain at the center of the lawfare spiderweb named Matthew Colangelo. Colangelo was the prosecutor who headed up Bragg's case against former President Trump. At one time he was a political consultant for the Democrat National Committee and a donor to Barack Obama. What's most interesting about Colangelo is he was ridiculously overqualified for this job, which should have raised numerous red flags.

Colangelo has a pristine resume. He went to Harvard Law School, served in the New York State Attorney General's Office, was a lecturer at Georgetown University Law Center, and earned social justice bona fides as director of the Economic Justice Group at the NAACP Legal Defense & Educational Fund. He worked at Obama's Department of Justice and, when President Biden was in power, rose all the way to principal deputy associate attorney general, the third-ranking official at the Department of Justice. Historically this position has been a springboard for ambitious lawyers, people like Supreme Court Justice Neil Gorsuch, FBI Director Christopher Wray, and U.S. Attorney General Merrick Garland. This is a plum job and requires extraordinary credentials to even be considered. With that on your resume, the world is your oyster. You can ascend to some of the most powerful positions in our government, or you can head to the private sector and make seven figures in private practice.

But not Matthew Colangelo.

He left Biden's DOJ and joined Alvin Bragg's office in December 2022. He went from number three at a prestigious government agency that has well over 100,000 employees to the job of a county prosecutor, a job that lawyers take straight out of law school—if they can't get a better post.

"It's the rough equivalent of like a four-star general in the army, quitting his job and enlisting in the National Guard as a private," said Will Scharf, one of Trump's attorneys.

To state the obvious, this is highly suspicious.

It's especially fishy when you look at the timeline of events. On November 8, 2022, the Democrats lost their majority in the House of Representatives. That meant the beginning of the end for their January 6th committee, which the Republicans would certainly shut down once they assumed power.

Donald Trump had made his intention to run for reelection clear, and the Democrats were about to lose their main vehicle for investigating him. On November 9, Joe Biden held a press conference and said, "We just have to demonstrate that he will not take power, if he does run, making sure he, under legitimate efforts of our Constitution, does not become the next president again."

As usual, Biden's diction was poor, but his message was clear: Stop Trump by any means necessary.

Just a few weeks later, Colangelo, who was known for taking on Trump and his family business at various times throughout his career, would leave the highest echelons of Biden's DOJ and arrive in Manhattan. As soon as he got there, the Trump investigation was renewed with tremendous vigor. Remember, Bragg's office was initially reluctant to pursue a case against Trump. But once Colangelo got to town, it was game on.

A few short months later, Colangelo went on to become the lead prosecutor and the difference-maker in the Trump trial. He was the star lawyer who delivered the victory.

The Stormy Daniels case was arguably the weakest case against Trump among any that I discuss in this book, yet it is the only one that hit its mark by landing the felony conviction; thirty-four felony convictions, to be precise.

Colangelo was a ringer from the Democrat elite and the Biden federal lawfare superstructure who descended on Manhattan to help Bragg bag Trump.

To this day, Biden has maintained that there was no coordination across the multiple prosecutions and the federal government. Given Colangelo's presence in Manhattan, this strains credulity and ought to be investigated. If there was no collusion, then that would mean there was a wild set of coincidences that occurred at exactly the same time.

On November 18, right around when Colangelo would have put in his two weeks' notice to the DOJ, Nathan Wade, prosecutor for and boyfriend of Fulton County District Attorney Fani Willis, was at the White House meeting with counsel for eight hours. Also on that day, Attorney General Merrick Garland's DOJ announced the appointment of Jack Smith as special counsel to investigate President Trump.

The lawfare war was about to expand on new, dramatic fronts.

CHAPTER 3

THE WOMAN CASE

D onald Trump doesn't refer to E. Jean Carroll by her name. He prefers "the woman" or "woman." He refers to the case as "the woman case." I've interviewed him multiple times about the case, and I never heard him use her name. I never asked him why he does that, because I know what he's thinking. She's not worthy of acknowledgment. And she's not so much the instigator of the case as she is a pawn of the lawfare superstructure.

The E. Jean Carroll civil case may be the purest example of lawfare against President Trump that I document in this book. Ultimately, the immediate stakes were the lowest of the major cases I profile herein, but this was full-blown legal harassment concocted by a political operative and rooted in virtually nothing.

The goal was to affix the "rapist" label to Trump's brand, despite the fact that he was a New York playboy for most of his life and had never been characterized as such.

Though women have accused Trump of inappropriate behavior in the past, no one had yet used the "r-word" against him—even after decades in the public eye.

Naturally one would hope that would mean the burden of proof against him was high. As we will soon find out, it meant the opposite.

In 2019, advice columnist and former *Saturday Night Live* writer E. Jean Carroll wrote an account in *New York* magazine alleging that Donald Trump sexually assaulted her in a Bergdorf Goodman department store dressing room in 1995. Or maybe it was 1996. She can't exactly remember.

Carroll claimed that Trump followed her into a fitting room at the store, shoved her against a wall, pulled down her pants, and forced "his fingers around my private area."

Interesting choice of words—"his fingers around my private area." Did he *grab* her by her private area, perhaps? This sounds a lot like the language Trump used on the infamous *Access Hollywood* tape.

Next, Trump "thrusts his penis halfway—or completely, I'm not certain—inside me," she claimed.

Ah, the old half-penis rape . . . that's definitely a real thing.

From this account of events, we are to believe that there were no other customers around, there were no employees nearby, the dressing room was left unlocked, and Carroll didn't scream.

Yet she wrote the interaction "turned into a colossal struggle." "I am wearing a pair of sturdy black patent-leather four-inch Barneys high heels, which puts my height around six-one, and I try to stomp his foot," she said.

She re-created this exact look for what I'm sure her handlers thought was a badass cover photo that graced *New York* mag in 2019, the year she publicly accused Trump.

Carroll is quite theatrical, to put it mildly.

"I try to push him off with my one free hand—for some reason, I keep holding my purse with the other—and I finally get a knee up high enough to push him out and off and I turn, open the door, and run out of the dressing room," she claimed.

Yet she doesn't remember when all this took place—as well as other key details in the encounter.

"I do not believe he ejaculates," she admitted casually.

Thanks for that attentive eye to detail, Jean.

A lot had transpired between 1996 and 2019. Bill Clinton's affair with Monica Lewinsky and subsequent impeachment rocked the country. Donald Trump became the biggest star in all of television with *The Apprentice*. By the time she voiced her accusation, Trump had won the presidency and served for more than two years, the #MeToo era had arrived, and dozens of big names in Hollywood, the news media, and the entertainment industry were taken down by accusations of sexual impropriety. Finally, in that context, seventy-five-year-old E. Jean Carroll decided to tell her alleged story.

The timing was perfectly logical, however, because the media cycle surrounding her accusations was in sync with when Carroll was promoting her new book about problems caused by men. She gave the book the wince-inducing and grammatically offensive title *What Do We Need Men For?*

There were a host of other problems with her claims. There is no surveillance video of the incident. There are no eyewitnesses. She claims that she was wearing a "black wool Donna Karan coatdress"; Trump's team (among others) have claimed the dress wasn't even made at the time.

Carroll also said, "The Donna Karan coatdress still hangs on the back of my closet door, unworn and unlaundered since that evening."

Unlaundered? So dramatic!

Since the dress was unwashed, surely she offered it up to the authorities so it could be checked for Trump's DNA, right?

Apparently not.

"The dress was great," Trump told me in an interview in 2025. "The dress was a Monica Lewinsky–type dress. Then when they found out there was nothing on the dress, so we wanted the dress, and the judge said 'nope.' We're not gonna let you show it."

Trump is correct that Judge Lewis Kaplan would not allow for it to be admitted as evidence. This would be a recurring theme of the trial.

The core question, though, is whether she was actually raped, not the status of the dress. And when push came to shove, not even Carroll herself was bold enough to say in court that she was raped. Her civil complaint does not mention rape. In fact, it focused only on defamation as the statute of limitations had run out. The word *rape* does not appear in the complaint.[1]

This would get incredibly awkward when she began to do media appearances to discuss the claim.

Carroll sat down for a long interview with CNN's Anderson Cooper (who evangelized on her behalf throughout the saga) in which she made wild and outlandish statements that seemed far more like performance art than a serious effort to discredit President Trump.

The interview starts with Carroll describing the alleged encounter, which was shaping up to be one of the best possible New York moments—a classic celebrity sighting at an iconic city location—until Trump trapped her in the dressing room. It was quite the story arc.

Carroll said she was "too panicked to be scared" as he ripped down her tights and assaulted her "against my will and it hurt and it was a fight."

At one point, she said she laughed at him to disarm him.

Then the interview crescendoed to the most absurd conclusion imaginable: a discussion of why she assiduously avoids calling what Trump did "rape," even though she claims he shoved his penis (or was it half his penis?) into her. She prefers the word *fight*. Why doesn't she use the word *rape* in favor of the word *fight*? She tried to explain:

> Sexual violence is in every county and every strata of society and I just feel that so many women are undergoing sexual violence and mine was short, I got out, I'm happy now, I'm moving on, and I think of all the women who are enduring constant sexual violence. So this one instant, this one, what?, three minutes in this little dressing room, I just say it's the "fight," that way I'm not the victim, right, I'm not the victim.
>
> I was not thrown on the ground and ravaged.

So, this wasn't a rape because other women who make less money in other countries get raped for a longer duration and are thrown onto the ground and aren't happy now. Get it?

Neither do I.

Cooper lightly pressed her on her distinction between the words *rape* and *fight*, and she delivered a line that would reverberate across media:

> The word *rape* carries so many sexual connotations. This was not sexual. It just, it hurt. I think most people think of rape as being sexy. Think of the fantasies.

Whoa. I think this statement says a lot more about Carroll than about society as a whole.

So, she was penetrated against her will, which is a "fight" and not a rape, because rapes are . . . sexy.

This is how E. Jean Carroll thinks.

If you're trying to find the clip online, you might have some trouble because CNN edited the YouTube video of the interview so as not to include this final portion.[2]

Her allegations somehow get more surreal.

Her narrative about the events is—not a joke—almost identical to the plotline of a 2012 episode of *Law & Order: Special Victims Unit*. In that episode, "Theatre and Tricks," one of the characters fantasizes about being raped in the lingerie section of Bergdorf Goodman, exactly where Carroll alleges she was raped by Trump. Carroll testified that she was aware of the episode but hadn't seen it.[3] Yet she claimed she is a fan of *Law & Order*—but not *Law & Order SVU*, which she said was "too violent."[4]

If Carroll hadn't seen that episode, it might have been because she was spending her time watching *The Apprentice*, which she raved about on the witness stand. "I was a big fan of the show. Very impressed by it," Carroll said, calling it "such a witty competition on TV, and it was about something worthwhile, competing."[5]

She was a Donald Trump fan, it appears.

Carroll also trafficked in the explicit, writing and tweeting frequently about "unusual" sexual practices.

"How do you know your 'unwanted sexual advance' is unwanted, until you advance it?" she tweeted in 2015.

Here's a pretty rapey tweet from 2010: "Sex Tip I Learned From My Dog: When in heat, chase the male until he collapses with exhaustion . . . then jump him!"[6]

If you aren't yet skeptical of her story, consider that she had joked about having sex in Bergdorf's in a 1993 column for *Elle*. An actual passage from one of her sexual advice columns:

> Begin by reading For Yourself by Dr. Lonnie Barbach. She'll give you excellent instructions on how to have an orgasm during intercourse. Then after 313 queenhell love-wiggles, move on to Gretta [*sic*] Garbo's favorite love position—the top. (In erotic scenes, Garbo is always above the man. So are Sharon Stone, Bette Midler and Katherine Hepburn.) Indeed, this location works better for women than the fourth floor of Bergdorf's.[7]

Carroll herself never made this rape (or is it "fight"?) claim against Trump public until the most convenient moment, which is especially suspicious, considering that she often wrote and spoke explicitly about sex and sexuality. (Carroll apparently told two friends about the alleged attack at the time but did not tell the police or anyone in media, despite the fact that she worked in Manhattan media herself.[8])

It's remarkable that a professional loudmouth could keep such a secret for so long.

And it wasn't her only secret. In June 2019, she fired a sexual assault allegation at former CBS News chairman and CEO Leslie Moonves. The timing seemed odd considering that Moonves had been ousted the previous year after a series of women came forward and alleged he had sexually assaulted them. Carroll also stayed quiet about this until just before her book was released in summer 2019.

VAGINA AND TITS

My favorite detail of the entire E. Jean Carroll saga is not that her recounting of the alleged events was almost identical to a network television episode, or that she can't remember what year it took place, or that she is clearly obsessed with sex at Bergdorf's.

In fact, it has nothing to do with the case at all. It has to do with what she named her pets.

"Her dog, or her cat, was named 'Vagina.' The judge wouldn't allow us to put that in," Donald Trump himself told a CNN audience, noting that Judge Kaplan tried to keep the courtroom G-rated, even if that meant Trump couldn't bring evidence to suggest that Carroll might be batshit crazy.

The cat's name was Vagina T. Fireball, to be exact. Carroll herself posts photos of Vagina T. on her Twitter[9] and Instagram[10] accounts.

When Trump revealed the cat's name, leftist journos accused him of smearing Carroll.[11]

A 2017 video that *Elle* put together of their beloved advice columnist should have been submitted to the court as evidence. In the video, it is revealed that Carroll lives alone in the woods in a home she has dubbed "The Mouse House." She gave it that name because of the rodents that live there. She decorated the outside of her property with garbage hung from string. At the time, she drove a polka-dotted Toyota Prius. She paints rocks.

We also learn in the video that Carroll claimed to have had a dog named Tits.[12]

When asked about her daily routine, she said that every afternoon when she wakes up (yes, a woman in her seventies says she wakes up at noon) and screams to the heavens "thank God I don't have children."

It's hard to disagree with that sentiment, but why is a childless woman who names her pets after female body parts and lets powerful rapists get away with it until it's time to sell books employed to give advice to people?

And why did much of America take her seriously?

Maybe I'll write in to *Elle* and "Ask E. Jean."

GEORGE CONWAY TAKES HIS SHOT AT TRUMP

Lawfare, at its core, is the weaponization of the legal system against a political target; the Carroll case is exactly that.

The goal with this case was clear: Brand Trump as a sex criminal (even though it's a civil case) and impose a severe financial penalty.

Trump could never be jailed for these alleged crimes; the statute of limitations had long run out. But he could be branded with a scarlet *R* for the rest of eternity, which is a powerful political weapon.

E. Jean Carroll didn't make these accusations spontaneously. There was an organized team around her that worked to make sure her account delivered maximum damage. The person who orchestrated the entire case was none other than George Conway, professional anti-Trump legal pundit and bitter ex-husband of Trump advisor Kellyanne Conway. He coached Carroll into pursuing a civil trial rather than criminal litigation. Carroll would cop to this on the witness stand.

Apparently, the two hatched the plot to take down Trump at a party. Conway went on to recommend a lawyer to the columnist.[13]

The plot led to a November 2019 suit filed in New York accusing Trump of defaming Carroll while denying her accusations of sexual assault.

Yes, you read that correct: Trump denying her allegation was deemed defamation. Apparently it's acceptable to deny an accusation, but if you're too animated in your defense, then you could get sued for that too.

Here is the entirety of the Truth Social post at the center of the case:

This "Ms. Bergdorf Goodman" case is a complete con job. . . . I don't know this woman, have no idea who she is, other than it seems she got a picture of me many years ago, with her husband, shaking my hand on a reception line at a celebrity charity event. She completely made up a story that I met her at the doors of this crowded New York City Department Store and, within minutes, "swooned" her. It is a Hoax and a lie, just like all the other Hoaxes that have been played on me for the past seven years. . . . She has no idea what day, what week, what month, what year, or what decade this so-called "event" supposedly took place. The reason she doesn't know is because it never happened, and she doesn't want to get caught up with details or facts that can be proven wrong. If you watch Anderson Cooper's interview with her, where she was promoting a really crummy book, you will see that it is a complete Scam. She changed her story from beginning to end, after the commercial break, to suit the purposes of CNN and Andy Cooper. . . . For the record, E. Jean Carroll is not telling the truth, is a woman who I had nothing to do with, didn't know, and would have no interest in knowing her if I ever had the chance.

This is a terrific summary of the events by President Trump, and I rather enjoy the way he takes artistic liberties when it comes to capitalization. The key details:

- He claims he doesn't know her and dismisses the one photo as a passing moment from a celebrity charity event.

- He notes that he has been consistently falsely accused of sexual assaults since he entered politics.

- He notes that Carroll has no specific recollection as to the time of the alleged attack.

- He notes that she changed her story throughout the course of an interview on CNN with Anderson Cooper.

Whether or not her story is true, it certainly has a lot of the hallmarks of anti-Trump hoaxes. For starters, the fact that it originated with George Conway is a dead giveaway that this was a political hit designed to harm Trump's brand, not achieve moral or legal justice. Conway frames his position on Trump as principled opposition, but that hasn't stopped him from flinging ad hominem attacks at him, like calling him "a narcissistic psychopath"[14] who is seeking "revenge on the United States." He also said that Trump represents the "worst of the human spirit."[15]

Unhinged.

Conway, who made a career embarrassing his then-wife in the media while she worked for Trump, championed Carroll in the press without making a legally persuasive argument. At one point he said that he rage-tweets at President Donald Trump so he doesn't "end up screaming" at his wife. (It's hardly a surprise that the marriage didn't make it.) Conway was also an early backer of the anti-Trump Lincoln Project.[16]

"Carroll's account is supported by the sheer number of claims that have now surfaced against Trump—claims in which women have accused Trump of engaging in unwelcome or forcible sexual conduct or assault against them," he wrote in the *Washington Post*. This is a legally fallacious argument in several ways. First of all, it is an example of the bandwagon fallacy where something is thought to be true just because it's seemingly popular. More importantly, it is an example of "affirmation of the consequent," a common fallacy when the presence of an allegation or allegations is considered sufficient to conclude guilt. If our legal system looked at crime through that prism, there would be no due process. In American civil law, the prosecution must provide a preponderance of evidence for the accused to be found liable, not a preponderance of hysteria.

It was all emotional and lacking in substance, and the fact that he wrote it in the friendly *Washington Post* shows that he was trying to win over the court of public opinion more than any potential jury.

"Finally, no controversy involving Trump would be complete without at least one utterly brazen, easily disprovable Trumpian lie," Conway wrote. "In his statement denying the rape allegation, he added the claim that 'I've never met this person in my life.' If Trump had even bothered to glance at Carroll's published account, he would have seen a photograph of himself and his then-wife, Ivana, from 1987—in which he was amiably chatting with Carroll and her then-husband."[17]

There you have it: Trump says he doesn't recall the one time he talked to her thirty years ago, which proves he is a liar, because we all remember every conversation we had thirty years ago, or something.

Conway isn't the only familiar anti-Trump name associated with the Carroll cases. Reid Hoffman, the Democrat megadonor who has been a primary subject of my research for years, bankrolled Carroll's efforts. Hoffman helped launch PayPal before cofounding LinkedIn in 2002 and is worth billions of dollars. He has funded a vast array of left-wing political causes through shadowy "dark money" nonprofits. He specialized in using nonprofits' lenient disclosure laws to make large contributions in relative obscurity.

Hoffman, known as "the most connected man in Silicon Valley," has been criticized for complying with Chinese censorship rules while his business operated in the country.[18] He has praised the Chinese tech sector[19] and appears to be the only American to regularly speak at China's World Internet Conferences, which are designed to amplify Xi Jinping's vision for the digital age and are closed to the press.[20] He also promoted fake news on behalf of Democrats, financing a left-wing online disinformation campaign targeting Republican Alabama Senate candidate Roy Moore in 2017; Hoffman issued an apology for this—after Moore narrowly lost his race.[21] A whistleblower claimed in 2022 that Hoffman's Orwellian-named Good Information Foundation offered him money to attack "Trump Republicans" online despite federal laws prohibiting such political behavior from 501(c)(3) organizations.[22] None of that bothered the powers that be in Joe Biden's America. Hoffman is on the board of Microsoft and was on the Pentagon's Defense Innovation Board through Biden's presidency. He has made big bucks from Facebook, Airbnb, and his venture capital firm, Greylock Partners.

Oh, and he admitted to visiting Jeffrey Epstein's island.[23]

Hoffman hates Trump, saying he would "spend as much as I possibly can and it takes" to beat him.[24] And he just so happens to have been the one shoveling coal into E. Jean Carroll's engine. Carroll's legal team, led by Roberta Kaplan, disclosed that they were funded by American Future Republic, a nonprofit primarily backed by Hoffman.

None of this is coincidental.

Naturally, Trump's attorneys suggested that this pattern reveals the true motive of the suit. And they were right. The story of the E. Jean Carroll lawsuit is simple: A far-left billionaire attempted to buy the election via lawfare involving E. Jean Carroll. Full stop.

Hoffman runs a shop full of rabid Trump haters. Dmitri Mehlhorn, Hoffman's former top political advisor, pushed a narrative that the assassination attempt on President Trump in Butler, Pennsylvania, in July 2024 was staged.[25] (He split with Hoffman days later to join the anti-Trump Lincoln Project.[26])

The team to take down Trump was coming together, but they faced a massive hole in their case: The statute of limitations.

THE NEW YORK JUDICIAL SYSTEM IS "FUCKED"

Carroll's attorney, Roberta Kaplan (no relation to Judge Lewis A. Kaplan), is a powerful lawyer for left-wing causes. She represents Joe Biden's daughter, Ashley, for example. She's better known as the cofounder of the Time's Up Legal Defense Fund, which raised tens of millions of dollars during the #MeToo era of sexual assault accusations. However, she ultimately resigned her role after a report claimed that she had tried to discredit a woman who accused Governor Andrew Cuomo of sexual harassment.[27] Specifically, she was said to have "weaponized [her] knowledge of survivors' experiences to help Governor Cuomo and his office retaliate against at least one of nearly a dozen women who were courageous in speaking up."[28]

Lawfare is a full-contact sport.

Yet Kaplan and Carroll had a serious problem with their case: This alleged assault happened so long ago that it theoretically wasn't eligible even for civil court.

So what did they do? What else could they do? They got the law changed. Not satisfied with merely claiming that Trump defamed Carroll, Democrats actually passed a law to enable the lawsuit to proceed, the Adult Survivors Act of 2022. This New York State law allowed for victims of sexual assault to file civil suits even after the statute of limitations for a criminal court had run out.[29] The law came into effect on November 24, 2022, and was immediately exploited by Carroll and her handlers. She literally filed suit against Trump that day. Those who supported the bill maintain this was to provide avenues for #MeToo victims to sue their alleged attackers.

It just so happened it was used on Trump before anyone else.

I asked both Trump and his attorney Alina Habba about this law, and they believe that it was passed specifically because Democrat Governor Kathy Hochul was targeting him.

Now, all of a sudden, after the new law passed, Carroll's story changed. She *was* raped by Trump, all of a sudden, or at least that's what she and her attorneys alleged. "Roughly 27 years ago, playful banter at the luxury department store Bergdorf Goodman on Fifth Avenue in New York City took a dark turn when Defendant Donald J. Trumps seized Plaintiff E. Jean Carroll, forced her up against a dressing room wall, pinned her in place with his shoulder, and raped her," the second complaint began. It also renewed her claim that Trump had made defamatory false statements.[30]

This was so confusing to people that even the Clinton-appointed judge in the case, Lewis A. Kaplan, couldn't keep it straight.

The first trial began in April 2023 in the U.S. District Court for the Southern District of York; Judge Kaplan presided over the proceedings. In May 2023, the anonymous jury deliberated for only a few hours before finding former President Trump liable for sexual abuse and battery. Trump was not found liable for rape. Carroll was awarded $5 million in civil damages against him—$2 million for sexual abuse, and another $3 million for defamation. Trump moved for a new trial, which Kaplan denied.

How could it have gone any other way? The judge was anti-Trump, and the nine jurors were based in New York City.

In an act of overt partisanship, Judge Kaplan allowed character evidence to be used against Trump, including the infamous *Access Hollywood* tape. The plaintiff's team used Trump's locker-room talk to try to prove that he committed the alleged rape. This defies logic and would have been legally inadmissible in a criminal case, but the judge allowed it here.

Judge Kaplan posed significant problems for Trump's defense as well. Recall that he would not allow the dress that presumably did not contain Trump's DNA as evidence, nor would he admit Carroll's contradictory interview with Anderson Cooper where she could not decide if Trump had actually raped her.

"The judge wouldn't allow anything," Trump told me, emphasizing the significance of Carroll's quote about how women fantasize about being raped. Trump also said he wanted to introduce that she called her black husband "ape," a racial slur, but wasn't allowed to do that either.

Trump told me Kaplan was the meanest judge he encountered during the series of trials I describe in this book, with Juan Merchan a close second.

"He's Bill Clinton's best friend," the president said.

His effort to control what evidence the court was allowed to see and hear enraged the Trump team. Habba told me that while the Trump team was considering putting the former president on the witness stand, "the judge made me tell him every single question that I was going to ask and what answers [Trump] was going to give me."

"I went ballistic," she told me. "I wouldn't relent."

"You are not allowing me to represent my client. This is so insane," she told me, reenacting the drama.

"I can't put in evidence that proves everything this woman says is a lie."

Kaplan didn't take kindly to the push-back. "You say one more thing and I'm going to throw you in jail," the judge said, according to Habba. (Trump corroborated her account to me, even suggesting the judge threatened to put her into cells underneath the courthouse that are seldom used.)

"I knew how fucked the state of New York's judicial system was at this moment," she told me.

"He wouldn't let her speak," Trump told me.

"You use the one weapon we have to fight back and you get threatened and silenced and threatened to be put in jail," she said.

Kaplan kept coming at Team Trump. In July, he released a "clarification" saying that Trump may be said to have "raped" Carroll, even though the jury specifically did not say he had done so.

"The finding that Ms. Carroll failed to prove that she was 'raped' within the meaning of the New York Penal Law does not mean that she failed to prove that Mr. Trump 'raped' her as many people commonly understand the word 'rape,'" Kaplan wrote.

"Indeed, as the evidence at trial recounted below makes clear, the jury found that Mr. Trump in fact did exactly that," according to the judge.

This is egregious and reveals Judge Kaplan's anti-Trump prejudice clear as day. (Correction: *alleged* prejudice. I don't want to get accused of defamation.) He went out of his way to redefine rape so it applied to Trump, even though the jury had not done so.

He also allowed Carroll to seek additional damages for supposed defamation and set a trial for January 2024, in the heat of primary election season.

In September, Judge Kaplan ruled that Trump was liable for defamatory statements against Carroll when she went public with her claims. In an odd twist, Kapan ruled that Trump was civilly liable for defamation. Typically a jury would make that determination at a trial, but Kaplan did it himself.

Kaplan relied on the jury that had found in May that Trump had abused Carroll. "The truth or falsity of Mr. Trump's 2019 statements therefore depends—like the truth or falsity of his 2022 statement—on whether Ms. Carroll lied about Mr. Trump sexually assaulting her," Kaplan wrote in a twenty-five-page decision. "The jury's finding that she did not therefore is binding in this case and precludes Mr. Trump from contesting the falsity of his 2019 statements."[31]

The jury had bought Vagina and Tits's mom's story, and now Trump wouldn't even be allowed to defend himself without having to pay millions of dollars.

"How many millions?" was the next question. Carroll had asked for $10 million because she said that he had hurt her twice as bad as last time because now he's president, or something.

The second trial was set for January 2024 and would focus on Trump's supposed defamation of Carroll in 2019, while he was president. It was another anonymous jury of New Yorkers, so Trump was in an unwinnable position from the start.

Yet this supposedly neutral jury had a special surprise for Carroll cooked up in January 2024: They settled on an additional $83.3 million, more than eight times what Carroll even requested. The federal jury ordered Trump to pay $11 million for reputational damages, $7.3 million for emotional harm, and $65 million in punitive damages, to go along with the other $5 million from the first trial.[32]

The number was absurdly excessive. It would have bankrupted any other president in history. Only Trump could possibly weather this.

Obviously, the judge and Manhattan-based jury sought to levy a penalty that would strike Trump hard enough that it would harm his reputation and tie up resources needed for his presidential campaign.

Carroll was beaming. She went on MSNBC's *The Rachel Maddow Show* and celebrated gleefully. "I had such, such great ideas for all the good I'm gonna do with this money," she said. "First thing, Rachel, you and I are gonna go shopping!" she exclaimed. "We're gonna get complete new wardrobes, new shoes, motorcycle for [attorney Shawn] Crowley, a new fishing rod for Robbie [aka Roberta Kaplan]." Then she offered to shower Maddow with gifts. "Rachel, what do you want? A penthouse? It's yours, Rachel! Penthouse and France? You want France? You want to go fishing in France? No?"

Classy.

Trump's effort to get the penalties reduced or rescinded didn't go anywhere. In March 2024, during the middle of one of the biggest presidential elections of our lives, the presumptive Republican nominee had to go out and secure a $91 million bond ($83 million plus 10 percent insurance) just in time to make a deadline.

This is how lawfare works. If you can't get him with the laws on the books, make a new one. And if you can't convict him in a criminal court, get a civil judgment with obscene damages.

Judge Kaplan continued to campaign against Trump in his courtroom and the court of public opinion, citing "evidence that Mr. Trump used the office of the presidency—the loudest 'bully pulpit' in America and possibly the world—to issue multiple statements castigating Ms. Carroll as a politically and financially motivated liar, insinuating that she was too unattractive for him to have sexually assaulted, and threatening that she would 'pay dearly' for speaking out."

The judge is referencing a point that Trump has made repeatedly: Carroll isn't even his type. (From what I know about Trump, this checks out.)

Trump was married at the time to the gorgeous Marla Maples, who was in her early thirties. He had a massive real estate empire and was a popular fixture in the New York social scene. And this judge is insisting Trump risked it all to put half of his penis into a fifty-two-year-old woman, who happens to be a known fabulist, in a department store.

And not only are we being told to believe he was attracted to her, we're told to believe he was so hot for her he couldn't even bring her to one of his own secure properties like, say, Trump Tower, which is across the street.

C'mon.

Kaplan clearly was a fan of Carroll's. He wrote that the jury was "entitled to conclude that Mr. Trump derailed the career, reputation, and emotional well-being of one of America's most successful and prominent advice columnists and authors."[33]

Maybe he wants to take Carroll to the Bergdorf fitting rooms.

An attempt by Trump's lawyers to overturn the decision was rejected in late December 2024, just before the president was set to take office.[34]

Trump did try one countersuit against Carroll for defamation, but it was quickly thrown out. He did have success suing ABC News anchor George Stephanopoulos. The former Bill Clinton communications director said in a March 2024 interview with Congresswoman Nancy Mace (R-NC) that "judges and two separate juries have found him liable for rape and for defaming the victim of that rape." Specifically, he was found *not* liable for rape (he was found liable for "sexual abuse" and defamation).[35]

Trump's attorney Alejandro Brito wrote in the twenty-page complaint that Stephanopoulos's statements were made "with actual malice or with a reckless disregard for the truth given that Defendant Stephanopoulos knows that these statements are patently and demonstrably false."

ABC News and Stephanopoulos agreed to settle the case and pay Trump $15 million plus attorney fees and issue a public apology.

In February 2020, Carroll's employer dismissed her from her advice-giving obligations. "Because Trump ridiculed my reputation, laughed at my looks, & dragged me through the mud, after 26 years, ELLE fired me," she tweeted.

She was picked up to write a five-part series on men she hates for

Laurene Powell Jobs's *Atlantic*, but she hasn't published there since late 2020. She also hasn't published any additional books. She has since launched a Substack where she posts generic pro-Democrat and anti-Republican memes with a distinctly baby-boomer–centric sensibility.

After Trump had won the election but lost a bid to overturn one of the Carroll cases, Carroll posted a brief message to her Substack complimenting her attorney, Robbie Kaplan: "You remind us: He can be beat!"

She's right, at least for now. The case is pending appeal as of spring 2025.

When I asked Trump about this case, he expressed frustration with his team, particularly lead counsel Joe Tacopina. Trump told me "I wanted to testify," but Tacopina said, "Sir, this is beneath you." He was harshly critical of Tacopina's handling of the trial, but he ultimately thought the point was moot. "If I had F. Lee Bailey in his prime it wouldn't have mattered," referring to the famed criminal attorney known for architecting O. J. Simpson's successful defense, among other high-profile cases.

The "woman" case was over as soon as the judge and the jury were set. Judge Kaplan saw to that.

"They tried to embarrass me before the election," Trump told me.

He certainly has a talent for pinpointing root causes.

CHAPTER 4

A VICTIMLESS CRIME

I look forward to going into the office of Attorney General every day, suing him . . . and then going home." Those were the words of Letitia "Tish" James. By "him" she meant Donald Trump, of course, whom she regarded as an "illegitimate president."[1] She made those comments on July 19, 2018, during a speech before the Bronx Democratic Party.

Earlier that year, Letitia James had announced herself as a new anti-Trump star on the national stage. But she had been on a steady rise through New York politics for the previous decade.[2] James had served as the Big Apple's public advocate, where her role in theory was to represent the public interest in court. In reality, it's hard to figure out exactly what she accomplished aside from garnering public attention, which she did do on a number of occasions, positioning her to pursue higher office.

Most relevant here, however, is that she used this perch to cut her lawfare teeth. "James' tenure as public advocate has also showed her interest in using the levers of the law to advance policy goals," according to Law.com.[3]

James won her election for New York attorney general that November and immediately announced her intentions: "We're definitely going to sue him. We're going to be a real pain in the ass. He's going to know my name personally," according to the *New York Law Journal*.[4]

She didn't take long to make good on that promise.

"We will use every area of the law to investigate President Trump and his business transactions and that of his family as well," James told NBC News in an interview. "We want to investigate anyone in his orbit who has, in fact, violated the law."[5]

She had a flair for the dramatic, even using props on occasion to make public events theatrical.

She also gravitated toward high-profile causes likes taking on Google, Facebook, the National Rifle Association, and of course, President Trump. Her tenure has featured a series of lowlights that has infuriated MAGA Republicans, including broad support for vaccine and mask mandates.[6]

To give you a sense of her personality, in a highly assertive move after she won the AG seat, she tried to strip control of the NYPD from Mayor Bill de Blasio, replacing his oversight powers with an "independent commission." This was ostensibly because the NYPD had been too aggressive under the far-left mayor.[7]

Though James was running for the top law enforcement position in the state, her slate of priorities seemed to have nothing to do with actual crime. Just a week before the 2018 election, she was asked by *Ebony*, "What is the most important issue you have heard from prospective voters?" Her answer is, frankly, horrifying, and tells you everything you need to know about Tish James:

> President Donald Trump and the threat to our democracy and our values. The fact that his policies have reversed all the progress that we made under President Barack Obama and others. There's an issue of public corruption in New York state; I will seek to restore confidence and integrity in public service. The foreclosure crisis is not behind us, students [*sic*] debt is a major issue, health care is a challenge since they repealed the individual mandate, people are having a difficult time with premiums that have increased and are often times deciding to go without medicine because of the costs, resulting in premature death and gun violence. The NRA holds [itself] out as a charitable organization, but in fact, [it] really [is] a terrorist organization. Women's rights . . . in New York, we have not codified *Roe v. Wade*, and last but not least, equal pay for equal work. We can address the feminization of poverty in the state.[8]

To recap, her biggest threat is Donald Trump, and her second biggest threat is public corruption in New York, aka Donald Trump (again), as well as Trump's friends and family. As New York attorney general, she made it clear that she's focused on student debt, health care, and abortion—none of which have much to do with crime. She considers the NRA, which represents citizens who believe in the right to keep and bear arms, to be a "terrorist organization." And she believes in something called "the feminization of poverty."

James barely pays lip service to addressing any criminality that doesn't have to do with Trump despite the crime wave that had swept through New York. She did, however, host a "drag story hour read-a-thon" while serving as attorney general.[9]

This is all shameless politics, and James herself is a political figure. She even briefly ran for governor during the events described in this chapter, announcing her candidacy in October 2021 before quickly dropping out.

James assumed office in January 2019 and immediately got to work looking for ways to be a pain in Donald Trump's ass, as well as his family's. We started to get a clear picture of exactly what she was up to in September 2022, just a month and a half from the midterm elections. It was then that James filed a lawsuit against Trump as well as his three eldest children, Donald Jr., Ivanka, and Eric, for alleged fraud. Other defendants included former Trump Organization chief financial officer Allen Weisselberg, former controller Jeffrey McConney, and ten related companies. Ivanka was dropped as a defendant due to the statute of limitations expiring on her alleged violations.

Much like James's comments before she even became New York State AG, this suit was the most militant lawfare we've encountered in the book. Just about every single key detail in the case suggests the entire process was political from the jump.

"The number one issue in this country is defeating Donald Trump. Nothing else matters," James said.[10]

Unlike most of the villains of lawfare featured in this book, I bet that Tish James would admit to your face that she had strictly political intentions and that she viewed the law as a political tool to take out Trump by any means necessary.

THE TOPLESS JUDGE TRIES TO BANKRUPT THE DON

The crux of James's suit against the Trumps was that they undervalued properties to gain better rates on loans, insurance policies, and tax rates. Who was the victim here of the evil Trump Organization? Apparently it was corporations, specifically multibillion-dollar financial institutions that loaned money to the Trump family.

So what did these corporations say when they filed complaints about Trump? Ah! But there were no complaints. The supposedly victimized banks and lenders liked working with the Trump Organization, so far as we can tell. It was James who brought the case on behalf of financial institutions that never claimed for a moment to be harmed.

The only harm in a business transaction is financial harm, and representatives of these institutions got onto the witness stand and under oath said they were not harmed and did not suffer.

This was literally unprecedented. It was the first time in state history that someone was accused of fraud even though no one believed that they had been harmed.

The judge in the case was a justice of the New York County Supreme Court, Arthur Engoron. (The New York County Supreme Court refers to their judges as justices, so I use the two words interchangeably regarding Engoron.) A New Yorker through and through, Engoron was born in Queens and educated at Columbia College and New York University; he drove a cab before he began his legal career.

There's not a lot of public information about his background, but we know that he bragged about being a "boisterous" Vietnam War protester.[11] He won elected office in New York and donates exclusively to Democrats.[12]

What is a shock is that Engoron has a penchant for posting half-nude photos of himself to a high school alumni newsletter that he controls. Marco Polo, a group of researchers best known for uncovering contents of Hunter Biden's laptop that had not been made public, unearthed the photos, which apparently were snapped after Engoron's seventieth birthday.[13]

When a leftist website contacted him about the pics, he reportedly said, "Sorry I can't comment. Bye."[14]

Only an extremely vain and unaware individual would engage in such behavior.

Those are not great traits for a judge in a high-profile trial that has no jury.

And that's precisely the scenario in which Donald Trump found himself.

In September 2023, Engoron issued a summary judgment that Trump had committed years of fraud while building his real estate empire. Engoron claimed that Trump had deceived banks and insurers by overvaluing his businesses to secure loans at lower interest rates and needed a hefty punishment. Several of Trump's business licenses would be rescinded, making it nearly impossible for him to do business in the state again, provided that Trump doesn't prevail during inevitable appeals.[15]

Engoron piled on, sanctioning Trump's attorneys and fining them for filing motions to dismiss the case that he deemed frivolous.

It was highly unusual and, frankly, inappropriate that Engoron made this judgment before Trump's team had even finished laying out their defense.

The origin of the investigation was claims made by former Trump attorney Michael Cohen, who accused Trump of "inflating his total assets when it served his purposes."[16] Cohen is hardly a credible witness, having already been convicted of lying to Congress.[17] Snitching on your own client as an attorney obviously breeches attorney–client privilege—and, among other things, gets you branded a "rat."

Much of the case hinged on the valuation of Trump's legendary Mar-a-Lago property in Florida. The resort and club, which is a National Historic Landmark and has been Trump's primary residence since 2019, was assessed a value in the range of $18 million to $28 million between 2011 and 2021. The court insisted these weren't his figures, but the valuation of a basic Palm Beach assessment. The appraiser's office is tasked with assessing property value for taxation purpose. Trump valued Mar-a-Lago as high as $739 million, according to the suit, which the judge declared was "an overvaluation of at least 2,300%, compared to the assessor's appraisal." Trump, on the other hand, testified that he believed the property is worth between $1 billion and $1.5 billion.[18]

Mar-a-Lago wasn't the only property Engoron put under the micro-scope. Engoron found that Trump inflated the value of the Trump Build-ing at 40 Wall Street, the Seven Springs Estate in Westchester County, New York, as well as Trump International Golf Links in Aberdeen, Scot-land, by massive margins.

While appraisal values are often fractionally lower than market val-ues, Engoron's numbers were absurd, and utterly baffling to the real estate community. Mar-a-Lago was opened in 1927 after years of con-struction and was home to packaged-foods mogul Marjorie Merri-weather Post, who was once considered the wealthiest woman in America. Its name means "sea to lake" in Spanish, as the property touches the Atlantic Ocean on the east and Lake Worth on the west. It is more than twenty acres in size and is in one of the most valuable residen-tial areas in the country.[19]

Trump says that Mar-a-Lago was built for $18 million in 1920, though reports estimate the number is closer to $7 million.[20] The latter number is approximately $110 million today, adjusted for inflation.

Despite the sheer magnitude and the historical significance of the lo-cation, Engoron and company asserted it was worth only a fraction of properties a tenth its size.

One-acre properties in the area routinely hit the real estate market in the $40 million price range, and two-acre homes in the area often are priced between $150 million and $200 million.

"Mar-a-Lago is such a trophy asset. It's in a completely different league of its own," said Dina Goldentayer, a South Florida realtor.

"If that property were on the market today, I would list it at around $300 million, minimum . . . at least," one real estate insider told the *New York Post*. Estimates of what rock-bottom pricing for Mar-a-Lago might look like ranged from $300 million to $600 million. Trump himself sug-gested the property could sell for $1 billion or more.[21]

It is important to note that these are all estimates. It's incredibly diffi-cult to prove that there is any fraud that's taken place because the proper-ty's true value will never be known until it is sold.

Engoron brazenly ignored this reality, relying on the county assessor without considering the value of comparable properties.

Trump was steaming mad about the whole thing. As he usually does, he took to Truth Social to spell it out:

The New York State Attorney General went before a Highly Politicized Democrat Judge, who refused allowing the case to go to the Commercial Division, where it belonged, to simply rule, despite all of the evidence on the contrary, that I committed fraud, which is both ridiculous and untrue. As an example, this Democrat Operative valued Mar-a-Lago, the most spectacular and valuable property in Palm Beach, Florida, to be worth as low as $18 Million, when in actuality, it could be worth almost 100 times that amount. He hated everything about me at a level that I have never seen before.

"This is a judge that should be disbarred," he said. "This is a judge that some people say could be charged criminally for what he's doing. He's interfering with an election, and it's a disgrace."[22]

But Tish James didn't care about any of this, nor did Justice Engoron. They believed that regardless of what the financial institutions that lent to the Trump Org said, the deals were not in the public interest.

Soon it became clear where all this was going: James and Engoron were trying to bankrupt Donald Trump. Or at least that's what Cohen predicted.[23]

"He's watching as his company, his 50-plus-year company, is in a death spiral. I mean, basically what Letitia James did, our unsinkable attorney general, she gave him the corporate death penalty. Judge Engoron is in agreement with Letitia James that the company should not be able to practice, neither should Donald,"[24] Cohen said on CNN.

"He cannot survive this. He cannot recover from this."

This was a witch hunt of the highest order.

SCHUMER'S GIRLFRIEND

There is a layer of irony to this case, being that it is a "civil" one. Of all the contentious and unpleasant Trump-related cases covered in the book, this one seemed the most contentious and unpleasant. Tish James set that tone before she even was elected. Trump hardly let his contempt for those involved with the case itself remain a secret.

On the second day of the trial, Trump shared a screenshot of a Twitter post that showed one of Engoron's clerks next to Senator Chuck Schumer (D-NY). "Schumer's girlfriend, Alison R. Greenfield, is running this case against me. How Disgraceful! This case should be dismissed immediately!!" the former president Truthed.

Nothing in that Truth was literal, but Engoron didn't take kindly to it and issued Trump a limited gag order. "This morning, one of the defendants posted to a social media account a disparaging, untrue post about a member of my staff," Engoron said, before imposing an order barring Trump from commenting on personnel involved in the trial. "Personal attacks of my staff are inappropriate and I won't tolerate them," he said.[25]

At the center of this dispute was exclusive reporting by *Breitbart News* on Greenfield, Engoron's top clerk. Matthew Boyle, our Washington bureau chief, reported on a complaint filed by Brock Fredin, who runs the activist Twitter account @JudicialProtest, that Greenfield had donated to Democrat candidates in amounts exceeding New York State ethics rules.[26] (There is no clear evidence that she was ever disciplined following the complaint, though Greenfield never denied making the donations.)

Trump's attorney Christopher Kise brought up our scoop in court, suggesting that it raised questions of impartiality and that the "defense will have to give serious consideration to seeking a mistrial." A frustrated Engoron denied the allegations and took a veiled dig at *Breitbart*. Yet the facts were on our side.

From Boyle's report: "In 2022 alone, Greenfield gave thousands of dollars in donations. The donations, which can be found in New York's elections database, total several thousand dollars." Court officials were not allowed to donate in excess of $500 in aggregate donations in a calendar year. The database suggested that Greenfield's donations exceeded that threshold many times over.

Anyone is free to verify our work in New York's elections database. The facts are there for anyone to see. It's just a matter of whether anyone will enforce the laws on the books.

Trump seethed with contempt for Greenfield during a 2025 meeting in a dining room adjoining the Oval Office. He told me "she was the one behind it," referring to the entire trial. Trump stated flatly that "she has total control over [Engoron]." Trump told me she had her future mapped out, and it started with a big victory against Trump. "She thought Biden was going to win," he said, and then she is "going to be a federal judge." He appeared to take a bit of pleasure in knowing that plan had been derailed.

During our meeting, Trump also raised questions about whether the White House was coordinating strategy with Letitia James. He noted that she had been regularly visiting the White House at this time. Publicly available records show that James visited the White House on April 8, 2022, for a celebration of Ketanji Brown Jackson; July 18, 2022, to meet with Kamala Harris along with other attorneys general; and August 31, 2023, for an event honoring black women. The establishment media were entirely dismissive that she could have also taken other meetings to discuss Trump's trial during these visits.[27] Trump remains unconvinced these White House visits were so innocent here.

Meanwhile, several members of Trump's family were under gag orders and would be fined or worse if they publicized our entirely accurate report.

Trump repeatedly attempted appeals to have the gag order removed, claiming that he was not able to defend himself with it in place. He was fined multiple times before the order was briefly suspended. The gag was quickly reinstated after Trump made a series of posts on Truth Social attacking Engoron's wife.[28]

Trump took the stand on November 6 and immediately began sparring with Engoron. The judge pleaded with Trump's attorneys to rein the former president in. "Can you control your client? This is not a political rally," he reportedly said at one point, and "control him, if you can" at another. Trump's attorneys dutifully defended their client, informing Engoron he should "hear what he [Trump] has to say."

Engoron snapped back, "I'm not here to hear what he has to say. He's here to answer questions."[29]

This became a familiar refrain, repeated a number of times. Alina Habba, an attorney for Trump, ripped Engoron for it, calling him "unhinged," and claiming that he slammed a table in court during Trump's testimony. Engoron "has already predetermined that my client committed fraud before we even walked into this courtroom," Habba said, accurately.

The squabbling continued throughout the largely meaningless proceedings. It was clear from the start that Engoron was going to find Trump liable. It was never fair for a minute.

A CRIMINAL TRIAL IN CIVIL COURT

One of the dead giveaways that Tish James was not even attempting to play fair was that she carried out the case like it was in a criminal court and that the Trump family were crooks—despite the fact that the case was filed in civil court.

There are several distinctions between civil and criminal law, but the most relevant here is that most criminal cases are prosecuted by officials who represent a state, country, or some other jurisdiction. Civil cases are typically brought by an aggrieved party who believes they have been the victim of some wrongdoing. In this instance, the chief law enforcement officer for New York brought a civil case, not a criminal one, against Trump.

She did that because there was no criminal wrongdoing alleged. Of the seven charges against Trump, the closest thing to a crime that is even mentioned is that he falsified financial statements with the intention of committing another crime.

So, who was the victim here? Again, no one knows. If Trump had done what Tish James is suggesting, then the plaintiff would be one of the financial institutions that did business with the Trump Organization. James argued that these ultrawealthy institutions were in fact harmed by Trump, and so it was in the public interest to prosecute him.

Yet none of them ever made complaints about Trump. In fact, they liked doing business with him! They got onto the stand and said so, under oath.

They. Were. Not. Harmed.

"The loan was perfect. it was perfect," Trump told me in a 2025 interview, emphasizing that the private company with which he had a private contract had not alleged any damages.

If they had been damaged by Trump, they would have spoken up. Financial institutions know when they are getting fleeced. That is their business. These banks do transactions worth hundreds of millions of dollars. They have teams of trained professionals that do their own diligence and complete their own ultrasophisticated appraisals of the properties in question.

Of course they do! Their investors would sue them for breaching fiduciary responsibility if they weren't able to adequately evaluate such things.

In every case raised by James, you can bet that these financial institutions completed thorough evaluation processes, asked intrusive questions, and determined that Trump's numbers were close enough to their own that it was worth doing a deal.

And Trump was an ideal business partner. He made every payment on time. He paid every dollar owed. The financial institutions made every nickel they expected to make from their dealings. Trump told me he even had a tendency to pay back loans early, even if he incurred penalties, ensuring that banks were happy with their relationship.

These businesses gave Trump the ultimate stamp of approval: They wanted to do business with him again. Deutsche Bank, for example, viewed Donald Trump as a "whale," that is, a client who had the potential to bring enormous revenue. "We are whale hunting," according to then-bank managing director Rosemary Vrablic. They landed him, and it paid off. The bank "eagerly cultivated a relationship that grew from $13,000 worth of revenue to $6 million in two years," according to an Associated Press report.[30]

What's more, these businesses are accustomed to litigation; they can afford the best lawyers in the country. If Trump owed them, they would have come after him, and they would have gotten what they were owed.

Disparities in valuations are ubiquitous in real estate. Businesses want a high value to get loans and a low value to keep taxes down. There is a game that is played, and there's no evidence Trump played unfairly.

If there was, there would have been a victim crying foul.

But there wasn't. Quite the opposite, actually.

"Yet the victims—the bankers who lent to Mr. Trump—testified that they were thrilled to have him as a client," reported the *New York Times*.[31] Trump told me that one bank chairman's glowing testimony infuriated Engoron so much that he verbally abused the banker in the courtroom.

Yet Tish James took the position that Trump had conned them. The tenor of the suit suggested that he was an evildoer and needed to be punished. What punishment did she deem appropriate? This is an interesting question, considering that no one was actually harmed and no money was actually denied to anyone else. The amount of financial damage done was clearly zero dollars. So Trump should have zero penalty. Let's say she wanted to make an example out of Trump and thought he should pay quadruple his ill-gotten gains: That number is quadruple zero.

He should have owed nothing.

Both Trump and Habba emphasized to me that Tish James was essentially creating a law out of whole cloth. She relied on New York Executive Law §63(12), which gives the authority broad power to investigate and prosecute civil fraud against consumers. It was typically used to go after con men who swindled sweet little grannies out of their savings, not real estate developers who sign agreements with sophisticated banks—banks who then told the court that they received every dime they were due, on time, and that they would do business with Trump again.

Yet the law does not require the AG to show intent to defraud anyone or even financial loss for the victim, which is very convenient for Tish James.

"They tried me on a statute like it was consumer fraud, like I stole a refrigerator," Trump told me.

This is where Trump and Habba have a point about the law's being applied uniquely—and more harshly—applied here than ever before. While §63(12) is typically used for injunctive relief, restitution, or smaller fines, in this case it was clearly being used to take down Trump's entire business empire.

CRUEL AND UNUSUAL PUNISHMENT

Trump was always going to lose (are you beginning to notice the pattern?), given the Democrat AG, the Democrat judge, and the absence of a jury. The brunt of the penalty for the victimless crime would be financial. Engoron and James came up with a number so obscene it reads like a joke: $354.8 million—plus interest!—adding up to over $450 million.

The math on how they got to this number is, of course, unintelligible. They plucked it out of thin air. It was bigger than anyone saw coming, more than four times the outrageous $80 million that Trump was ordered to pay E. Jean Carroll.

The penalty was intentionally confiscatory to the extreme. It was higher than the entire gross domestic product of several countries![32]

During a conversation with President Trump in 2025, he emphasized the irregular nature of the size of the fine: "I borrow $125 million, I get a $500 million penalty. It was a perfect loan." "The judge found nothing wrong with the loan, but 'I'm charging you $500 million,'" he said, channeling Engoron.

James wasn't done yet. She called for lifetime bans for Trump and other Trump Org officials from participation in the New York real estate industry or serving on other corporate boards or as officers. She asked for Trump's eldest sons, Donald Trump Jr. and Eric, to get five-year bans.[33] Engoron obliged. He barred Trump from serving in top roles in New York, including some at his own companies, for three years, among other penalties.

As if the penalties weren't enough, Engoron took one last chance to scold Trump, criticizing him and the other defendants for "complete lack of contrition and remorse [that] borders on pathological."

Trump was faulted for refusing to admit wrongdoing.

Had anyone considered that he hadn't done anything wrong?

Even the anti-Trump *New York Times* noted that this last bit was "unconventional."[34]

James and Engoron had abandoned the legal foundations of civil law and assessed a fine that imitates a criminal penalty, and, I argue, a fundamentally cruel and unusual one. Nearly half a billion dollars in a zero-damages situation is an excessive amount that is seemingly chosen at random.

While it's customary for public elected officials to maintain a poker face and an air of seriousness in situations like this, James was visibly enjoying herself as she made President Trump and his family suffer. She seemed to have a permanent grin plastered to her face during the trial, unable to conceal her glee, even sporadically laughing during testimony. Her indecorous demeanor was widely criticized in conservative media, but the establishment press seemed to have no problem with it.[35]

And why would they? She had campaigned on going after Trump, and that's exactly what she was doing. But unlike Bragg, who at least acted professional while he was committing lawfare, James mugged for the camera, letting the whole world know how pleased she was with herself.

George Washington University law professor Jonathan Turley was unflinching in his analysis of the penalty handed down to Trump:

> The court has done everything short of ordering that Trump be thrown into a wood chipper. He's imposed almost the maximum

amount that James requested. He's barring him from doing business in the city where he's an iconic business figure, barring him from getting loans. The last part is particularly ironic because the banks not only said that they were not victims and did not complain about the alleged fraud, but they said that they wanted to do more business with Trump. They described him as a "whale" client. So this is all being done essentially in their name as victims, even though no one lost any money.[36]

After the verdict came down, James grew more flagrant. She began to taunt Trump by posting daily updates to the X social media platform on the gargantuan interest payment he was required to make.[37]

James even threatened to seize Trump's assets if he does not pay off the judgment.[38] And according to New York State law, it was presumed that he would have to pay off the entire sum before he was allowed to appeal.[39]

Donald Trump's main assets are real estate. James's implication is that she would have sent New York officials to seize one or more of his properties. Had she done that, it would have been one of the most dramatic moments in the history of lawfare, and something that we are accustomed to seeing only in movies and television.

The Democrats were giddy. Joe Biden's joke writers created a zinger about Trump's predicament that the president delivered at the annual Gridiron Club dinner:

Our big plan to cancel student debt doesn't apply to everyone. Just yesterday, a defeated-looking man came up to me and said, "I'm being crushed by debt. I'm completely wiped out." I said, "Sorry, Donald, I can't help you."

The room of journalists erupted in applause.

You see, it's all fun and games.

Trump got a minor miracle in late March when the New York Supreme Court Appellate Division—the intermediate court in New York—reduced his bond to $175 million. Trump said, "It will be my honor to post" it,[40] before calling out the lawfare apparatus with clarity:

"This is all about election interference. This is all Biden-run... meaning Biden and his thugs because I don't know if he knows he's alive," Trump said, before opining that Biden "can't win an election because of the borders, because of energy prices, because of inflation, because of Afghanistan." "So what they do is they do election interference," Trump concluded.

As of my March 2025 Oval Office interview with Trump, they still have his money. Yes, the $175 million bond was still up as of Spring 2025.

The appeals continued to play out in courts while the Trump Organization and the various defendants are apparently on the hook for $87,502 per day in interest, should they ultimately lose.

Though Trump won a resounding victory with the electorate, he is not out of the woods yet in the New York civil fraud case. "The ordinary burdens of civil litigation do not impede the President's official duties in a way that violates the U.S. Constitution," New York Deputy Solicitor General Judith Vale wrote in a letter to a Trump legal representative, adding that there is "no merit" to a claim that Trump's official duties as president impede his ability to appeal the case.[41]

James, naturally, has made clear that she will pursue this case interminably.

TRAMPLING ON THE CONSTITUTION

In the United States of America, at least until this point, the main ambition of law enforcement has been to protect society, not to achieve political objectives. We look down on countries like Venezuela, Brazil, and Russia for a politicized justice system where those who are out of power are punished for thought crimes and organizing a political opposition.

With the notable exceptions that fill this book, this is still not the norm here. But if Americans continue to empower people like Tish James, then the notion of impartial, blind justice will seem as farcical as a $450 million fine for a victimless crime.

One thing that is clear from this case is that the Supreme Court needs to shut down these pseudo-civil cases. This was a civil case that was treated as a de facto criminal case and ended with a punishment that was both cruel and unusual.

The fact that this was allowed to go on is outrageous. The fact that it took place during the middle of a presidential election is a national disgrace.

It's on the Supreme Court to make sure something like this never happens again.

Trump ought to pursue the appeal all the way to our nation's top court. At a minimum, I expect the Supremes to rule that penalizing him half a billion dollars for a victimless violation violates the Eighth Amendment's Excessive Fines Clause. "Excessive bail shall not be required, nor excessive fines imposed, nor cruel and unusual punishments inflicted," the amendment reads. Notice how the language does not specify whether the excessive fine is related to a criminal or a civil matter, so Trump's attorneys can certainly use this argument.

In the 2019 case *Timbs v. Indiana*, the U.S. Supreme Court held that protection from excessive fines is "fundamental to our scheme of ordered liberty" and "deeply rooted in this Nation's history and tradition." Justice Ruth Bader Ginsburg traced the lineage of this opinion back to the year 1215! "As relevant here, Magna Carta required that economic sanctions be proportioned to the wrong and not be so large as to deprive an offender of his livelihood," Ginsburg wrote.

Yet the case isn't entirely a slam dunk for Trump for one reason that ought to unsettle us all: "The only reason there is no case on the books that already makes it clear that Engoron's fine is unconstitutional is because no one has done this before," then–Breitbart Senior Legal Contributor Ken Klukowski wrote of the case. (Klukowski worked during the first Trump administration as an attorney in the White House Office of Management and Budget and then in the Justice Department. As of early 2025, he works for Senator Mike Lee in the Senate Energy and Natural Resources Committee.) He added a somewhat comforting addendum: "When no one has tried something in more than two centuries, it could be an indication that what they are trying to do is not allowed by the Constitution."[42]

Hopefully his read is accurate here.

There is a great irony to Tish James's and Arthur Engoron's efforts to punish Trump in New York civil court for alleged fraud, considering that their conduct bears all the hallmarks of what we nonlawyers colloquially refer to as "a fraud."

This New York attorney general has always sought to destroy Trump and is clearly abusing her power to do so. The judge in this juryless case does not seem to be operating on a rational plane. First he was prone to outbursts in the courtroom and then leveled a fine that seems intentionally incongruous with any damages suffered by any person or company. That is, if there even were damages at all (because the supposed victims said there were none).

"Since everyone made money here and none of the lending institutions are complaining—in fact, they made it clear in court that they are happy with the business they did with Trump—this $464 million is appallingly excessive," according to Klukowski. "It shocks the conscience, which is a red line in the law."

The most powerful law enforcement officer in a massively powerful state used her power to target and attempt to character-assassinate one of the state's most successful residents on naked political grounds. It wasn't merely excessive; this was a low moment for our country.

Justice must be served, and Trump must win his appeal.

Then Tish James ought to be prosecuted for conspiracy against rights.

In April 2025, the Trump administration referred James for criminal potential prosecution over suspected mortgage fraud. William J. Pulte, director of the Federal Housing Finance Agency (FHFA), alleged that James falsified records to secure a favorable home loan for a house in Virginia, which she claimed was her "principal residence" (sic) in 2023. That timing is suspicious, given that not only was she still serving as New York attormey general at the time, she cosigned the mortgage just weeks prior to the beginning of the civil fraud case against Trump.[43]

Pulte also claimed that James misrepresented a five-family dwelling she purchased in Brooklyn in 2001. She "consistently misrepresented the same property as only having four units in both building permit applications and numerous mortgage documents and applications," he wrote in a letter to Attorney General Pam Bondi and Deputy AG Todd Blanche.[44]

James hired Abbe Lowell, an attorney famous for representing Hunter Biden and Jared Kushner, among others, who denied all of Pulte's claims in a letter to Bondi. Regarding the Virginia property, Lowell maintains that James informed the mortgage loan broker that the property would not be her primary residence and Pulte's claim was based on a paperwork mistake. Regarding the Brooklyn home, Lowell cites New York City records from 2011 that lists the dwelling as a four-unit property.[45]

This matter is ongoing at the time work on this book is completed in the spring of 2025, but it is irresistible to point out the potential for even more irony if James is determined to have falsified records to obtain a favorable loan. It would render her efforts targeting Trump the ultimate example of projection, or falsely accusing someone of something that is actually your own trait or behavior.

It remains to be seen if James will be charged with criminal fraud, or if there will be any consequences for her past actions.

But as Tish James is fond of saying, "[N]o one is above the law."[46]

CHAPTER 5

THE CONSPIRACY TO PROVE A CONSPIRACY

If you thought that the point of the E. Jean Carroll and Stormy Daniels cases was to entertain MSNBC-viewing voters, Georgia's election interference trial was an attempt to turn their most arousing fantasies into a reality.

However, this case became such a mess for the prosecution that even the most dependable lawfare enthusiasts knew this one was not going to succeed.

The saga begins with one of the fake news stories of the century: when Donald Trump supposedly called then–Georgia Secretary of State Brad Raffensperger and told him to "find me the votes" to overturn the state's election results in 2020.

This fake event was at the center of a criminal prosecution of Donald Trump and myriad associates by Fulton County District Attorney Fani Willis. The media has often advanced the falsehood that Trump told the Georgia secretary of state to "find me the votes." Famed investigative journalist Michael Isikoff even named a book about Willis's case against Trump *Find Me the Votes*. It made the *New York Times* bestseller list.

The transcript of the conversation, however, shows that Trump didn't say that at all. He said, "I just want to find 11,780 votes, which is one more than we have because we won the state."[1]

Fake reports of this conversation were repeated so often, it was clear the establishment media just stopped checking the stories for accuracy before going to publication. A January 9, 2021, story from the *Washington Post*, for example, was headlined "'Find the Fraud': Trump Pressured a Georgia Elections Investigator in a Separate Call Legal Experts Say Could Amount to Obstruction."

They would later issue an embarrassing correction: "Trump did not tell the investigator to 'find the fraud' or say she would be 'a national hero' if she did so. Instead, Trump urged the investigator to scrutinize ballots in Fulton County, Ga., asserting she would find 'dishonesty' there."[2]

Oh, I see.

This didn't stop the media from repeating the lie over and over.[3] In fact, Democrats' House impeachment managers treated the "find the fraud" hoax as if it were real. (Is this not falsifying evidence in the Senate?)

Georgia underwent a lot of controversial last-minute changes, ostensibly due to the coronavirus. As I documented in *Breaking the News*, Raffensperger, along with a group run by radical Democrat Stacey Abrams, came to an agreement that allowed for considerably less restrictive verification regulations on absentee ballots. This alone appeared to have swung the state from Trump to Biden and the Democrats.

Trump went to bed on election night 2020 thinking he had won the state and woke up knowing he was not likely to be declared the winner. You can bet he found this not just upsetting but shocking.

Trump wanted there to be 11,780 more votes out there somewhere, but he didn't call on anyone to do anything illegal.

During the course of the call, Trump said that he believed he had probably won the state by 500,000 votes, but that all he needed to do was show that he had won it narrowly. He was clearly illustrating that he believed he had to show only a small increase in his percentage of the vote to see a different outcome. This obvious interpretation of the conversation was summarily ignored in the vast majority of media reports that I reviewed during the scope of my research for this book.

Trump didn't command Raffensperger to do anything, no matter what the media and Trump's haters insisted. Yet insist they did, suggesting that it was incontrovertibly evident that Trump had committed election fraud by pressuring an election official to overturn his defeat in the state.[4]

The content of the call seems even less outrageous when you consider that while Trump was contesting the result, Georgia Democrats went door-to-door *after* the election to cure ballots; that means they helped their voters "fix" mistakes that absentee voters may have made to make sure their votes counted.

It was a big mess across the country, and the messiest of all the states was arguably Georgia (see *Breaking the News* for more details).

Trump had every right to be perturbed by it all.

Yet it became clear that Willis's investigation was going to lead to a criminal indictment.

THE MOST ICONIC MUG SHOT IN HISTORY

Fani Willis knew she was going to prosecute Trump on her first day in office.[5] It was her singular ambition.

Willis has lawfare in her blood. She was raised by her father, John C. Floyd III, who was a top member of the Black Panthers and later became an attorney himself.[6] He had a love affair with radical Marxist and Black Power revolutionary Angela Davis.[7] Willis has stayed close with her dad, who was a crucial character witness on her behalf.[8]

On August 14, 2023, a ninety-eight-page indictment came down against Trump and eighteen other codefendants. It contained forty-one counts, thirteen of those against Trump.

Fani did not run a tight ship. Initially there was a false alarm when the Fulton County court website displayed a document listing thirty-nine charges against Trump, before it was quickly removed. Attorneys for the former president called it a "glaring constitutional violation" and a violation of his due process rights. Trump supporters hoped this would lead to an immediate mistrial, but the frenzy quickly subsided.

The leak was not just messy and embarrassing, it was an indication that the indictment was going to happen even before witnesses had testified or the grand jury had a chance to complete their deliberations. The district attorney's office never fully explained the fumble.

The indictments were a long time coming. In fact, Willis's top prosecutor, Nathan Wade, would reveal in a bombshell deposition to the House Judiciary Committee that Willis had planned the prosecution even before she took office.

Trump's codefendants included State Senator Shawn Still; attorneys John Eastman, Sidney Powell, Jenna Ellis, Bob Cheeley, Ray Smith III, and Kenneth Chesebro; former Assistant Attorney General Jeffrey Clark; GOP strategist Michael Roman; former Coffee County elections supervisor Misty Hampton; former Coffee County GOP chairwoman Cathy Latham; Atlanta bail bondsman Scott Hall; publicist Trevian Kutti; Illinois pastor Stephen Cliffgard Lee; and Harrison Floyd, who served as director of Black Voices for Trump.[9]

The Trump campaign released a blistering statement, calling Willis a "rabid partisan who is campaigning and fundraising on a platform of prosecuting President Trump through these bogus indictments." The statement also accused Willis of intentionally stalling the investigation so it was timed to "maximally interfere with the 2024 presidential race."

"Call it election interference or election manipulation—it is a dangerous effort by the ruling class to suppress the choice of the people. It is un-American and wrong," the statement continued.[10]

Fulton County Superior Court Judge Robert McBurney, who signed off on the charges, was spotted joking around with journalists right after he had done so.[11]

Trump immediately and vociferously objected to the indictment. The media tried to inoculate Willis from criticism by emphasizing her blackness and womanhood. MSNBC's Andrea Mitchell said among a panel of women on *Katy Tur Reports* that a "strong black woman standing up to Donald Trump" was something to behold.[12]

Trump made a comment on Truth Social that had CNN commentators Alyssa Farah Griffin, Kaitlin Collins, and Jake Tapper seeing phantom n-words: "They never went after those that Rigged the Election. They only went after those that fought to find the RIGGERS!" "That the use of the word 'rigger' is not unintentional, Mr. Trump has certainly been accused of racist language before," Farah Griffin said.

You see, "rigger" rhymes with a word you can't say, which makes Trump a racist.

Call it a *hate rhyme*.

The media couldn't help themselves: They made it crystal clear that this was a political persecution and that the alleged conspirators were being targeted for their politics. Attorney and former Senator Claire McCaskill (D-MO) said on MSNBC, "The good news is we finally have Rudy Giuliani indicted. Whoo-hoo! That makes me very happy."[13]

The internet calls that "saying the quiet part out loud."

It was clear from the jump that this was a selective prosecution and a violation of the Equal Protection Clause, which mandates equal justice under the law for all citizens. "A selective prosecution claim is not a defense on the merits to the criminal charge itself, but an independent assertion that the prosecutor has brought the charge for reasons forbidden by the Constitution," according to the Supreme Court in *United States v. Armstrong* (1996). Among those forbidden reasons is political alignment.

Willis is a politically ambitious Democrat. How ambitious? She launched a fundraising website days before the indictment came down.[14] She's that brazen.

Still, it was game on, yet again.

Lawfare skeptics immediately raised First Amendment concerns, noting that the indictment seemed to treat merely pointing out flaws in the 2020 election as a crime. Trump had every right to express himself to Raffensperger, which he did, and Raffensperger had every right to do nothing about it, which he did.

Where is the crime?

Like the Bragg case in Florida, this was another instance where they were trying to bust Trump for federal election crimes in a county court.[15] You can't do that, theoretically.

Yet for Trump haters, it was another moment to celebrate, maybe now more than ever, because Fulton County Sheriff Pat Labat promised them something that none of the other lawfare functionaries had: a mug shot. "Unless somebody tells me differently, we are following our normal practices, and so it doesn't matter your status, we'll have a mug shot ready for you," Labat said.

The point of a mug shot is to help the public, especially victims, identify the arrested person. In Trump's case, he was the world's most famous man and there were no victims of these supposed crime, but they would make him go through the ritual anyway.

What's more, it wouldn't just be Trump who had to pose for a booking photograph; everyone who was indicted alongside him would have to go through the ignominious procedure as well.

Willis and company were out to humiliate their political foes.

Some defendants used the mug shots to portray themselves as rebels, dissidents, or political prisoners. Others made a mockery of the whole broken system by posing with ear-to-ear grins. Others looked quite sad, haggard, or rattled.

Trump himself took perhaps the most iconic mug shot in history. It turned into a multimillion-dollar marketing and merchandise campaign that no doubt did his campaign more good than harm.

Yet the president didn't view it as a joke or a stunt. He knew exactly what was being done to him.[16]

"It was a terrible experience. I came in, I was treated very nicely, but it is what it is. I took a mug shot, which I never heard the words *mug shot*. They didn't teach me that at the Wharton School of Finance. I have to go through a process. It is election interference," Trump told Newsmax host Greg Kelly just hours after being booked. "But it's a very sad experience, and it's a very sad day for our country. This is a weaponized Justice Department and all of these indictments and cases."[17]

EVERYTHING BUT THE KITCHEN SINK

Willis was taking the "kitchen sink" approach—throwing everything but that at the supposed wrongdoers. She tried to stick Trump and company with election fraud and conspiracy to defraud the state, among a smorgasbord of other alleged crimes.

The charges go well beyond the Raffensperger phone call. For example, Trump associates were accused of stealing data from voting machines seeking evidence of fraud. Trump and his associates were accused of making false statements about election fraud, elected leaders, and an election worker. They allegedly filed false documents, committed perjury, and recruited people "to convene and cast false Electoral College votes."[18]

"The indictment alleges that rather than abide by Georgia's legal process for election challenges, the defendants engaged in a criminal racketeering enterprise to overturn Georgia's presidential election result," Willis said at a press conference when the indictment was released.

Rudy Giuliani was accused of making felony false statements.

Attorney Sidney Powell allegedly entered a written agreement under which a computer forensics firm breached election equipment.

Former dean of Chapman University law school John Eastman was indicted over a memo explaining the process through which Trump could conceivably remain in power, so long as a long series of dominoes fell sequentially. First, Vice President Mike Pence would have to choose not to certify some of the states over irregularities. At that point, certification reverts to the various state legislators to sort out the true results. If they believe the initially determined result was inaccurte, via recounts, contested ballots, legal cases, etc., then the state can send an alternative slate of electors to the Electoral College.

This was not an attempt to create "fake" or "fraudulent" electors, as the Democrats and the media claimed, but rather to provide a legal pathway in the event the results were overturned. Trump needed to assemble the electors in case that happened.

It was a long-shot (I wrote in *Breaking the News* that I didn't think it would work),[19] but it wasn't entirely without precedent. It was the Democrats, in fact, who used this strategy in the 1960 election contest between Vice President Richard M. Nixon and Senator John F. Kennedy. Even left-wing *Politico* acknowledged this:

> Nixon's Hawaii electors met and cast their three votes in an official ceremony. But nearby, Kennedy's three elector nominees gathered and signed their own certificates, delivering them to Washington as though Kennedy had won the state.
>
> Until now, it's been unclear whether the 1960 case of the Kennedy electors was truly analogous to 2020 Trump electors. But the unofficial Democratic certificates,[20] obtained by POLITICO from the non-digitized files of the National Archives, show the three Kennedy electors signed documents that are remarkably similar to the false Trump-elector certificates. . . .
>
> Instead, the Hawaii Democrats used virtually the same language that the false [*sic*] Trump electors in five states used in their effort to upend the 2020 race.[21]

Eastman (and Kennedy) relied on the Electoral Count Act of 1887. Both parties agreed to change that statute in 2022 with the Electoral Count Reform Act. But the fact that it was necessary to change the law proved that Eastman and Trump's plan was probably legitimate.

But that didn't matter to those who sought to destroy Trump and anyone else who helped devise his strategy to contest the 2020 election results. They had to destroy John Eastman for advancing contestable—if unorthodox—legal theory.

A lawyer is obliged to give his or her client the best possible advice to their knowledge. Your interpretation of "best advice" could mean advice that you think has the most likely chance of a positive outcome for the client, or it could mean providing a path to the client's best-case scenario. That's between attorney and client. I can't read Eastman's or Trump's mind, but clearly Eastman was trying to serve the interests of his client.

Yet John Eastman's law license was revoked amid an ethics probe surrounding the 2020 election; it could lead to permanent disbarment.[22] And so as he waits for an ultimate ruling, he doesn't have the ability to ply his trade to earn money to pay his exorbitant legal bills.

The overreaction to Trump attempting to use lawyers to achieve victory was as hypocritical as it was blatant. Joe Biden and the Democrat Party had assembled some six hundred election lawyers and volunteers to find any alleged improprieties in the election—and bragged about it.[23] If they had lost a close contest, we would have seen election denialism that would have been as bad as—if not worse than—what we saw after the 2016 election. This time they were more organized, and they had a larger, heavily funded army of lawyers ready to find the necessary votes themselves.

They're no different from Trump, aside from being organized and protected by the press.

RICO

Willis charged Trump under Georgia's RICO statute, which is typically used to dismantle organized-crime enterprises. Trump led a "racketeering enterprise to overturn Georgia's presidential election result," according to the indictment.

Willis has made a name for herself charging RICO violations, having used it to bust rapper Young Thug and his Young Slime Life gang.

However, just because this worked against the YSL gang doesn't mean Trump and his supporters were part of an organized criminal organization.

RICO stands for and derives from the federal Racketeer Influenced and Corrupt Organizations Act. The bill was passed in 1970 and introduced a new tool at the federal level to take down organized criminal syndicates, that is, the mafia. In essence, if you are in a group that exists in large part to commit illegal acts, being a part of said group is illegal in and of itself. Individual members of the group can be held accountable for crimes committed by the syndicate.

The prosecutors tried to lump all of MAGA into one prosecution and call it an enterprise so that they could get enhanced penalties. Fani Willis had done what so many of the "progressive" proponents of lawfare have in the past: She invented new uses of RICO, civil liberties be damned.

Georgia's RICO law has come under attack from members of the legal community for being more expansive than the federal government's, which is itself quite elastic.[24]

"Somebody could go to JCPenney, shoplift a pair of socks, walk next-door to Sears and shoplift a second pair of socks, and they can be charged with RICO," according to Georgia-based trial attorney and RICO specialist Chris Timmons.[25]

Willis had already pursued eleven RICO cases since she assumed the role of DA a year and a half earlier. She used it against everyone. She used it against actual gang members. She used it against schoolteachers who she thought were cheating to inflate standardized test scores. RICO was her hammer, and potential cases presented themselves to her as nails.

But there was one glaring hole in the RICO case she built against Trump: For it to work, she would have had to read Trump's mind.

Theoretically, Willis would have to prove that Trump had honestly thought he lost the election and thus participated in a criminal conspiracy to illegally overturn it. If Trump sincerely believed that he had won the election and that it had been stolen from him, then her case was doomed. With RICO, Willis was suggesting Trump was knowingly participating in a criminal enterprise. So, what was the crime Trump knew that he was committing? From Trump's vantage point, he was merely trying to rectify an unjustly decided election result. Willis would need to prove Trump was trying to illegally alter the outcome of an election.

Willis's main problem boiled down to this: There is no evidence to suggest Trump didn't truly believe that the election was rigged. He has been utterly consistent in this regard. If there was even one quote or one eyewitness testimony claiming Trump believed all along that he had lost and wanted the election overturned anyway, we would never stop hearing about it. He'd be in jail today, or worse, I guarantee it.

But there's no evidence to suggest that Trump doesn't really believe with his heart and mind that he won the 2020 election and that it was stolen from him.

Thus, Fani Willis was never going to prove that he intended to join a conspiracy to knowingly commit a crime.

What's more, Willis was clearly overstepping her jurisdiction. She was effectively attempting to prosecute a federal RICO case at the state level. The indictment includes allegations that the conspiracy to undermine the election included conduct in other states like Pennsylvania. This is totally out of bounds in this particular court and a sign that Willis was making a national *political* case, not a case about supposed violations of Georgia law.

Yet these points would all prove to be moot. As far as this case was concerned, it didn't matter whether she had a strong case or a weak one. It didn't matter if it was legal or political.

That's because Fani Willis did the single dumbest thing she possibly could have done, and it had nothing to do with Donald Trump himself: She indicted Mike Roman.

FANI GETS ROMAN'D

As Willis's case wore on, several codefendants yielded to the agents of lawfare. As legal bills pushed into the six-figure range for many people caught up in the dragnet, many broke and exhausted codefendants cried uncle and took plea deals.

In so many words, some blinked.

Modern-day American politics is not for the faint of heart. It's not enough to merely be innocent. You also must be willing to fight a brutal and relentless opposition. And you must be able to see things clearly—that is, that your cause is righteous—under intense pressure. In my view, caving was understandable, but not excusable.

Thankfully, not everyone did. Some chose to stand their ground, like

Georgia Republican Party Chair David Shafer, who was indicted for being one of the alternate electors, or, in other words, merely for being the top Republican in the state.

A man named Mike Roman went a step further. Not only did he refuse to confess to crimes he knew he hadn't committed—he fought back.

Roman is described in media as "a former Trump campaign aide," an "operative," or an "opposition researcher." All of that is true, but in my line of work, he's just "Roman." He resides in that ultraproductive gray area of political activism and journalism.

He is one of the few true badasses walking among us.

In my seventeen years at *Breitbart News*, fewer things have gotten me more excited than hearing that one of my editors or reporters has a new piece of information they "got from Roman." Whenever I hear those words, I know that whatever they tell me next is going to be substantive and accurate, and—most relevant—that someone who deserves some scrutiny is going to be very upset when they learn that we have this information. If you get in his (figurative) gun sights, Roman will comb every document, every detail, every old social media post, and every court document that bears your name until he gets what's he's looking for.

Whenever I think of him, Harvey Keitel's character in *Pulp Fiction* comes to mind: the Wolf. Professional, unafraid, and absolutely zero bullshit. What the Wolf does isn't rocket science or brain surgery; he handles more practical yet urgent matters, like scooping bits of bone and brains out of the back seat of a Chevy Nova. Theoretically, anyone can do it, but they won't, and even if they can, they can't do the job efficiently and stealthily. He doesn't do glamorous work. He doesn't get the spotlight. Yet he's the coolest character in a film filled with cool characters. He's calm enough to figure out what's actually useful, and he gets it done. That's Roman.

His specialty, unfortunately for Fani Willis, is helping conservatives figure out who is committing fraud.

When I saw that Willis had indicted him, I said to myself, *I don't know about that.* The thought went through my mind that she'd better be squeaky clean, because if she had as much as an unpaid parking ticket, Mike Roman was going to find it and haunt her dreams.

As it turned out, she wasn't clean. Not even close.

Fani was about to get Roman'd.

Roman zeroed in on her relationship with Nathan Wade, her boyfriend and colleague in lawfare on this very case.

Roman, the consummate investigator, filed a motion alleging that Willis had a romantic relationship with special prosecutor Wade. What's more, Wade's law firm had used county funds, aka tax dollars, to take Willis on an exotic vacation. Willis appeared to be embezzling taxpayer money to go on luxury trips with her boo, who also happened to work for her. Roman dropped this bombshell scoop in a court motion.

Wade was a family law attorney—that means his area of law is divorces and prenuptial agreements—with no prosecution experience. He was appointed by Willis to the Trump World cases without any checks or oversight that would have questioned his qualifications. He had zero background in RICO law. In fact, he admitted that he had to study up on it.

Wade filed for divorce from his wife the day after he signed his deal with Willis,[26] which was apparently sometime after their affair began.

With county funds, Willis paid Wade handsomely, far more than other prosecutors on the case.[27] She directly benefited from these payments too. They traveled together to California's Napa Valley to go wine tasting, they cruised the Caribbean, and they holidayed in Florida, according to Roman's research.

Call it a kickback by another name.

While public prosecutors don't tend to earn the big salaries that corporate lawyers can fetch, Fani and Nathan were milking MAGA's pain for all it was worth.

They were living the high life.

"The Fulton County district attorney never had legal authority to appoint the special prosecutor, who assisted in obtaining both grand jury indictments," according to Roman's filing.

Everything was starting to make perfect sense.

It's ironic that it was Willis and Wade who were using RICO to charge Trump when they were the ones working together in a legally suspect manner.

"The district attorney and the special prosecutor have violated laws regulating the use of public monies, suffer from irreparable conflicts of interest, and have violated their oaths of office under the Georgia Rules of Professional Conduct and should be disqualified from prosecuting this matter," wrote Roman's attorneys.[28]

Devastating.

As the internet might say, Fulton County Fani effed around with Mike Roman and got found out.

You knew she was in trouble when she cast "racial aspersions" toward Roman. That was Judge Scott McAfee's phraseology, not my own. The judge rebuked her for "playing the race card."[29]

Nevertheless, she persisted, refusing to step down.

A slow burn of controversies and setbacks followed after she got Roman'd. For example, it became clear that the Fulton County District Attorney's Office colluded with the January 6th Committee in Congress. *Politico* reported that Willis's team received guidance from J6 committee investigators and was allowed to review evidence against Trump and his allies compiled by the committee. The J6 committee destroyed its records, rendering them nondiscoverable for Trump and the eighteen codefendants. There were strenuous efforts to conceal the evidence from the court and the public.[30]

But wait, there's more.

Nathan Wade met with the White House counsel at least twice. He billed the Fulton DA's office for eight hours from the White House on at least two separate occasions: May 23, 2022, and on November 18, 2022, both before Trump was indicted. The case should have been thrown out in January 2024 when this was revealed, but honestly it is more of a scandal for Joe Biden and his administration than it is for Wade. Wade has refused to say what was discussed in these White House meetings, but it's hardly a mystery. Of course the subject du jour was the indictment of Trump. Wade's career to that point was completely unimpressive. He was a nobody. There is no plausible reason he would have had multiple eight-hour meetings at Biden's White House if they weren't working on something big together.

It wasn't until January 2024 that we would learn that Fani Willis herself reportedly had a five-hour meeting at the White House with Vice President Kamala Harris months before the indictment. The meeting occurred on February 28, 2023, months after Wade's meetings but months before the August indictment.[31] It is, again, unknown what was discussed at the meeting, but it would boggle the mind if anything of substance other than Trump was discussed.

This means that the lawfare to undo Trump didn't just happen spontaneously, it came from inside the White House. If the executive branch tried to use the legal system to disqualify its main political rival—and it did—that is pure election interference. Lawfare at its very worst.

In retrospect, of course there was coordination. There was no way a Fulton County DA would prosecute a former president of the United States without seeking approval of the White House.

So, who would be the liaison between the White House and Willis's team?

Enter Jeff DiSantis. In March 2024, *Breitbart News* broke news of financial disclosures revealing that Fulton County's Deputy District Attorney Jeff DiSantis worked with Joe Biden's reelection campaign and was a former Biden White House aide.[32] Sources told us that he was planted inside the Fulton County DA's office specifically to target Trump. DiSantis became the primary spokesperson for Willis's team in regard to the Trump investigation.[33]

DiSantis was an intern for President Bill Clinton, was on staff for Senator Zell Miller (D-GA), and worked on behalf of Democrats in dozens of states.[34] He was a veteran of Georgia's Democrat machine, having led the state party, and was on Fani Willis's transition team after she was elected.

He also was a professional communicator and messaging expert.

Sources insisted that DiSantis was responsible for coordinating with the White House to target Trump. "DiSantis did this," a source told *Breitbart News* about the Trump case. "He's the one. He is the one pulling all the strings. . . . He was in every important meeting. He is the brainchild behind this. That is the connection to the White House."

Breitbart News's sources speculated that DiSantis might have been involved in selecting grand jurors. The source did not provide any direct evidence to support the claim but did assert that that "there's not one conservative person on that grand jury."

He was the Democrat establishment's political operative hiding out within Fani Willis's DA office. He was positioned to be the Matthew Colangelo of the Georgia case against President Donald Trump. He could be the ringer brought in to secure the victory.

Only in DiSantis's case, it was not meant to be.

FANI GETS SLOPPY

The judge went on to throw out three criminal charges against Trump because Willis did not specify the nature of the alleged felonies. The counts "fail to allege sufficient detail regarding the nature of their commission, i.e., the underlying felony solicited," Judge McAfee wrote. "They do not give the Defendants enough information to prepare their defenses intelligently."

It was the latest in a string of sloppy errors by Willis.[35]

Simultaneously, the Trump team attempted to get the case thrown out due to Willis's apparent misconduct with Wade. McAfee said the case could continue, but not if Wade was a part of it. Wade quickly resigned.[36]

This was good news for Trump, but it was still a half measure by the court. Saying that she could continue on the case so long as Willis and Wade weren't working together is a textbook non sequitur argumentative fallacy. If both of them were acting unethically, why punish one and not the other?

Even former Assistant U.S. Attorney and MSNBC star Andrew Weissmann said he'd seen enough and called on Willis to recuse herself in order to save the case. "She clearly has no credibility with this judge," he said on television.[37] Frustration ricocheted across the anti-Trump legal punditry. CNN talking head Jeffrey Toobin, himself a former assistant U.S. attorney, said, "This case is going nowhere."[38]

Things were starting to get silly, literally. Nathan Wade, presumably a single man free to speak his mind, decided to discuss his relationship with Willis with comedian Marlon Wayans, of all people. Only, it wasn't really Marlon Wayans, it was a character Wayans plays called Quon. As you can imagine, the conversation quickly turned from his position under Willis to . . . his positions under Willis. "Young Black men need a role model," said Wayans's Quon. "What's your advice to kids in the hood that's out there that wanna grow up and have their dick potentially in democracy?"

Wade cut the interview at this point.[39]

In September 2024, Judge McAfee dismissed two counts against Trump for a lack of jurisdiction. Willis's error was trying to enforce a federal law in a state court.

By McAfee's logic, that means "[i]f federal courts and tribunals exist to enforce federal campaign finance laws, or to punish false filings, then arguably it is unconstitutional for a state court to preempt the FEC or federal court, and Trump's conviction should be tossed," *Breitbart News* editor and Harvard-trained attorney Joel Pollak wrote.

Willis got a vote of confidence from her constituency on November 5, 2024, when she was reelected Fulton County district attorney. But it was Donald Trump who got the last laugh that day, winning back the presidency despite Willis's strenuous efforts.

On December 19, Fani of Fulton County was disqualified from the Trump case. "After carefully considering the trial court's findings in its order, we conclude that it erred by failing to disqualify DA Willis and her office," a three-judge panel wrote in its opinion. "The remedy crafted by the trial court to prevent an ongoing appearance of impropriety did nothing to address the appearance of impropriety that existed at times when DA Willis was exercising her broad pretrial discretion about who to prosecute and what charges to bring," the decision continued.[40]

This was a huge win for Trump, but it could have been bigger. "It's disappointing that the appeals court didn't go the extra mile to also dismiss the underlying indictments as unconstitutional, essentially punting on that issue without analysis," then–Breitbart News Senior Legal Contributor Ken Klukowski said.

Once Mike Roman figured out that she had hired her unqualified boyfriend at a sweetheart rate and then received financial benefits from the arrangement via luxury vacations, the whole case should have gone away and investigations into Willis should have begun.

So many conflicts of interest went undisclosed.

So much taxpayer money was funneled back to Willis.

The case was going nowhere. It was never going anywhere for a number of reasons. It ought to live in infamy in our historical records as a national disgrace. Yet its death throes lasted for weeks on end.

In January 2025, Willis announced her intentions to get back onto the doomed case: She asked Georgia's highest court to review the lower court's decision to remove her. This raises the stakes, but is potentially good news for Trump. Sure, Willis could potentially get reinstated, which would nullify the victory of her getting removed in the first place, but it's likely that a higher court will cement the lower court's decision, giving Trump another positive day of news.

Yet the dream scenario for Trump supporters is that a court issue a more sweeping rebuke of Willis and her tactics. We could see a judgment that clearly states that the deliberate targeting of the leader of an opposition party violates the Due Process Clause of the U.S. Constitution. Willis had, after all, specifically campaigned on a promise to take down Trump. If that happens, and a court like the Georgia Supreme Court holds that it is illegal to use the law specifically to take down your political enemies, then the New York courts and courts across America would have to take notice.

Yes, Willis's appeal could potentially lead to the dismissal of the entire case, which would provide an important precedent that would need to be considered across all of the prosecutions of Donald Trump and any politician who finds him- or herself on the wrong end of a massive lawfare campaign.

This includes the Stormy Daniels case, the one case that ended in a criminal conviction.

CHAPTER 6

DEPARTMENT OF INJUSTICE

It wasn't long after Joe Biden was sworn in that the efforts to pursue Trump began in earnest. In fact, they hadn't really stopped, considering that he was impeached over virtually nothing, was investigated by Special Counsel Robert Mueller, and then impeached again after January 6, 2020. One entity that was always lurking in the background and occasionally on full display in the foreground was Merrick Garland's Department of Justice.

Garland has a picture-perfect resume. He got two degrees from Harvard before clerking at the United States Court of Appeals for the Second Circuit for the legendary Henry Friendly, perhaps the most influential circuit judge of his era, and Supreme Court Justice William J. Brennan Jr. In 1997, he was appointed to the nation's most prestigious federal appeals court, the United States Court of Appeals for the District of Columbia Circuit, by President Bill Clinton. He would eventually serve as its chief judge.

He is known as a gentleman. Reasonable, not venomous or harsh. Yet he became a prime example of an old-school liberal Democrat judge who was forced to try to metamorphize into a militant member of the new woke Democrat Party, ultimately betraying his own past yet falling short of sufficient militancy to satisfy his party base.

Things got very interesting for Garland at the very end of Barack Obama's second term. As I wrote in *Breaking Biden*:

Garland achieved political martyrdom in 2016 when he was nominated by Barack Obama to fill the Supreme Court seat vacated by Justice Antonin Scalia upon Scalia's death in February of that year. Senate majority leader Mitch McConnell (R-KY) vowed that the Republicans would not consider filling the seat until after the presidential election. Obama tapped Garland anyway, but that nomination expired with the end of the congressional session in January 2017. Donald Trump went on to win the 2016 election and nominate Neil Gorsuch to fill the seat, and Gorsuch was confirmed.

Garland would have been a shoo-in for confirmation, that is, if he got a vote. He did not.

Upon election, Joe Biden installed Garland as attorney general. Biden gave him the nod, according to establishment media reports, because of the insistence of longtime advisor and eventual White House chief of staff Ron Klain.[1] It was a role that was certainly a much worse match for him than the U.S. Supreme Court. Garland, the mild-mannered, largely apolitical liberal, went from running a small office of fewer than ten people to controlling a vast bureaucracy of well over 100,000 people.

Immediately it raised a legitimate question: Who was driving the bus over at the DOJ?

Garland's top two deputies did not share some of his aforementioned positive character traits. Deputy Attorney General Lisa Monaco and Associate Attorney General Vanita Gupta had reputations for far-left activism. It would have been highly unusual if Garland had not signed off on the appointment of his top two deputies, so he is not free from blame for the events that unfold in this chapter. Ultimately, the buck stops with him. However, I want to note at the outset that the most egregious examples of lawfare documented here likely came from the minds of Monaco and Gupta, not the affable Garland. But he certainly didn't stop anything.

Occam's razor suggests that it was Monaco and Gupta who were the likely masterminds of the Biden DOJ's lawfare against Trump.

Monaco, a reliable Biden-world crony, became deputy attorney general overseeing Trump and J6 cases. Previously, she served in Obama's White House as a homeland security adviser. She also worked at Secretary of State Antony Blinken's shadowy consulting firm WestExec. WestExec brokers deals between the public and private sector. For example, WestExec helped Google land lucrative Defense Department contracts. It is a prime example of consultant-class culture in Washington that is essentially legal corruption. Consultants cut deals with the government to benefit corporations and bag millions in the process, then they go into the government and enact policies that benefit those same companies and consultancies. The cycle continues. It's the proverbial revolving door. Monaco, for example, held an off-the-record meeting with tech industry titans amid DOJ lawsuits against Google and Apple; Apple was a client of hers, and WestExec had a big contract with Google.[2]

Monaco is also close with Andrew Weissmann, to the point that President Trump told me, "Weissmann is her boss," referring to the Trump-deranged former general counsel at the FBI and top official for then–Special Counsel Robert Mueller.[3]

After Biden tapped Gupta to be the DOJ's No. 3, she felt compelled to issue a face-saving apology for her "harsh rhetoric" toward conservatives.[4] In the aftermath of the *Dobbs* decision that overturned *Roe v. Wade*, Gupta expressed urgency to target pro-lifers who protest at abortion clinics. She relied on the Freedom of Access to Clinic Entrances (FACE) Act, a law passed in the 1990s that prohibits threats, violence, or obstruction of abortion facilities. The FACE Act was designed to counter a wave of violence at clinics, but it was clear that Gupta was using it to go after the nonviolent. Biden's DOJ made a habit of arresting and prosecuting protesters who would pray and sing at clinics while urging women to not go through with having abortions. Not only did the Department of Justice characterize these actions as FACE Act violations, but as felony "conspiracy against rights," which carried severe penalties. The Biden DOJ racked up a series of convictions that carried years in prison and fines up to $250,000.[5]

While Vanita Gupta cracked down on peaceful Christian pro-lifers, pro-abortion militants were engaging in a sustained campaign of violence and getting away with it.

A rash of violence at crisis pregnancy centers during the "Days of Rage" saw over one hundred attacks against pro-life organizations nationwide led by a group called Jane's Revenge.[6] In one instance, pro-abortion radicals firebombed a conservative advocacy group.[7] The attacks were systematic,[8] including sustained campaigns of harassment and intimidation. In many instances, the left-wing militants would promote the violence on Twitter (now known as X).[9]

If Monaco or Gupta did anything to address Jane's Revenge, I could not find a public record of it.

Their DOJ had other priorities, namely Donald J. Trump and his movement.

I spoke to Trump several times about his ongoing legal battles throughout the 2024 election cycle, and he pointed the finger directly at Monaco.

"Lisa Monaco, she's really running the Justice Department, rather viciously and rather illegally, and that will be found out over the next year and a half, I predict," Trump told me in January 2024.[10]

Investigate her he should. Start by examining communications between Garland's, Monaco's, and Gupta's respective offices.

Interestingly, Trump theorized in conversation that even above Monaco in the actual hierarchy of Biden's DOJ is Andrew Weissmann. The MSNBC contributor and lawfare architect who took a star turn as a top official in Special Counsel Mueller's investigation into Trump appears in several chapters of this book. If there is lawfare going on against President Trump, it's a safe bet that Weissmann has coordinated it, praised it on TV, or both.

Biden's team was quickly assembled with Garland at the top. The DOJ probes into Trump began immediately. It wasn't until 2022, though, that we got the coup de grâce: a federal special counsel probe into Trump.

Merrick Garland was going to try something Robert Mueller could not.

THE FBI'S PANTY RAID

With the Republicans poised to win the congressional majority in November 2022, the Democrats had a binary choice.

The first option was to admit defeat and drop all investigations into Trump. The voters had rejected (albeit by a narrow margin) the Democarts' agenda for the first half of Biden's term; lawfare against Trump via the J6 committee was fundamental to that. So they could simply walk away from the tactic and start fighting fair. There were legal headaches in New York and Georgia that were going to proceed anyway, so Trump wouldn't be off the hook entirely, the Dems could have allowed the voters to decide his fate at the ballot box, as has been our democratic tradition until recent years.

If you know anything about the modern-day Democratic Party, though, they were never going to go with that option.

They were going to double (triple? quadruple?) down on lawfare.

The base demanded Donald Trump's blood, and with Joe Biden's administration limping along, the last thing the Democrats and the establishment media was going to do was take their boot off Trump's neck.

To this point, the Democrat lawfare efforts against Donald Trump were rooted in civil law. This is the realm of investigations and subpoenas, hearings and fines, even the occasional impeachment. It was an effort to damage his brand, shame him with scarlet letters, and waste his time and money with incessant legal carpet bombing.

(Fani Willis's Georgia election inference case was the lone criminal case to this point.)

There was simply no reason to pursue him unless they believed he had done something criminal. There is nothing left to look at. He's not subject to any regulator body as he was out of government. There were no victims of other (assuredly fake) crimes who had come forward. Thus, if they weren't prepared to move on, they had to charge him.

But for what?

The DOJ had two known investigations into Trump that had plodded along to that point: one into alleged efforts to overturn the results of the presidential election, the other on the handling of classified documents. They would try to get him for both.

The general public had no idea about these investigations until the most dramatic lawfare moment of this entire book: an unannounced predawn raid on Trump's home at Mar-a-Lago on the morning of August 8, 2022. It was an explosive, made-for-TV moment. The visuals were surreal: flashing red and blue lights, agents in full tactical gear with heavy artillery. You'd have thought they had found a missing terrorist cell or most-wanted fugitive hiding out in a casita on the property.

This wasn't just unprecedented, it was unthinkable. No former president had ever been treated in such a way.

Eric Trump offered some details to Fox News's Sean Hannity: "[t]hirty FBI agents, actually, more than that descend on Mar-a-Lago." He confirmed that there was no notice given before they started "ransacking an office, ransacking a closet." "You know, they broke into a safe," Trump's second-eldest son said. "He didn't even have anything in the safe. I mean, give me a break. And this is coming from, what, the National Archives?" The final comment was in reference to classified documents in Trump's possession.

The Trump family watched much of the search from New York via their security camera system.

Naturally, President Trump was perturbed by the incursion: "These are dark times for our Nation, as my beautiful home, Mar-A-Lago in Palm Beach, Florida, is currently under siege, raided, and occupied by a large group of FBI agents," Trump posted to social media. "Nothing like this has ever happened to a President of the United States before."

"Hillary Clinton was allowed to delete and acid wash 33,000 E-mails AFTER they were subpoenaed by Congress. Absolutely nothing has happened to hold her accountable. She even took antique furniture, and other items from the White House. I stood up to America's bureaucratic corruption, I restored power to the people, and truly delivered for our Country, like we have never seen before," continued the president.[11]

He isn't wrong about anything here.

It was instantly clear to anyone watching that this wasn't about getting the documents, it was about getting Trump.

Biden's then–White House Deputy Counsel Jonathan Su paved the way for the raid by waiving Trump's claim of executive privilege surrounding the documents in Trump's possession. Su had worked as a liaison between the January 6 committee and the Biden White House. While working as an attorney with Latham & Watkins, he represented Antony Blinken during his effort to deflect responsibility for the fifty-one officials who falsely said the Hunter Biden "Laptop from Hell" had all the hallmarks of Russian disinformation.[12] Former CIA Deputy Director Michael Morell told the House Judiciary Committee in 2023 that Blinken was the impetus for the letter.[13]

Magistrate Bruce Reinhart approved the FBI raid. Reinhart was almost entirely unknown to the public, but it quickly became well-known that he had previously worked for the U.S. attorney's office in South Florida. He left that role and represented employees of convicted pedophile Jeffrey Epstein, including his pilots, his scheduler, and a woman who was reportedly his sex slave.[14] (I believe everyone is entitled to have a strong defense in the United States of America, but this is certainly a colorful group, to say the least.) To the shock of literally no one, Reinhart had donated to Barack Obama.[15]

Interestingly, it took the FBI several days to act on the warrant. It is not known exactly why there was such a long lag time, but there are several possible explanations. First, the bureau did not regard the matter as so serious that it required immediate action. However, if that was the case, why the blockbuster-movie-style surprise raid? Another theory that makes more sense to me is that Garland was less than comfortable with the whole thing and dragged his feet. The *Wall Street Journal* reported that he deliberated over the search of Mar-a-Lago for weeks, perhaps because he thought it was too severe a tactic given the legal dubiousness of the eventual case against Trump. Maybe he knew this could backfire and lead to massive scrutiny if and when Republicans ever regained power.

Either way, he slow-walked it, before he eventually approved the raid.

Or maybe he didn't personally approve it after all. It took Garland three full days to come out and take ownership of the historic raid.[16] Why did he wait to explain this to the public? Perhaps Garland wasn't aware of what actually happened and took responsibility only in order to look like he was in control of his own Justice Department. If that scenario is in fact the truth, Republican investigators should try to ascertain who really was behind this unparalleled act of lawfare.

The details of the raid made it all the more ridiculous. President Trump's lawyer, Emil Bove, said they searched a room used for Barron Trump's Peloton stationary bike. There was even a rumor the FBI raided Melania Trump's lingerie drawer.[17]

When I first heard that account—true or not—I came to believe that it was all but certain Donald Trump would win the 2024 presidential election. The violation of privacy was that flagrant.

The FBI must have been feeling the public pushback, because they released a photo of all the supposedly illicit documents. The FBI had staged the photo shoot, scattering the documents as if that was how Trump had left them, strewn across the carpet in Mar-a-Lago. If the documents were so sensitive, why display them like this? What's more, these documents had nothing to do with making a case to a judge; it was an obvious media play to try to convince a skeptical public Trump really had warranted the harsh treatment.[18]

The publicity stunt backfired. The raid and aftermath was largely viewed as making a mockery of the legal system and the concept of classified documents itself.

In retrospect, it was all kind of amusing.

What was less amusing is that the FBI agents were authorized to use "deadly force" if necessary during the raid, according to the "operations order" for the seizure.[19]

If Biden's Justice Department was willing to kill Trump over these documents, there must have been something really, really secret in there, right?

As far as we can tell, not really. There were thirty-three boxes taken in all, including 13,000 government documents, several hundred of which were classified. This included at least four dozen empty folders with CLASSIFIED banners on them; it's unknown what happened to the contents of those files.

Not all classified documents are created equal. There are various levels of classification, and just because a document has a certain classification status, that does not necessarily mean it contains info that will greatly harm the nation if not handled according to National Archives and Records Administration (NARA) guidance. (NARA is the independent government agency charged with preservation of documents for the historical record.)

The media keyed in on thirty-one documents related to national defense, suggesting that Trump had been reckless with nuclear secrets about America as well as foreign countries.[20]

It is still unknown to the public exactly what Trump was harboring or why.

What was also far from certain, and more relevant: Was Trump's conduct actually illegal?

The Biden DOJ was about to start trying to prove that case, both in a court of law and to the American voting public.

NOVEMBER 18, 2022

Franklin Delano Roosevelt, a hero to Joe Biden, once said, "In politics, nothing happens by accident. If it happens, you can bet it was planned that way."[21]

I think about that quote when I think of the events of November 18, 2022. The midterms were over, the Democrats had lost, and the J6 committee was doomed. This meant that Congress was powerless to do much against Trump. What were the Democrats to do?

On November 9, 2022, Joe Biden held a press conference in the State Dining Room at the White House and told the press corps exactly what the Democrats intended: "Well, we just have to demonstrate that he will not take power by—if we—if he does run. I'm making sure he, under legitimate efforts of our Constitution, does not become the next President again."[22]

Well, that's fairly explicit.

Biden simply stated plainly that his administration intended to use the law to take down his political opponent.

He should have been impeached and removed from office on the spot, but I don't think enough Republicans took him seriously enough to understand the gravity of what he had just stated.

It was at exactly that point that lawfare kicked into overdrive.

After the Democrats hijacked Trump's first administration with the Russia collusion hoax and two impeachments, and after the first two years of his postpresidency featured the J6 kangaroo court and the beginning of the civil cases against Trump, the Democrats still found another gear for the back half of Biden's administration: They were finally going to try to lock Trump up.

And Joe had just given them the go-ahead.

It was the DOJ's turn. Garland was no longer allowed to ponder. To this point, Biden had harbored resentment that the Justice Department was slow to prosecute Trump while pursuing his son Hunter.[23] Things had to change.

And they did on November 18.

This was at the exact same moment Matthew Colangelo suspiciously resigned from his plum gig as a senior DOJ official for a vastly inferior post in Alvin Bragg's Manhattan DA office. It was the same time Nathan Wade went to the White House to visit the special counsel's office for something he just couldn't recall (presumably, prosecuting Donald Trump).

It was at this moment that Garland did his boss a solid and appointed Jack Smith special counsel to investigate Donald Trump.

Typically, a special counsel would be appointed to investigate an incumbent president for the obvious reason: To investigate a past president looks like an act of retribution or a preemptive strike. In this case it was clearly both.

Special counsels are expected to bring charges. This meant a prosecution of Trump was all but a guarantee, carried out by Joe Biden's Justice Department using his own political employees.

It should have been the scandal of the century.

Unless, of course, the special counsel really did deliver the goods.

YOU DON'T KNOW JACK

Jack Smith represents the type of snob who thinks America isn't good enough. He has spent large chunks of his life trying to undermine Republicans, then left the country to work for the International Criminal Court in The Hague, Netherlands. He was the guy the Biden's lawfare superstructure decided was the right person to take the final big swing at Donald Trump before the voters would decide the former president's ultimate fate.

Smith is a Harvard Law graduate (naturally) who worked as a prosecutor in the Manhattan (New York County) District Attorney's Office, the same office led by Alvin Bragg, which had Trump under indictment at the time Smith was appointed. Smith moved up in the world at the U.S. Attorney's Office for the Eastern District of New York in Brooklyn before taking a gig in the Public Integrity Section of Barack Obama's DOJ, which was run by lawfare pioneer Eric Holder.

Smith became "the lead person at the Justice Department looking for ways to target and prosecute the very people looking into who Lois Lerner went after," according to Representative Jim Jordan (R-OH).[24] Lerner is a former IRS official who had gained infamy for targeting conservative groups' tax-exempt applications.

During that time, Smith oversaw prosecutions of major political figures, many of which ended in resounding defeats. I mention two of them here because they are relevant to his efforts to take down Trump.

First was John Edwards, the former North Carolina U.S. senator and 2004 Democratic vice presidential nominee. Smith argued that if you spend money to protect your reputation, it is a campaign expense. The case was remarkably similar to the Stormy Daniels case described in great detail earlier. Edwards was accused of violating the Federal Election Campaign Act by paying off a mistress. He was acquitted on one count and a mistrial was declared on all five others, granting Edwards a big win and a huge loss to Smith.

The most famous of Smith's high-profile prosecutions was of former Virginia governor Robert McDonnell, a Republican. Smith, on behalf of the Obama administration, tried McDonnell for violating the federal bribery statute. In this case, McDonnell and his wife had received some gifts and loans from a businessman seeking his help, which may have been unsavory or unseemly, but not necessarily criminal. Smith, however, had ambitions of a criminal conviction. He used a bribery statute to prosecute his case even when there were no allegations of bribery.

Smith got his conviction, but it was overturned by a unanimous, 8–0, Supreme Court decision. The court could see that Smith had weaponized the law against a Republican target. "There is no question that this case is distasteful; it may be worse than that," Chief Justice John Roberts wrote in the opinion. "But our concern is not with tawdry tales of Ferraris, Rolexes, and ball gowns. It is instead with the broader legal implications of the Government's boundless interpretation of the federal bribery statute," he added. "A more limited interpretation of the term 'official act' leaves ample room for prosecuting corruption, while comporting with the text of the statute and the precedent of this Court."[25]

The emphatic SCOTUS opinion was a massive embarrassment for Smith (8-0!), but it was little solace for McDonnell, whom Smith had tormented. Leaks from Smith's office to the *Washington Post* had put McDonnell in the eye of a political storm for years. He was victorious in the end, but his promising political career was over thanks to Smith's lawfare.

"That stretch was exceptionally painful; three-and-a-half years from the investigation until we got the unanimous vindication by the U.S. Supreme Court," McDonnell told Mark Levin in an interview. "I knew in my heart from the very beginning—I'm a lawyer, obviously, looking at the law and the facts—that these charges were completely wrong," he continued. "And yet they persisted and pulled the trigger and the indictments started."[26]

What's more, not only did Smith's overzealous approach lead to an eventual defeat at the Supreme Court, but the ruling weakened the federal bribery statute.[27] In the end, Smith hurt his own cause. That's bad lawyering.

Smith had a few other headline-grabbing cases. He prosecuted the obviously corrupt Democrat Bob Menendez of New Jersey on public corruption charges. He failed, though, and that case ended with a mistrial. Years later, the senator would finally be convicted on federal bribery and corruption charges, well after Jack Smith swung and missed.

Smith also prosecuted a Republican Arizona congressman and father of twelve children, Rick Renzi. In this case, Smith got a conviction and a prison sentence; Trump granted Renzi clemency in his first term.

Smith eventually left the Justice Department and, as noted above, landed at the International Criminal Court (ICC) as a war crimes prosecutor.

The ICC was established in 2002, ostensibly to prosecute war crimes, crimes against humanity, and genocide. The United States is not a part of the ICC because it gives foreign nationals sovereignty over our citizens, including military personnel, among other objections. The ICC has been roundly criticized for failing to effectively prosecute high-ranking officials, pursuing prosecutions for political purposes, and being generally slow and expensive.

(After Trump's reelection, he would sanction the ICC's top prosecutor for peddling the lie that Israel is committing a genocide and that its leaders are war criminals.[28] The ICC is known for falsely equating Israel and its jihadi adversaries.[29])

The International Criminal Court is a partially realized globalist fantasy whereby world elites determine the law for all of humanity.

I regard it as a total farce, but it's the perfect place for a guy like Jack Smith. After habitually overcharging Americans, he fled the country to prosecute people in the world community's kangaroo court.

He couldn't even come back right away when Merrick Garland appointed him as special counsel due to a bicycle accident. Smith had been struck by a scooter while cycling around The Hague and had to launch his investigations from there while he recovered.

It was an inauspicious beginning.[30]

Weeks after the scooter collided with his Huffy, Smith arrived in

Washington, D.C., to the standard media fanfare. *A fearless, dogged investigator, open-minded, famous for his attention to detail.* When he's not busting the bad guys, he's completing a triathlon.[31]

Democrats welcomed home a savior.

Or so they thought.

DOUBLE TROUBLE: DARK TIMES FOR THE DONALD

On June 8, 2023, in Miami, a grand jury in the U.S. District Court for the Southern District of Florida indicted Trump over the documents found at Mar-a-Lago. Thirty-seven counts were announced that day, including thirty-one under the Espionage Act.

Yes, Jack Smith was suggesting President Trump was a spy against his own country. It was overwrought, yet it was taken deadly seriously by most of the establishment media and the Democrat Party.

Trump and aide Walt Nauta (who was charged with six counts) were accused of hiding boxes that contained classified documents. The documents contained information about past attacks on the United States and foreign countries' nuclear arsenals.

The indictment had one portion that did appear to be quite bad for Trump. He had allegedly said he could have declassified a document in his possession but hadn't. Prosecutors were quick to claim that meant that Trump knew the document was classified and he never intended to declassify it. That certainly makes it sound like slightly more than an innocent mistake.

Still, much of the indictment is made up of mundane details. It laid tracks for prosecutors to argue that Trump had misled his lawyers about the whereabouts of the documents so that they would remain in his possession. Nauta reportedly misled federal investigators about the location of the boxes.[32]

Trump faced a potential sentence of four hundred years if he was convicted on all counts and the judge chose to impose those sentences to run consecutively.[33] (One of our attorneys at *Breitbart* thought Trump probably faced twenty-five years in prison, but for a man in his late seventies, that's a difference without a distinction.)

Three more counts were tacked on on July 21, bringing the total to forty. This time Trump was accused of showing guests at his Bedminster, New Jersey, golf club a U.S. military plan to attack Iran. Those guests "did not have security clearances," according to the indictment.[34]

These last few indictments provide a perfect political Rorschach test. To the Trump hater, this looks like a smoking gun. *Jack Smith caught the Bad Orange Man breaking the law!* But to those who know Trump and give him the benefit of the doubt, we know exactly what was happening: Trump was showing off to his guests, who never were going to do anything with the information Trump flashed them. Silly stuff really. Trumpian braggadocio, nothing more.

Nonetheless, Smith saw a path to get Trump in handcuffs.

Trump spokesperson Steven Cheung blasted the Justice Department, calling their move a "continued desperate and flailing attempt by the Biden Crime Family and their Department of Justice to harass President Trump and those around him."[35]

Trump instantly saw the weaknesses in Smith's resume and character.

"The prosecutor in the case—I will call it OUR case—is a thug. I've named him Deranged Jack Smith," he said to a crowd of supporters.[36] "He's a behind-the-scenes guy, but his record is absolutely atrocious. He does political hit jobs."

"He's been known to viciously arrest a certain governor. You know the governor, Bob McDonnell of Virginia, and absolutely ruined his life, and the life of his family. Only to have the case overturned eight–nothing by the Supreme Court," Trump continued.

Trump caught some good luck on the documents case when he got dealt Judge Aileen Cannon of the Southern District of Florida, a judge he appointed and who was not easily cowed by media pressure.

She was going to have to show some serious spine because she wasn't just running into Jack Smith; she was going to have to weather the heat of the entire anti-Trump media.

Undeterred, Smith brought a second case against Trump, this time connected to January 6th. Smith was also investigating Trump for allegedly attempting to overturn the 2020 election. Smith made the case that Trump plotted to overturn the election with a slate of fake electors and intended to disrupt Congress's certification of the results. (Notably, they never charged Trump with "insurrection," the most intense buzzword in

Democrat political circles to describe Trump's actions leading up to the certification of the election on January 6, 2021.)

On August 1, a grand jury empaneled in the District of Columbia issued a four-count indictment of Trump for conspiracy to defraud the United States, obstructing an official proceeding, conspiracy to obstruct an official proceeding, and conspiracy against rights.

The more details we got, the more things really did look like a witch hunt.

Karen E. Gilbert, one of the lead prosecutors for Smith, donated to Barack Obama, Joe Biden, and the Democratic National Committee, according to the FEC.[37] David Rody, another DOJ veteran tapped to advise Smith, had donated to Joe Biden, lawfare specialist Representative Dan Goldman (D-NY), Kamala Harris, and other Democrat-connected causes.[38] Smith's wife, Katy Chevigny, not only donated to Biden, but also cut a check to Friends of Rashida Tlaib, which is a committee for one of the most radical leftists in the history of the U.S. Congress. Chevigny also produced a Michelle Obama documentary, *Becoming*.[39]

Trump pounced on that last fact, panning the documentary in a rant to supporters at his club in Bedminster. Even liberal critics panned the doc as "bland," "self-celebratory," and "paper-thin."[40]

The lawfare was so in-your-face, we learned that Biden's legal team threw caution to the wind and met with a Jack Smith aide before the indictment.[41]

Trump wasn't nearly as fortunate with his D.C. judge, Tanya Chutkan. Chutkan, an Obama appointee (and donor), had revealed extreme bias against Trump supporters in a prior sentencing when she said the Capitol riot "was nothing less than an attempt to violently overthrow the government, the legally, lawfully, peacefully elected government by individuals who were mad that their guy lost."[42]

She even compared January 6th to the terrorist attacks of September 11, 2001, and the Boston Marathon Bombing in 2013, revealing herself to be a hysteric or just plain stupid.[43] Trump came to believe that she sincerely wanted him in prison.[44]

Trump's team asked her to recuse herself from the case, but she refused.[45]

After enduring seven years of lawfare and still standing, Trump somehow found himself in his toughest spot yet.

TRUMP'S TAXES: A LAWFARE BRIEF

Indulge me a brief aside that connects back to Jack Smith's prosecution of Trump in a crucial way.

As far as I can tell, of all the things that have bothered the left about Donald Trump, his unwillingness to relinquish his tax returns to the public might be the issue that has caused them the most indignation.

This tradition in American life is a fairly recent addition to the public's presidential vetting process and is by no means the standard over time. After all, the income tax didn't exist until the Sixteenth Amendment was ratified in 1913. No president released their returns until Richard Nixon prior to the 1972 election. While every president from Carter to Obama did release returns, there is no law demanding Trump do the same.

I've long been a vocal proponent that presidents need not reveal their tax returns. I've yet to see a correlation between a clean tax return (what are we even looking for anyway?) and a successful presidency. It fosters a culture of voyeurism and discourages people with any sense of privacy and shame (both deeply human traits!) from running for the highest office in the land.

The left has long wanted to get Trump's tax returns so that they could prove once and for all . . . something. I don't know what, exactly. I assume they want to undermine the notion that he's a savvy businessman. Maybe he's not charitable enough. Maybe they think they'll find some sort of cheating. Who knows, but they want them.

They want them so bad that someone actually stole some of them and sent them to Rachel Maddow. In 2017, MSNBC's most conspiratorial star shared illicitly obtained Trump tax records from 2005 with her audience, garnering a frenzy of attention for her show. After dragging out the opening of her daily broadcast for nearly a half hour, she finally revealed that Trump had made more than $150 million in income that year—and paid $38 million in income taxes. As *Breitbart*'s Economic and Finance Editor John Carney reported at the time, he was paying at an effective rate of around 25 percent, which is much higher than normal for the very, very wealthy.[46]

So, what's the big deal with these tax returns? If you're a Democrat, everything Trump does is suspicious, so his breaking a tradition (albeit a relatively new one) is certainly going to have them scheming to figure out why. Naturally, the Democrats turned to their lawfare playbook to try to get the returns. This took the form of two cases that would not get settled until reaching the Supreme Court during Trump's first term.

The first case was *Trump v. Vance*, as in Cyrus Vance Jr., the former Manhattan DA who fruitlessly investigated the Trump Organization before Alvin Bragg took over for him. Vance, a Democrat, had tried to subpoena Trump's tax returns for this investigation, but issued a bad-faith, overly broad subpoena that Trump's attorneys accurately described as an "arbitrary fishing expedition."[47]

In the second case, *Trump v. Mazars* (a private accounting firm), the Democrat-controlled House of Representatives had subpoenaed financial records from Trump and his family in order to investigate the president over alleged past wrongs. The case went all the way to the Supreme Court, where Trump was victorious, 7–2. Chief Justice Roberts made clear that this effort was in defiance of the basic concept of separation of powers. Specifically, the House has broad authority to subpoena documents in order to carry out the legislative process, not to harass a rival politician over their personal finances.[48]

Justice Clarence Thomas added that Congress can go after these documents in the context of an impeachment, but this was not such an incident. This was congressional Democrats trying to find some way to get Trump's tax documents out into the public or perhaps gain momentum to change disclosure and ethics laws.

The Democrats then waited until Trump had left office, when they believed that they would have more leeway to go after him using criminal law. The locus shifted from Congress to prosecutors.

I include the above vignette, an attempt at lawfare by the Democrats that summarily failed, in this section of the book, because the tax return obsession is where Jack Smith started digging into President Trump.

RANK HYPOCRISY

The classified documents case was always the most dangerous for Donald Trump on its merits. The case against him didn't rely on unprovable allegations that were hidden for decades, or supercharged misdemeanors well beyond the statute of limitations, or strained claims that Trump had somehow formed a criminal mafia (in all his spare time). The other cases against Trump addressed in this book had deep internal weaknesses. They either ultimately have failed, will fail, or have succeeded only due to deep institutional rot. But with the classified documents, prosecutors had a serious argument based on the broad nature of the law at issue.

Yet it's still somewhat strange that they actually decided to pursue it. While it's easy to see Jack Smith's argument—Trump had classified documents that he didn't formally declassify—it was highly unusual to go after something like this with such intensity, given precedent.

First of all, people on both sides of the aisle in Washington will privately tell you that we tend to overclassify documents in this country anyway, mostly as CYA measures for those doing the classifying. When in doubt, classify. If you show any classified documents to anyone who shouldn't see them, or if you store them improperly, you run the risk of a criminal penalty, though those are rarely assessed.

Additionally, presidents simply are not scrutinized at the level Smith was scrutinizing Trump. There was no pretext for a figurative public colonoscopy on this level.

Consider how many high-profile instances of mishandled classified documents led to little or no penalty.[49]

The worst example, by a mile, in my opinion, comes from former Secretary of State Hillary Clinton, who maintained a private email server while serving as our nation's top diplomat, which she stored in a bathroom closet in a loft in Denver, Colorado. The server included classified information. She also used thirteen (!) mobile devices to send and receive email on the server, as well as five iPads, some of which were eventually destroyed with a hammer.

Any honest person would admit that there was no legitimate reason to maintain this server and extra devices.

The Clintons had a history of leveraging their power into massive sums of money for themselves and their family foundation, and there was reasonable suspicion that was exactly what she was doing with that server.

Clinton claimed she didn't know that classified emails were marked with a C when asked if there had been any digital erasure of the server, she joked about wiping her server "with a cloth."[50]

In other words, she was lying to our faces and knew she would get away with it.

There was also no reason to destroy the devices with a blunt instrument other than to evade laws and regulations and future Freedom of Information Act requests to unseal her communications. Smash them, and the public will be none the wiser forever. Simple, yet corrupt.

She was investigated by the FBI. Even then-director and Never Trump stalwart James Comey said that it was possible that foreign enemies accessed her email. He let her off the hook because he said she did not appear to intend to break the law, which is both implausible and irrelevant. The applicable portion of the Espionage Act does not include an intent requirement.[51]

Long story short: The "lock her up" chants were 100 percent legitimate. She probably wasn't even the only Clinton to mishandle classified documents.

Bill Clinton hid seventy-nine tapes of conversation he had with a historian in a sock drawer after he left the White House, claiming them as personal even though they were created while he was president. A judge believed there was likely classified information, particularly about diplomacy and international relations, on the tapes, but the National Archives was powerless to get them, as was the DOJ. The prevailing belief was that Clinton was entitled to the tapes, as a popular interpretation of the Presidential Records Act of 1978 (PRA) stated that the president himself has sole discretion to decide what is or is not part of the "presidential record."

A compelling defense for Trump himself!

Long before he became president and had the unilateral ability to declassify documents, Joe Biden took classified documents from the Senate Sensitive Compartmented Information Facility (SCIF). He stored the papers pretty much everywhere, including in his Delaware garage next to his beloved classic Corvette, the Penn Biden Center at the University of Pennsylvania, and the University of Delaware. Hunter Biden, famous for his drug addiction, business ties to foreign governments in China and Ukraine, and full-spectrum bad behavior, stayed at the house with the Vette and state secrets, giving him easy (and presumably illegal) access to them.

The Penn Biden Center regularly receives foreign visitors, and the

University experienced a massive uptick in Chinese donations after part-
nering with Joe Biden.[52]

An important distinction between Biden's documents and Trump's:
The Big Guy never had the authority to declassify any of these until he
became president, more than a decade after the docs went missing. A
special counsel investigation found grounds to charge Biden but declined
to do so because of difficulties related to Biden's obvious mental decline.

As Joe would say, "Not a joke!"

No agents raided Biden's home or sifted through Dr. Jill's intimates
trying to find them.

Even Barack Obama behaved similarly *vis-à-vis* state secrets. The
Obama Foundation kept classified documents, likely illegally, in a private
facility for more than a year after leaving office.[53]

Obama administration officials also made it a common practice to
leak sensitive information to the media to make him look tough, such as
details of the raid that ended in the death of Osama bin Laden, Obama's
"kill list" of foreign national security threats, and details of the Stuxnet
computer virus program used to cyberattack Iranian nuclear facilities.[54]
Even the late Democrat Senator Dianne Feinstein of California complained about this pattern.[55] Neither Obama nor anyone else in his administration was ever held accountable, despite the fact that during his
presidency Obama was very harsh on "leakers" he did not control, like
Bradley "Chelsea" Manning and Julian Assange.

Former FBI director James Comey leaked records of his interactions
with Trump in order to gin up the phony Russiagate controversy. He dis-
closed a memo to his friend Daniel Richman, a professor at Columbia
Law School, with a plan to have him share it with the *New York Times*.
Comey's intention was to prompt a special counsel investigation into
Trump's supposed ties to Russia.[56]

Former Vice President Mike Pence had classified documents at his
house in Indiana. Recall that vice presidents do not have broad declassi-
fication powers. That DOJ investigation resulted in no charges.[57]

Another former head of the CIA under Barack Obama, Leon Panetta, revealed top secret information about the raid that killed Osama
bin Laden to a Hollywood screenwriter.[58]

Clinton's National Security Advisor Sandy Berger was caught stealing and destroying documents regarding the Clinton administration's

handling of antiterrorism efforts from the National Archives. He claimed that it was a "sloppy" mistake, but there was widespread speculation at the time that the information in the documents could be damaging to Clinton's legacy when reviewed by the 9/11 Commission.[59] He received a fine and two years' probation.[60] His boss, President Bill, laughed it off. "Well, that's Sandy for you," Clinton told the *Denver Post*. "We were all laughing about it."[61]

Former President Lyndon Johnson directed Walt Rostow, his national security adviser, to gather up sensitive records, some with details on surveillance done by himself and former President Richard Nixon. In 1973, after Johnson's death, Rostow gave the records to the Lyndon B. Johnson Presidential Library in Austin, Texas, on the condition that they keep them sealed for fifty years. The library opened them in the 1990s and found classified material.[62] Johnson also ordered the destruction of at least one classified document.[63]

All these examples were punished with a wrist slap or less. But with Jack Smith on the case, Trump could be looking at the rest of his life behind bars, even though at one point he had the right to declassify any of the documents in question.

TRUMP'S LEGAL CASE

The legal team of every president negotiates with the National Archives about documents. They may be used for memoirs, they can be mementos, they may be used for something else, but it happens after every administration. It isn't just common, it's automatic.

But until now, it had never been a potential criminal violation.

Why is that?

The arguments Trump's attorneys would make in this case were more numerous and more subtle than other cases in this book. So it's worth breaking down some key ones:

Objection 1. One objection to Smith's charges relies on the notion of a "classified" document itself. Perhaps the presidency itself is foundational to the concept of a document being "classified." The president has godlike powers when it comes to determining if a document remains classified. Thus it is a precondition for the manifestation of a classified document that there is a president and that president wants that document to be classified. Whether a document is classified or not is subject to his discretion, first and foremost.

While there is a process to declassify a document that Trump didn't follow in these instances, there is a legitimate question of whether that process is actually necessary.

(Notably, Trump undercut this argument himself by saying at one point, "As president I could have declassified, but now I can't," according to a report from ABC News.[64] I note this here to provide full context. Still, Trump's understanding of the law is irrelevant to the law itself.)

Objection 2. The next objection is the rule of lenity. The rule comes from *McBoyle v. United States* (1931): "[I]t is reasonable that a fair warning should be given to the world in language that the common world will understand, of what the law intends to do if a certain line is passed."

In essence, this says that there is often more than one way to read a criminal law. When that happens, the rule of lenity dictates that you read it in a narrower sense, which decreases the risk to the defendant. In other words, when interpreting a law that is either unclear or ambiguous, the benefit of the doubt ought to go to the defendant. This is applicable here because the thrust of Jack Smith's classified documents case uniquely applies to the presidency, and it is far from clear given past criminal statutes.

Smith was attempting to choose the most damning possible interpretation of the law, which violates norms. (This is a common lawfare tactic. Robert Mueller was also criticized for not taking a more restrained approach, for example.)[65]

Even if a court ultimately concluded Trump's conduct was illegal, they could also determine that he did not have fair warning of what the law intends.[66]

The bottom line is that there are simply no comparable cases. Of my list of famous classified documents disputes, the one most similar is probably Obama's documents that were kept in a private warehouse. Despite conservative media trying to get energy behind the story, it never led to any charges.

By that standard, Trump's shouldn't have either.

Objection 3. This is a corollary to the rule of lenity objection. It is also the law that the president is entitled to take personal documents with him into his postpresidency. And it can be reasonably argued that it is impossible for the president of the United States to separate entirely their personal documents from things that are more sensitive in the eyes of the government. The office is all-consuming. It defines you throughout history. So, when a personal document is also classified, what wins out: the fact that it's personal or the fact that it's classified?

We have never had to even consider this fact until this point. One reason is that if we had, it would effectively allow most if not all presidents to be prosecuted. Maybe we're considering it now for the first time only because Jack Smith and the lawfare superstructure hate Donald Trump.

Objection 4. The next objection is regarding separation of powers. Outside authorities, such as an appointed special counsel of a subsequent administration, have little established authority to review what gets classified, yet that is essentially what Smith was attempting to do here. There certainly isn't anything resembling the tactics used by a known partisan like Smith that establishes any precedent for the intensity with which this case was prosecuted, and for good reason.

Objection 5. The next issue is that it's difficult for a reasonable prosecutor to have determined that Trump had willfully broken the law. Typically, being ignorant of the law is not generally an excuse to get out of obeying it, but Joe Biden had gotten away with having classified documents of his own for exactly this reason. Recall that Biden had classified documents in his possession when he had been vice president—not president. A vice president does not have broad authority to declassify documents, yet Joe skated.

Some of Biden's docs went back to his Senate days, where he served from 1973 to 2009. He shouldn't have had any of those documents. He didn't have his own SCIF. He doesn't have secure facilities that also house his classic car. Why did he even take these documents home? We were never told. My guess is so he could use them for memoirs, ginning up foreign business for his family, or both.

Yet in the eyes of the law, he had done nothing criminal. Eventually, Biden's own classified documents case was given up because prosecutors could not determine his willfulness.

Trump's case is murkier, which favors Trump, considering he was the original source of classification of the documents in question, unlike Biden, who was merely a senator at the time. Given Biden's example, a reasonable prosecutor would have determined that it is impossible to sufficiently establish Trump's willfulness to break the law.

There was one final objection to Smith: the only one that truly mattered.

THE EPIC DOWNFALL OF JACK SMITH

As it turned out, none of the previous five objections were necessary. Neither was anything that took place in Tanya Chutkan's D.C. court. All these points were moot.

The sixth and most powerful issue facing Smith's prosecution is the one that actually did him in: His appointment was unconstitutional because, according to the U.S. Constitution, his office must have been "established by Law," which it was not. The Constitution establishes that major officers of the United States must be appointed by the president and confirmed by the Senate. Inferior officers, whose positions are established by Congress, are able to be hired at will by the executive. Principal officers include the attorney general and the ninety-four U.S. attorneys.

The Supreme Court in *United States v. Nixon* (1974) allowed the DOJ to appoint a special prosecutor to investigate the president, effectively allowing an investigator to look into his or her own boss. Biden's DOJ naturally pointed to this when justifying the existence of the Jack Smith special counsel. However, two years later, *Buckley v. Valeo* (1976) ratcheted down nonpresidential appointments. This case is considered the beginning of modern Appointments Clause (Article II, Section 2, Clause 2 of the Constitution) jurisprudence. Subsequent cases built out that area of the law, especially *Lucia v. Securities and Exchange Commission* (2018).

Lucia specified that when exercising significant authority, that power must be vested in an officer of the United States government and not an employee. An officer means someone appointed by the president alone, appointed by the president and approved by the Senate, or appointed by a department head alone.

The Appointments Clause says that there is no statute on the books for the appointment of special counsels. A special counsel is created with a regulation, not a law, and there isn't anything in the Constitution about special counsels. In other words, Jack Smith's job doesn't exist.

There is some essential recent historical context: The Ethics in Government Act of 1978 established the framework for appointing independent counsels and special prosecutors. It sunsetted in 1999, but Janet Reno, then–attorney general for Bill Clinton, created a provision allowing special counsels under the authority of the DOJ. But there is a catch: Reno created this rule via regulation, not law, which legal scholars with whom I consulted argue is illegitimate. Special counsels cannot be "inferior officers" as described in the Appointments Clause (U.S. Constitution Article II, Section 2, Clause 2), i.e., hirable at will by a department head without Senate confirmation, due to the fact that they were created by a regulation and not a law. Thus, a non–Senate-confirmed special counsel cannot legally exist.

All of this is to say, this special counsel, whether it be a saintly, politically neutral figure or a fervid partisan like Jack Smith, was created only by trying to exploit a vague loophole of the law that many legal scholars believe does not actually exist.

What's more, even if the job existed in a legal sense, Jack Smith was operating with powers that had superseded U.S. Attorneys, who require Senate confirmation. Special counsels are typically chosen from the current crop of U.S. Attorneys, who are confirmed by the Senate. Not only was Smith not a U.S. Attorney and not confirmed by the Senate, but he had left the country after Trump was elected to police the international community from the Netherlands.

He had all the powers of a U.S. attorney but was conducting an operation that was nationwide in scope and had no supervision by superiors. U.S. attorneys are bound by one of their ninety-four districts, and they are fully supported by layers of supervision.

Smith seemed to be bound by nothing, which is clearly illegal.

Jack Smith was either coordinating with the Biden administration on his Trump investigations, which is blatant election interference, or he wasn't coordinating with anyone, i.e., he had no oversight. Smith's team claimed that cooperation with the Biden administration was nonexistent, of course, but that just meant that Smith was a power unto himself, which is clearly unlawful.

Luckily for Trump, a genius lawyer who worked closely with his team figured this out, a man who happens to be a friend of mine and my former colleague at Breitbart News: Ken Klukowski.

Some big guns came in and backed up Klukowski's argument, and

Trump's legal team adopted it. Trump's field general Todd Blanche, and Blanche's brilliant deputy Emil Bove, incorporated this argument into their filings and presented it to the judge.

Beginning in December 2023, Klukowski and other lawyers from the law firm Schaerr Jaffe filed friend-of-the-court briefs representing former Attorneys General Ed Meese and Michael Mukasey, arguing in multiple courts that only Congress can create federal offices such as Smith's. Those lawyers' argument was based on groundbreaking academic work published by two top legal scholars, Steven Calabresi, the cochairman of the Federalist Society, and prominent constitutional law professor Gary Lawson. Calabresi and Lawson joined Attorneys General Meese and Mukasey on the briefs. David Bossie's Citizens United likewise joined the brief and funded this effort to derail the unconstitutional lawfare against Trump, and Bossie's lawyer Dan Jorjani teamed up with Klukowski as they worked with Blanche and Bove.

Meese and company's lawyers also made the additional argument that Smith has so much power that he is a "principal officer" under the Constitution, which specifically requires a presidential nomination and Senate confirmation, making his appointment even more illegal. Ultimately, "he has no more authority to represent the United States in this Court than Bryce Harper, Taylor Swift, or Jeff Bezos," they wrote.[67]

Smith was operating as if he had all the powers of a U.S. Attorney with a broader scope and none of the checks necessary. Yet he lacked the authority to do even a fraction of what he had set out to do.

This wasn't a real job. It was a concoction of Joe Biden's DOJ to harass Trump.

While it would have been interesting to see the courts take on the first five objections to Smith's cases above, we'll never get that chance. It's just as well, because they could have gotten it wrong, as Juan Merchan and his New York jury did, as well as Judge Arthur Engoron.

The momentum began to build in Trump's favor. In June 2024, Judge Aileen Cannon scheduled a hearing on arguments made by Meese and company that Smith's appointment was unconstitutional.[68] Klukowski's team appeared alongside Trump's team in the courtroom, with Mukasey and Bossie in attendance and the senior partner of Schaerr Jaffe, Gene Schaerr, participating in oral argument. NBC's lawfare operation immediately began an astroturfed effort to get liberals to file complaints about

Cannon. They had to stop her before she put the (figurative) knife into Smith. But Cannon was not deterred.[69]

Meanwhile, Trump continued to notch wins in the J6 case. On June 28, the Supreme Court ruled that the January 6th defendants could not be prosecuted under 28 U.S.C. § 1512(c)(2), the "Enron" statute, for generally obstructing "an official proceeding." Attorney Joel Pollak summed it up at Breitbart:

> Section 1512(c)(2) was passed after the Enron scandal, when it was discovered that federal law had a loophole: it was illegal to instruct others to destroy evidence, but not illegal to destroy evidence oneself. Consequently, Congress passed a law prohibiting tampering with witnesses or evidence that is to be used in an "official proceeding." The Department of Justice used that law to prosecute participants in the Capitol riot based on the idea that they had "obstructed" an official proceeding—i.e., the certification of the Electoral College vote in the 2020 presidential election. But critics said that 1512(c)(2) had never been intended to apply to protests or other First Amendment–connected activities. . . .
>
> In order to continue a prosecution under the Enron law, the prosecution would have to show that the defendants not only invaded the Capitol, but that they also impeded the delivery of documents or objects needed for the proceeding.[70]

Smith's team at the DOJ didn't show that the protesters impeded anything, and just like that, one of his four charges was over.

There was one Easter egg in Justice Clarence Thomas's concurring opinion on that matter that foreshadowed bombshells yet to come: Thomas suggested that Smith's appointment was likely unconstitutional and in violation of the Appointments Clause of the Constitution. He echoed Klukowski's argument for the attorneys general and scholars, expressing serious doubt that "any office for the Special Counsel has been 'established by Law,' as the Constitution requires." "Those questions must be answered before this prosecution can proceed," Thomas continued. "We must respect the Constitution's separation of powers in all its forms, else we risk rendering its protection of liberty a parchment guarantee."[71]

This was the beginning of the end of Jack Smith's special counsel.

Two weeks after Justice Thomas's opinion provided top cover, Judge Cannon would throw out the whole damn thing, ruling that the appointment of Jack Smith was unconstitutional.

"The Special Counsel's position effectively usurps that important legislative authority, transferring it to a Head of Department, and in the process threatening the structural liberty inherent in the separation of powers," she wrote in a ninety-three-page order.[72] It's noteworthy that Cannon granted the defense team's request to dismiss the case without even evaluating the substance of Smith's allegations against Trump.

"The dismissal of the classified documents case is a seismic development. From the beginning of all of these cases, I have said that the Mar-a-Lago case was the greatest threat to the former president. It is now dismissed," according to Jonathan Turley, a George Washington University law professor and popular legal commentator.[73]

He's correct on all points.

Smith immediately announced that he would appeal Judge Cannon's decision, but it was clear he was done for.

This was seemingly the most dangerous case against Trump of all the cases documented in this book, and the most aggressive prosecutor of them all was the one bringing it. Yet it resulted in a dismissal.

LAWFARE NEVER DIES

The Democrats were cooked, but they had to save face. Even though he was out of a job, Jack Smith and Tanya Chutkan weren't going to give up so easily. Chutkan unsealed a trove of documents on the J6 cases. Briefs of this nature are typically capped at forty-five pages, but Smith, always above the law, turned one in more than four times that length. This is known as an oversized brief.[74]

With the cases hurtling toward a legal dead end, it was clear that Chutkan, who was known as the most partisan judge on the D.C. Circuit, and the radical Jack Smith were going to dump as much anti-Trump info as they could while voting was already taking place.

The biggest "October surprise" of the 2024 election was given to us by Smith and his lawfare operation. In typical Smith fashion, this maneuver appeared to violate the Department of Justice's own guidelines. The "sixty-day rule" is an informal custom that federal law enforcement does not take actions that could influence a presidential election within sixty days of said election. The Democrats cite James Comey's testimony before Congress on the Hillary Clinton email server probe just days before the 2016 election as a breach of this.

Though the rule is unofficial and nonenforceable, it is well-known that federal prosecutors should try their best to avoid influencing election outcomes.[75] It is not their job, nor is it why they have their jobs.

Yet Smith and Chutkan don't even care to follow inconvenient laws that are on the book, so they certainly weren't going to honor informal customs.[76] After all, they still had time to stop Trump!

Their brief was not effective, despite the fact that it was oversized. It was heavily redacted, and there wasn't a single revelation that became indelible in the American consciousness.

Smith had failed.

Trump had just survived two assassination attempts, including one where a bullet took off a piece of his ear. He had survived all the lawfare. He won the election on November 5.

On November 8, Smith began to wind down his operation. He asked Judge Chutkan to end her January 6th cases against Trump, knowing that even if Smith won his appeal (that is, if it was determined his entire operation wasn't illegal after all), he had no shot at concluding his case before Trump was sworn in as president. DOJ policy strictly prohibits prosecutions of sitting presidents. That's a law clear enough that even Jack Smith would abide by it.

Trump's final triumph took place on November 25 when Smith filed a motion to dismiss all the cases.

"This is a huge victory for President Trump and the rule of law," said Klukowski. "Jack Smith's appointment as Special Counsel was unconstitutional from the outset, and Smith's surrender here is long overdue."[77]

Trump vanquished the Democrats and the lawfare superstructure, and his victory reverberated across the Washington swamp.

Smith, Chutkan, James, Bragg, Merchan, Willis, and all the rest had failed.

Lawfare had failed.

The winning was just beginning.

News reports indicated that DOJ and FBI and bureaucrats intended to voluntarily leave their respective departments before Trump returned to our nation's capital.[78] I refer to this phenomenon as Deep State "self-deportations." For this to occur is a huge triumph for Trump and his America First agenda, which was slowed and often outright blocked by permanent bureaucrats who worked against Trump's priorities from inside federal agencies during his first term.

Smith was the hunter, but he may now be the hunted. *Rolling Stone* magazine reported that he and his team immediately started lawyering up themselves in anticipation of possible retribution from Trump.

Still, he had one final move he could play: Release his report on the classified documents case. Smith wanted this information out so that his work wasn't entirely in vain. Even if his office wasn't legit, maybe he could prove ex post facto that Trump really did violate the law. Maybe the report could fuel a wave of anti-Trump media attention that could harm Trump politically. That was the goal all along, wasn't it?

And, of course, it would make Jack Smith look tough and good.

But it was not meant to be. Smith was foiled by Judge Cannon yet again. She blocked its release.

Days later, on January 11, having accomplished nothing other than harassing Trump and further normalizing lawfare in America, Jack Smith resigned from the DOJ.

Despite his resignation, the contents of Smith's report could eventually leak out.

But will anyone care? That's anyone's guess.

There's a common expression attributed to Stalin-era Russia: "You show me the man, I'll show you the crime." There're a lot of variations of it, but what it means is that we're all guilty of something; it's just a matter of whether a prosecutor is sufficiently motivated to figure out exactly what it is, charge us with it, and follow through all the way.

The phrase might be associated with Stalin, but it ought to be associated with Smith. He built a reputation for overcharging people. He didn't flinch when he was summarily rejected and embarrassed by the Supreme Court. And in his prosecution of Donald Trump, Smith seized authority, took the coercive power of government, and wielded it in a way to incarcerate people and ruin their lives.

He takes the approach, *I have a gun and a badge, so I might as well use them.* This is the opposite of the principles that ought to govern a free society.

A reasonable prosecutor would not have pursued these cases at all. First off, they would have determined that it is impossible to sufficiently establish Trump's willfulness in committing any alleged crimes. Regarding the January 6th case, Trump has consistently maintained that he won the 2020 election. He has vigorously protested the results with his words and via social media, but he hasn't done anything remotely close to obstructing anything, much less engaging in "insurrection," whatever that even means. Regarding the documents case, the lack of "willfulness" to commit a crime is exactly how Joe Biden got off.

This is what we talk about when we talk about presidential immunity. Without it, every president would be vulnerable to prosecution in their postpresidency.

That goes against our basic democratic principles.

Joe Biden trampled our democracy when he announced that Trump "will not take power" and that he would make sure Trump did not become president again.

Merrick Garland, Lisa Monaco, and Vanita Gupta interfered in our democracy when they unconstitutionally appointed Jack Smith.

And Smith meddled in the election by virtue of leading the illicit special counsel investigation and by releasing documents designed to harm Trump right before the election.

All of it is lawfare at its most aggressive.

It was also election interference.

Thankfully for the country, Smith was illegitimate, both in the eyes of the courts and the voting public.

Defeating Smith was Team Trump's most resounding victory documented in this book. They had a tough case and a maniacal prosecutor who believed he had the full force of the federal government behind him, yet they secured a 360-degree win. Still, this was also the scariest case in this book. The relentlessness of Smith combined with the pure partisanship of Biden's government meant that Trump was likely headed for a colossal downfall—if not for a fearless judge, some brilliant legal maneuvers, and the hard work of warriors who stood and fought not just for one man, but for the concept of democracy itself.

CHAPTER 7

THE LEFT HATES DEMOCRACY

Taken collectively, the goal of these cases was not simply to stop Donald Trump. It was to subvert democracy itself. Trump had been president, and, as we now know, always intended to run again in 2024. The leftist mind could not comprehend that. It never could, from the moment he came down that escalator in 2015.

After the series of impeachment attempts—two of which were successful—and the obsessive effort to use the courts to disqualify him from becoming the president again, the evidence is clear that the left did not want to run the risk that Donald Trump could be democratically elected.

The left purports to be the stewards of democracy. They are the champion of the system of government defined by the concept "rule by the people." They constantly claim that "democracy" is under attack from conservatives.

But do they practice what they preach?

As I will demonstrate in this chapter, the answer is a resounding no.

First of all, in order to have a functioning democracy, citizens must value its core tenets, which I believe are legal equality, political freedom, and law and order.

We know from the first chapter of this book that the left hates law and order.

You cannot hate law and order and still genuinely believe in democracy, so I could end the chapter right here, having already proven my point. Still, I'll take the time to present my full case.

It's worth keeping in mind that the United States of America is not a democracy in a literal sense. In their infinite wisdom, our Founding Fathers effected a system that is superior to a pure democracy. We live in a constitutional federal republic. There are particular facets to how our American republic functions, as enumerated in our Constitution. Unlike direct democracies, we have a federalist system of states that are independent of the federal government in important ways. However, for the purpose of this book, there is no need to dwell on the differences between "democracy" in general and America's specific form of government. "Democracy," in the colloquial sense, is when the voting public meaningfully and directly contributes to important decisions, either as individuals or via representatives. Though it is technically inaccurate, Americans tend to discuss democracy and republicanism interchangeably. Some readers may lament that imprecision, but this chapter is not meant to correct semantic disputes within our culture. So, please indulge me here.

Still, whatever you want to call the system that we have, the left has contempt for it. And they know it too.

DEMOCRATS RIG THEIR OWN PRIMARIES

The fact that the left really hates democracy began to dawn on me when the Democrats rigged their primary in 2016 to ensure that Hillary Clinton won the party's nomination. Nothing that I had read or saw with my own two eyes prepared me for that. I was shocked, and realized that year that the Democrats hate democracy. Everything I've seen since has only made that more clear.

You don't have to take my word for it. In 2017, famed Democrat strategist and interim Democratic National Convention chair Donna Brazile wrote about this for *Politico* under the headline "Inside Hillary Clinton's Secret Takeover of the DNC."

Brazile wrote that Hillary Clinton was essentially given control of the party committee and thus the nominating process in 2015 in exchange for her help fundraising. All of this was done well before the unexpectedly close primary, which ended in Clinton triumphing over socialist Bernie Sanders. Brazile discovered that the DNC and Clinton solidified the arrangement in August 2015, four months after Clinton announced her run for president and a year before she officially secured the nomination.

Brazile claimed that then–DNC chair Debbie Wasserman Schultz gave the Clinton campaign command of financing, strategy, and hiring decisions.

This is, of course, outrageous and should be considered completely unacceptable in a democracy. Party resources ought to go to the winner of the primary after she has earned the nomination. In a democracy, the party ought to be neutral until the contest is over. Brazile saw that clearly.

"The funding arrangement with HFA [Hillary for America] and the victory fund agreement was not illegal, but it sure looked unethical. If the fight had been fair, one campaign would not have control of the party before the voters had decided which one they wanted to lead. This was not a criminal act, but as I saw it, it compromised the party's integrity," Brazile wrote in her book *Hacks*.[1]

Brazile was not alone in framing the primary as "rigged." Massachusetts Senator Elizabeth Warren, who is on the hard left of the Democrat Party but had campaigned with establishment apparatchik Clinton, said that she agreed the primary had been "rigged."[2]

"What we've got to do as Democrats now, is we've got to hold this party accountable," Warren said.

Spoiler alert: There was never any accountability.[3]

Donald Trump, as he often does, cut to the quick with a withering tweet: "Pocahontas just stated that the Democrats, lead [*sic*] by the legendary Crooked Hillary Clinton, rigged the Primaries! Let's go FBI & Justice Dept."

(Trump mockingly refers to Senator Warren as "Pocahontas" because she has falsely claimed to have American Indian ancestry.)

He also told reporters of Clinton, "She basically bought the DNC and stole the election from Bernie."[4]

Where is the lie?

The Democrats never brought in outside auditors, so the public will never get a full accounting of the vast left-wing conspiracy to deliver Hillary Clinton the party's nomination in 2016. The incident should have been a warning sign to Democrats that their leadership was not practicing the values they preached.

Then again, most Democrat voters are probably unaware the rigging actually took place. Establishment media outlets were reluctant to cover the event. Brazile's allegations should fit anyone's definition of a "bombshell," yet neither NBC nor ABC nor CBS covered the allegations on the nightly news the day it broke.[5]

DNC Chair Tom Perez was asked about the allegations in an interview with CNBC and evaded the question entirely. "We're moving forward," he said, before describing his desire for fairness and transparency.[6]

"Fairness and transparency," but not when it comes to the election the Clintons just rigged with the help of the DNC, apparently.

At least Perez had the decency to avoid the question entirely. Howard Dean, himself a former DNC chair, stated flat out that "no one has said the primaries were rigged." He said this a day *after* Brazile had made the claim that the primaries were rigged and Warren had backed her up on it.[7]

That level of dishonesty takes some real chutzpah.

Brazile's admission should not have come as a complete surprise. A class action lawsuit was filed against the DNC and Chairwoman Debbie Wasserman Shultz in 2016 claiming she had rigged the primary in favor of Hillary Clinton and against Bernie Sanders. Even Senate Minority Leader Harry Reid admitted in July of that year that "I knew—everybody knew—that this was not a fair deal."

The lawsuit was dismissed in August 2017, not because the primary wasn't rigged, but because the court could offer no legal redress. "In evaluating Plaintiffs' claims at this stage, the Court assumes their allegations are true—that the DNC and Wasserman Schultz held a palpable bias in favor of Clinton and sought to propel her ahead of her Democratic opponent," read the court order from federal Judge William Zloch. So, the primary was rigged, but ultimately it was not within the court's jurisdiction to do anything about it ex post facto.

In other words, as the *Observer* summarized in a brilliant headline, "Court Concedes DNC Had the Right to Rig Primaries Against Sanders."[8]

In the aftermath of Brazile's bombshell, Sanders himself went wobbly. He backed off calling the primaries rigged, essentially letting the DNC and the Clintons off the hook, giving the green light to lawfare aficionados everywhere.[9]

Somehow, things in the Democrat Party are even less democratic than people know. In what can only be described as a threat to democracy, the Democrats allowed for 15 percent of the 2016 convention voters to fall under the "superdelegate" designation. Superdelegates are a group composed of party insiders and elected officials and can change their preferred candidate at will. Hillary Clinton claimed 572.5 of those voters, or more than 80 percent of the available 712, despite the fact that she received only about 55 percent of the current primary vote total across the country. Bernie Sanders got a mere 42.5 superdels, or about 6 percent, despite earning about 43 percent of popular support nationwide.

There is a word for what this is, and it's not *democracy*: It's called *rigging*.

DEMOCRATS DENY ELECTION RESULTS

Aside from rigging primaries, Democrats have a tendency to deny the results of general elections they don't win. The 2016 contest is a perfect example of this.

This was not an isolated event.

While the left did not allow for "democracy" to truly play out in their 2016 primaries, when it played out in the general election, they simply could not accept it.

The rampant election denialism was rooted in a consensus among influential Democrats that Russian operatives, especially President Vladimir Putin, rigged the election on behalf of Trump.

Hillary Clinton was the queen conspiracist. She told CBS News in September 2019, "I believe he [Trump] knows he's an illegitimate president."

She cautioned other Democrats that they could "have the election stolen from you," implying that that's what happened to her.

In October 2020, well after the Russian-collusion narrative had been thoroughly discredited by the Mueller Report, she said that "there was a widespread understanding that [the 2016] election was not on the level."[10]

It's an audacious statement considering that she had rigged the primary to get the nomination. It's also false; there was no "understanding" the election wasn't legitimate, much less a "widespread" one.

I could spend dozens of pages citing Democrats who denied the results of the 2016 elections, but I'll add just a few more here.

Former President Jimmy Carter said, "There's no doubt that the Russians did interfere in the election, and I think the interference, although not yet quantified, if fully investigated would show that Trump didn't actually win the election in 2016. He lost the election, and he was put into office because the Russians interfered on his behalf."[11]

The late Representative John Lewis (D-GA) told *Meet the Press*: "I do not see this president-elect as a legitimate president. I think there was a conspiracy on the part of the Russians and others that helped him get elected. That's not right. That's not fair. That's not the open democratic process." He then boycotted Trump's inauguration.[12]

Representative Jerry Nadler (D-NY) called Trump's election "illegitimate."

Democrats from at least ten states, led by Los Angeles–area congresswoman Maxine Waters, objected to the certification of the states' votes. The numbers were far less than those who raised concerns about Trump's 2020 defeat four years later, but it was Waters and company who set the precedent.[13]

Every one of these comments erodes our democracy, which is precisely why the Democrats make them.

The left hates democracy, after all.

As I noted in *Breaking the News*, "After the Russia hoax hysteria (mostly) ended with the whimper of the Mueller report, the *New York Times* refocused its newsroom." That means their entire newsgathering operation prior to the report was organized around anticipating that Mueller's special counsel would confirm that Russia had rigged the election.

The country's most prestigious paper is run by delusional, hysterical leftists who denied the results that our democracy had yielded. Of course, there was no evidence of Russian collusion between any elements of Trump's campaign or America's government to rig the election, but that didn't stop some Democrats from hanging on to the notion that the 2016 election was rigged.

The most enthusiastic purveyors of fake Russian–collusion news in our intelligence community landed jobs within the establishment media, where they continued to frame public perception. Former CIA Director John Brennan, former Director of National Intelligence James Clapper, and former Deputy FBI Director Andy McCabe are the most prominent examples.

The media felt no remorse over getting this story completely wrong.

If anything, the biggest hoaxsters got rewarded. Journalists won prestigious prizes, while resistance bureaucrats in the Deep State got fancy media and think-tank sinecures. Adam Schiff, who was chairman of the House Intelligence Committee during the most feverish moments of the Russian-collusion hoax, was promoted to senator by California voters.

To say that Schiff showed no remorse is an understatement. When asked by CNN's Jake Tapper in November 2024 if he still believed "there was evidence of collusion between Trump's campaign and Russia," he said that he did. "It wasn't an overstatement," Schiff said. "There is evidence of collusion."[14]

He's not alone. Other prominent House Democrats, in particular Maryland's Representative Jamie Raskin, has stayed on the Russia hoax narrative like a dog on a bone.[15] Meanwhile, the establishment media continued to debase themselves. MSNBC's Steve Benen, one of the most popular (and partisan) writers in online news, wrote in 2023 that Republicans were pretending the scandal wasn't real.[16]

In the 2024 election cycle, the Dems and their media allies tried to run the same playbook. In February 2024, NBC published the headline "Russia's 2024 Election Interference Has Already Begun." And guess which party the Russians were targeting with disinformation? The Democrats and Joe Biden, of course.

Tech publication *Wired* published a series of articles accusing Kremlin-connected entities of trying to rig the election, peaking with this doozy from November 5: "Russia Is Going All Out on Election Day Interference."[17]

The implication in all this is that the American people didn't elect Donald Trump, Russian operatives did. Liberals simply could not comprehend that the people rejected the arch-establishmentarian Hillary Clinton and voted for the outsider businessman Donald Trump. Likewise, in 2024, they couldn't believe that voters had turned against President Biden and Vice President Kamala Harris.

Either that or they were just lying about it flat out.

Their failure to accept the results of the 2016 election was a rejection of the democratic process, yet few powerful voices within the Democratic Party have shown any remorse.

That's because they view America's electoral system and the people who make it possible with disdain.

I offer a brief interlude here to note that President Trump and many of his supporters did not *fully* accept the results of the 2020 election. I use the word *fully* because President Trump ultimately peacefully relinquished power on Inauguration Day; he did not lead the January 6th Capitol riot, he did not encourage any violations of the law, and he repeatedly told supporters to remain peaceful.

That said, Trump has consistently maintained that the election was stolen, though he did acknowledge that he lost "by a whisker" on the campaign trail in 2024.[18] Once.

Perhaps Trump has been less than literal with his opinion of what really happened in 2020. It could be strategy: The trolling fires up the die-hard supporters who power his movement and brings out the worst in his political foes. However, Trump has consistently maintained that he won in 2020. A full examination of all the odd occurrences in that election are beyond the scope of this book. I offer more of my thinking in both of my prior ones.

I still feel compelled to mention it here because clearly in this one instance, much of the Republican Party did not accept the results, and I don't want any haters and losers who read this book to think I have ignored that fact.

However, if you look at the quantity of evidence I compile throughout this chapter, this is the exception that proves the rule that, by and large, Republicans and conservatives respect democracy while the Democrats respect it *if and only if they win.*

DEMOCRATS RIGGED THE 2024 PRIMARIES

Given that the Democrats rigged their own primary in 2016—and then claimed for years that the general election that year was rigged by Russia—it should not have surprised anyone that they did not allow their nomination process to proceed democratically in 2024.

(It's a mystery why the Democrat rigging machine seemed to take the cycle off during the 2020 race. Or did it? The world may never know.)

Joe Biden got the rigging going in December 2022 when he penned a letter to the DNC asking for changes to the nomination process. One of the changes he wanted was a reordered primary calendar. The party apparently didn't need much time to deliberate—the next day, they made South Carolina the first state to vote. Iowa has traditionally been the first primary or caucus day for each party, but Biden wanted to reward South Carolina, the state that got his then-struggling 2020 campaign on track, and make the Palmetto State first up.

New Hampshire, which set its primary date before the other states nonetheless, was punished. The DNC brought the hammer down on the Granite State: No New Hampshire delegates would be seated at the 2024 convention. This was a power move by Joe Biden and the party establishment. New Hampshire voters dissed him in the 2020 primary when he finished in fifth place and earned no delegates.

For some reason, the party was determined to clear the way for eighty-one-year-old Biden, who had presided over an open border, historic levels of inflation, increasing geopolitical tensions, and intense national division. Not to mention that his clear mental and physical decline hardly made him the ideal leader of the strongest and most vibrant country in the world.

There was a plan in 2018 to limit the amount of controversial "super-delegates," but they were still around as of 2024, rebranded as "Party Leader and Elected Official Delegates" (PLEOs).

Robert F. Kennedy Jr., the only serious challenger to enter the arena against Biden, wrote in the *Wall Street Journal* that not a single PLEO backed him despite his impressive resume and elite family pedigree. He would change his party affiliation to Independent after Biden was annointed.[19]

"In the Democratic presidential primaries in Indiana, Alaska, Ohio, Mississippi, North Carolina, and Montana, all other challengers to Biden were blocked from being named on the ballots, and the Democratic presidential primaries were outright cancelled in Florida and Delaware," reported the *Washington Examiner*.[20] Would-be Democrat challengers faced "roadblocks" in Tennessee and Massachusetts, according to ABC News.[21]

"Roadblocks" is quite the euphemism for disenfranchising the millions of Democrat voters who reside in these states.

Naturally, Biden did not agree to debate potential rivals. This was certainly a smart political strategy, but it is at odds with the party's claim to fight for American democracy itself.

All of this subversion to protect the man whom Special Counsel Robert Hur called "an elderly man with a poor memory."[22]

KAMALA, FOR THE DONORS

An already oligarchic process got even less democratic once Joe Biden chose to drop out of the race in July 2024. After a debate performance against Donald Trump that was so abominable it had to be seen to be believed, the party was left in an impossible position: They had to stick with Biden, who was doomed to lose the election, or somehow push him out and anoint a nominee who did not win a single primary vote.

To continue with Biden was tantamount to a concession, or "taking the L," as the kids say these days. Losing was inevitable, but the loss could have been blamed solely on old Joe and his selfish decision to run despite his deteriorating mental function and shoddy record.

Modern Democrats don't take L's, so a coup was performed. Mark Halperin, who seemed to have the best sources who knew the inner workings of the Biden campaign of any mainstream reporter, told Tucker Carlson that Nancy Pelosi was "determined to get him out."[23] Months later, we learned that Chuck Schumer, the top Senate Democrat, also urged him to drop out.[24] It also became apparent that Barack Obama wanted Biden to step down when George Clooney published his *New York Times* op-ed "I Love Joe Biden. But We Need a New Nominee" on July 10.[25]

Since when does an actor have the power to lead a coup to oust a sitting president? Good question. He doesn't. The piece was certainly blessed by Obama, one of Clooney's closest friends. Obama has had a reputation for being passive-aggressive throughout his political career, so it's not hard to connect the dots: Obama, via Clooney, was soft-pitching throwing out Joe Biden.

Also consider that Democrat super–power player Laurene Powell Jobs, Steve Jobs's widow, is one of Kamala Harris's best friends. Jobs inherited billions and has spent lavishly on a vast portfolio of left-wing media outlets and political causes. She runs the *Atlantic* magazine via her Emerson Collective organization. She has dreamed of Harris in the White House for years.

Pelosi. Obama. Jobs. Schumer. The coup dream team had been assembled.

Yet swapping him out still carried its own substantial risks. First and foremost, Biden and the Democrats did not have an heir apparent. This was a central premise of *Breaking Biden*: Joe named Harris, a mediocre political talent, as vice president partially to protect himself against a possible coup. It would have been much easier for party bosses to swap in a popular and dynamic second in command. That was not Kamala Harris. But the best-laid plans of mice and men often go awry, as the poem goes.

It probably would have been an even tougher task to introduce a completely new candidate. The new candidate would have been lesser known than Biden or Harris (unless they could convince Michelle Obama to run, which they didn't; I believe she doesn't actually like this country and does not want to lead it). Name recognition is valuable for any candidate, but especially for a Democrat running a shortened campaign because they need to mobilize as many low-propensity voters as possible to win. An alternate candidate would have been chosen in a process that didn't remotely resemble the democratic process, which would make the pitch to low-propensity voters even tougher. That made Harris the de facto choice.

Perhaps none of those calculations mattered anyway. Media reports suggested that Biden quickly endorsed Harris as a "middle finger" to the other Democrat Party elite who pushed him out. Obama, Pelosi, and Schumer supposedly wanted to hold a "mini primary" before the convention where they would sort out exactly who the nominee would be, but it was not meant to be. Joe Biden exerted control one last time and assured it would be Harris.[26]

From my vantage point, she was the only viable option. She had at least gotten primary votes as vice president, was a multiethnic woman, and a donor darling. She also was next in line, so anyone who would have vaulted over her could have thrown the party into even more disarray. What's more, Harris was the only potential replacement who could seamlessly access Biden's $96 million campaign war chest, which he had already amassed. Harris would go on to raise more than $1 billion herself.[27]

Once it became clear that Joe would relent to the pressure, the co-conspirators gathered in a smoke-filled room, or maybe it was at a Martha's Vineyard beachfront mansion, or maybe it was on an eco-friendly Microsoft Teams meeting, and decided what to do next: abandon any pretext of "democracy" and anoint Harris.

While the Democrats made the state of our "democracy" their signature issue on the campaign trail, 12 percent of Donald Trump's voters said that democracy was their key issue, according to an NBC poll.[28] If NBC's math adds up, then roughly 10 million Americans who thought threats to democracy were more important in this election than the economy or immigration or any other issue voted for Donald Trump and not the Democrat ticket.

No wonder. The entire nomination process denied Democrat voters their voice. Instead of acknowledging Biden's clear mental decline, they lied about it for years. Then at the last minute Biden's age became an undeniable political problem, the donors and party bosses swapped him out.

Amazingly, now that the results are in, it is unclear whether Biden would have performed worse than Kamala Harris. She lost the Electoral College, the popular vote, and all seven key battleground states.

In retrospect, kicking Biden out was clearly a mistake!

Harris's slogan, "Kamala for the people," was laden with irony, invoking her time as a prosecutor when she would represent the citizens ostensibly from society's evil machines. This time the *people* rejected her after the donors and Democrat Party elite imposed her on the nation. Those who guide the Democrat apparatus do not see it as their job to respond to "the people." Rather, the party elites believe they have the right to coerce their voters, manipulate the system to try to achieve victory, impose their will on us all, and then claim that's what *the people* wanted all along.

They'll use every weapon at their disposal, including lawfare, to achieve their ends.

It's poetic justice, I suppose, to see the Godfather of all lawfare himself, Joe Biden, have his career ended in the most undemocratic way possible. He built the system, it was wrestled away from him, and then it was used against him.

Yet maybe Joe got the last laugh. Instead of single-handedly having to shoulder the burden of the disastrous election night for his entire party, the blame is now shared. Nancy Pelosi, Barack Obama, George

Clooney, Laurene Powell Jobs, the *New York Times*, White Dudes for Harris, myriad celebrities, ineffectual liberal podcasters, establishment journos, and so many others all played a role. They were all part of the attack on democracy that failed to deliver the Democrats the White House but did reveal what they really think of the people whom they intend to govern.

BY ANY MEANS NECESSARY

While the Democrats fought among themselves until nearly the last minute choosing who they would nominate on their own ticket, there was never much of a doubt about whom the Republicans would place atop theirs.

Or was there?

Though Donald Trump was by far the most popular Republican politician, many prominent Democrats and the left were bound and determined to keep him from actually being able to run.

Consider their insistence that Trump is an existential threat to democracy. If that's the case, then surely it's appropriate to keep him off the ballot, right?

And there are only two ways to keep him off the ballot.

The first one was tried in Colorado, where they literally tried to remove his name from the ballot. In 2023, the Colorado Supreme Court disqualified Trump, citing the Fourteenth Amendment's Section 3 "Insurrection Clause," which states that no public official who has engaged in "insurrection or rebellion" against the United States can hold federal or state office thereafter.

As a reminder to anyone who thinks that prime-time MSNBC is real life, no court ever held that Trump was guilty of "insurrection," which literally refers to a violent uprising or rebellion against the government.

The U.S. Supreme Court unanimously overturned the Colorado ruling on the grounds that only Congress can deny a candidate ballot access.

If SCOTUS had not weighed in on Trump's behalf, states would have been able to disqualify any candidate deemed too dangerous.

Scary.

This was not a good-faith effort to protect the republic, it was a shameless power grab by Democrats to subvert the will of the people and control federal elections.

Again, this is blatantly antidemocratic, as proven by the fact that Donald Trump would go on to win the Colorado primary, the national popular vote, and the Electoral College by a wide margin.

Even though Colorado's efforts failed, the fact that Democrats even attempted so brazen a political trick suggests that state ballot rules could become a battleground for lawfare in years to come.

But this was just a legal, procedural way to make sure President Trump didn't run.

There was, of course, a guaranteed way to keep Trump from returning to the Oval Office. Thomas Matthew Crooks tried that method in Butler, Pennsylvania, in July 2024 when he attempted to assassinate Trump, shooting him in the ear and nearly killing him. Two months later, Ryan Wesley Routh was indicted for another effort to end Trump's life. Since then there have been repeated efforts to break into Trump's properties. The motives of the suspects remain unknown, but you can bet they weren't planning on working on their short games.

Considering the left's insistence that Trump has been waging an insurrection and the suggestion that he's a closet Nazi, it's a miracle that only two people have gotten close to taking him out.

After all, we had all heard nearly a decade commentary that labeled Donald Trump "an existential threat to the country," as author Bryan Walsh wrote for leftist Vox Media just days before Crooks shot Trump in the head.[29] "If the stakes of the 2024 election are as great as the party says," he went on, "there's no excuse for inaction."

Yikes.

This sentiment was shared by Joe Biden, who suggested that Trump ought to be imprisoned. "We gotta lock him up," Biden said in October 2024, days before the election. We had known for years that Joe Biden and his government wanted to throw Trump in prison, but they never outright admitted it before. The comments, notably, came right after Vice President Kamala Harris warned that Trump desired to prosecute his opponents—a practice that had become commonplace for Democrats in the Biden-Harris era and was not something that Trump had done in his first term as president.

Sadly, left-wing violence is nothing new. At *Breitbart News*, we tracked over six hundred examples of harassment and violence against conservatives at the beginning of Trump's first administration. We stopped updating the list in November 2018 because we thought that we had made our point. The most well-known example from that time was when Steve Scalise was shot and nearly killed by a Bernie Sanders supporter in June 2017.

Senator Rand Paul (R-KY) and his family have been attacked and have received death threats on a regular basis since 2017. At one point he was assaulted by a neighbor and suffered six broken ribs. Paul was also attacked by what his wife, Kelley, described as a "bloodthirsty" mob just a block from the White House in August 2020. "The threats were to f— you up, to you know, to kill you," Paul said at the time.[30]

It's not just high-profile individuals who have been targeted for supporting Donald Trump. Here are a few examples from October 2018 alone: A Republican candidate was punched in a Minnesota restaurant, a woman threatened to slap an eleven-year-old for wearing a Trump costume, and vandals attacked and shot at GOP headquarters across the country.[31]

The establishment media, most notably the *New York Times*,[32] regularly fantasized about Donald Trump getting assassinated long before Thomas Matthew Crooks took his shot. The *Times* even published a fictional essay by author Zoe Sharp where Trump gets taken out with a Glock by a Secret Service agent. A faux–Donald Trump figure was added to a Central Park production of the play *Julius Caesar* in 2017—and assassinated. That same year Madonna yelled on the National Mall that she dreamed of "blowing up" the White House. *Taxi Driver* screenwriter Paul Schrader considered assigning his students an assignment to detail a plot to kill President Donald Trump.[33] There are endless examples.

These people are sick freaks, and their radical acts of violence are far too numerous to list them all here.

Representative Bennie Thompson (D-MS), the leader of the January 6 select committee, introduced legislation in April 2024 that would take away Trump's Secret Service protection upon a felony conviction.[34] Thompson introduced this legislation just as Joe Biden was ramping up his framing of Trump as a "dictator" and Nancy Pelosi had demanded that Trump "must be stopped."

Taken together, the only conclusion one can draw is that prominent Democrats want Trump either in jail or dead.

First Trump himself, then his allies and supporters.

RFK Jr., who represents a massive threat to the Democrat establishment, told Tucker Carlson that his Secret Service protection was pulled when he suggested voters support Trump in states in which Kennedy himself was not on the ballot.[35]

Can we agree that for democracy to function, step one is making sure the standard-bearer of one of the two major political parties doesn't get murdered?

This is so easy to understand that even scholars and "experts"—a dependably liberal set of people—are starting to get it.

"A healthy democracy is supported by voting access, equality before the law, protection of individual liberties, and freedom of expression," according to Johns Hopkins University. "When violence in the form of threats, intimidation, or physical harm is aimed at these rights and freedoms, it can undermine the ability of democracy to function properly." Exactly.

Yet only one side is behind almost all recent examples of political violence: the side that claims that they are the caretakers of democracy itself.

DIVINE INTERVENTION

I spent Saturday, July 13, 2024, with my family in Santa Barbara, California, an idyllic beach town that Ronald Regan used to call home. It's about an hour and a half from my house in northern Los Angeles County. It was only a day trip and I don't have a fixed front-page shift at *Breitbart News* on Saturdays, so I had no real expectation of logging any keyboard time that day. Yet I had a premonition that it was going to be a big news day, so I dragged my laptop with me to the beach.

It turned out to be the biggest news day of the whole election cycle, and arguably one of the biggest days in the history of the republic.

That afternoon, Donald Trump was shot in the ear at a rally in Butler, Pennsylvania.

There are many unanswered questions about that day. How did the U.S. Secret Service allow for Thomas Matthew Crooks to scale a building, perch himself on a roof with a rifle, and get off an unobstructed shot at the once-and-future president from a relatively short distance? Then–Secret Service director Kimberly A. Cheatle offered an explanation so absurd that it certainly raised more questions than it answered: She said that it would have been unsafe to secure the building because "we wouldn't want to put somebody on a sloped roof."[36]

When I heard that explanation, it was clear to me that Donald Trump should have died that day.

Yet by the grace of God, he didn't.

I spoke to him about it a month later in his office at Mar-a-Lago. We sat behind a panel of impossibly thick bulletproof glass that had been designed especially for him. He said that had he not turned exactly a certain way at exactly the right moment, he would have been dead. His salvation was a chart showing illegal immigration trends. "The poster is never used early [in the speech, when Crooks got off the shot], and it's never on the right, it's always on the left. If you take the odds of this whole thing, it's like ten million to one and you only have an eighth of a second," he told me and my colleague Matt Boyle.

"This is an amazing phenomana [sic]. It's millions to nothing. There's about an eighth of a second where I'm good. The rest of the time you're dead."

I had chills.

He also noted that the fact that he was hit in the ear caused him to go down as eight bullets flew over his head. If he had not been nicked, perhaps he would have stayed standing and the would-be assassin would have had another clear shot.

Trump told us that if the bullet had actually hit its intended target, "my head would have exploded like a watermelon," and America's adversaries would have used it as propaganda against our country. "How about if you had that on slow-motion instant replay?" Trump said, darkly but hilariously.

"Couple of things just to think of it because it's got to be divine intervention."[37]

Exactly.

Anti-Trump media figures immediately objected to the characterization that "they" tried to kill Trump, insisting that it was only the one individual.[38] To frame it this way is disingenuous and intentionally avoids the reality that they have always wanted to stop Trump by any means necessary. And this *was* "any means."

It was only a matter of time.

The media could portray Trump as a Nazi and a threat to democracy and agent of a hostile foreign power for only so long before someone actually believed them.

While Thomas Matthew Crooks tried to end Trump with a gun, God apparently had other plans.

This was the moment I knew his election was inevitable (to be honest, I thought it was already over when the FBI searched Melania's undies, but it was *really* over at this point), despite all the lawfare. As it turned out, I was correct.

CHAPTER 8

MAPPING THE SUPERSTRUCTURE

While the Democrats ironically don't support democracy, they support what I refer to as "the superstructure," a term I have used periodically throughout this book. By that I mean the constellation of principles, people, and entities that the left has used to break our legal system as we once knew it.

Though there are many examples of weaponization of the legal system that occurred under presidents before Joe Biden, the superstructure began to rapidly expand during Trump's first administration and had amassed immeasurable amounts of power by Joe Biden's term.

This chapter lists the key elements of the lawfare machine as I see them. It will need updating over time. Some items mentioned require deeper investigation beyond what I can accomplish as an independent journalist without subpoena power. Yet I believe elected leaders and concerned citizens alike will find this list compelling.

Readers will recognize these tactics from the cases discussed at length in this book. These are the people, tactics, organizations, and entities that comprise the lawfare industry.

Novel Interpretations: In each of the major cases examined in this book against President Trump and his supporters, the left used a "novel interpretation" of the law in order to legitimize their political objectives. In the Stormy Daniels case, the court invented a new type of fraud that had never existed. It is exceedingly rare for a Manhattan DA to even bring a falsification of business records charge, and it was previously inconceivable that a payout to keep a scandal out of the news would be considered some kind of an election crime.

The E. Jean Carroll case extended the definition of defamation to merely defending yourself against charges that appear to be entirely bogus. What's more, the arbitrary and extreme nature of the fines themselves were, in a word, novel.

In Georgia, Fani Willis's case extended the bounds of RICO, and Jack Smith ferociously prosecuted Trump for a common violation that had traditionally been treated like a minor offense.

This is beyond "Show me the man and I'll show you the crime." If you show the superstructure "the man," they'll invent a new crime with which to charge him, then apply a ludicrously large penalty to it.

Coordination Across the Democrat Ecosystem: It is an indisputable fact that there was coordination between Joe Biden's White House and the various prosecutions of Donald Trump. The extent to which there was coordination, however, is unknown and ought to be the subject of extensive investigation. Start with the key date in the lawfare timeline: November 18, 2022, the moment Matthew Colangelo suspiciously left the DOJ for Alvin Bragg's Manhattan DA office, Nathan Wade visited the White House obviously to discuss the Trump case, and Jack Smith was appointed special counsel.

The thought that this all happened serendipitously beggars belief. To understand the coordination in the immediate aftermath of the Democrats' loss of the 2022 midterm elections and the inevitable end of the J6 committee is to understand the absolute nadir of America's system of justice. This is the moment that the law itself was officially broken.

It is my suspicion that no one individual acted alone. It was all coordinated. Consider how anti-Trump cable news fixture George Conway provided the impetus behind the E. Jean Carroll civil case, then repeatedly championed it in the media. Carroll had sat on her hands throughout numerous Democratic administrations, throughout #MeToo, and then finally came out at a moment that could potentially inflict maximum damage to Trump. To think this was a triumph of feminism and not a coordinated effort among anti-Trump political forces is to reveal yourself to be a sucker.

The deeper the investigation, the more corruption will be uncovered. Everyone involved must be exposed, or there will be no lasting justice.

The Department of Justice: When we talk about the Deep State, it's not just the State Department, the FBI, or the CIA. It's the entire bureaucracy. The permanent bureaucratic class in Washington—the unknown men and women who work to subtly push collectivism, statism, corporatism, globalism, and above all, anti-Trumpism within our bureaucratic agencies—are the foot soldiers of the modern Democrat Party. This is the group of people who do the heavy lifting to keep conservatives on political defense while Democrats skate on their crimes and corruption. The loudmouths on cable news hog the attention and the glory, but it is the behind-the-scenes bad actors—who are mostly anonymous—who truly execute the lawfare agenda.

Though Merrick Garland was clearly out of his depth, Biden was arguably wise to put him in charge of the DOJ. He's a friendly and familiar face not known for bomb-throwing. He also proved to be either exceedingly weak, a patsy, or every bit as radical as his deputies. Garland presents himself as reasonable and professional, but looming one notch lower on the DOJ hierarchy were Lisa Monaco and Vanita Gupta, the four-star generals of lawfare.

Garland could have blocked many of the most egregious examples of lawfare listed in the book. He could have boldly stood up to Monaco, Gupta, Biden, and the rest. Instead he rubber-stamped everything—or guided it himself. Regardless of who wielded the most power, ultimately it was Garland's DOJ, and his DOJ seemed far more focused on hobbling Trump and Republicans than on fighting crime.

Not until we get a full review of communications across the DOJ will we know the full story.

One minor retort to my overall argument about Garland's DOJ is that it did investigate Hunter Biden. But consider this: Of all the potential crimes committed by Hunter Biden, who had foreign entanglements with business closely tied to foreign adversaries of the United States government, and who received hundreds of thousands if not millions of dollars in anonymous payments for his alleged "art" from what are certainly foreign entities, he was investigated by the DOJ for only a minor gun charge.

This was certainly a head fake. It gives the DOJ a veneer of bipartisanship while Hunter got to skate on what were assuredly his biggest crimes.

And after he was pardoned by his father, he got to skate on that too.

I believe if we were to investigate his business dealings with foreign entities—some of which are no doubt ongoing as of Spring 2025—and payments for his artwork, we would find that he had specifically traded access to Joe Biden and the presidency for money.

Even the *New York Times* acknowledged that the DOJ blocked U.S. Attorney David Weiss from bringing additional charges against Hunter Biden.[1] Weiss's office accused Hunter of influence-peddling after uncovering payments made to Hunter back to at least 2015 by Romanian oligarch Gabriel Popoviciu,[2] who had begun cooperating with federal prosecutors. Hunter had structured the deal in such a way that he avoided filings required under the Foreign Agents Registration Act (FARA).[3] We did not learn about this until August 2024. He got that full and unconditional pardon four months later, rendering any investigation moot.

Of Hunter's many indiscretions, the one time he got busted, it had nothing to do with Joe or any foreign oligarchs.

It was all a big ruse. And the DOJ orchestrated it all. Biden even claimed, hilariously, that he resented Garland for investigating Hunter.[4]

He was either trolling or in a bout of senility.

The DOJ's handling of Hunter Biden's crimes perfectly illustrates the dangers of a politicized Justice Department. Yet my deeper concern remains the extent of the systemic rot. The DOJ has well over 100,000 employees. How many of them believe they are obliged to dismantle MAGA?

The Law Schools: When I wrote *Breaking the News*, my book examining the threat of the establishment media poses to our republic, what loomed large over my research is that so many of the worst actors in the press were educated at the same top-tier colleges, particularly journalism schools. Similarly, many law schools fashion normal young people into warriors for the lawfare cause. Until this reality changes—and it won't anytime soon—the Democrats' lawfare fighting forces will always be able to regenerate themselves.

Law schools tend to attract liberals. Only 17% of law students supported Donald Trump as of May 2024, according to the Buckley Institute (which was launched by Yale students to honor conservative intellectual William F. Buckley).[5] Only 8% of law school faculty backed Trump, according to an *Inside Higher Ed*/Hanover Research poll released just prior to the election.[6] It is also an observable truth that the teaching profession attracts people who want to indoctrinate other people. Law schools are thus incubators of left-wing activism. Aging liberals teach younger ones how to change the world by suing people and entities they consider villainous by defending their heroes. This is where young attorneys learn to become activists. Law school is lawfare boot camp.

Law journals have also largely been taken over by the left. Unlike scientific journals (which are far from neutral in many cases), law journals do not require data or peer review, yet they maintain incredible prestige and are often cited by the Supreme Court.

The practice of law is meant to be adversarial, yet it appears that law schools have forgotten this in favor of discrimination and censoriousness. Stop censorship, make sure young originalist and conservative attorneys compete for important clerkships, and foster the next generation of diverse legal talent. Diversity is more than just race/gender/sexual orientation. It's about encouraging heterogeneous thought and opinion.

A few examples to illustrate my point out of many:

- UC Berkeley Law Dean Erwin Chemerinsky admitted that the school has long factored in race in its admissions.[7] He even admitted that campuses were becoming breeding grounds of antisemitism.[8]

- In 2020, mobs chased down a Cornell University professor for criticizing Black Lives Matter.[9]

- Another woke mob targeted a University of Virginia student for criticizing BLM.[10]

- Another mob, this time at Stanford University, shut down a Federalist Society event.[11]

- Georgetown suspended libertarian law professor Ilya Shapiro and chased him across campus for criticizing Joe Biden's racialization of the Supreme Court. Biden had pledged that he would nominate only a black woman to SCOTUS.[12]

- After Yale Law students shut down a free-speech event at the school, a wave of judges said they would not hire any students from the school.[13]

It's clear that the most recent crop of law school graduates are being taught to shut down debate and try to win not with argumentation but through brute force. This is precisely the point of lawfare: The left cannot win on the battlefield of ideas, so they shut down the debate entirely. Generation Woke has already started entering the workforce—taking jobs at elite firms, clerking for top judges, and entering the federal bureaucracy.

This is why, if we don't change course fast, lawfare will become a generational issue. Taking on law schools is going to take hard work and a lot of time.

The Establishment Media and the Social Media Giants: The media class have been incentivized to provide support for lawfare's wildest arguments and most aggressive proponents. George Conway, Rachel Maddow, Andrew Weissmann, *The View*'s Sunny Hostin, and so many others waged a political persecution of Trump in the court of public opinion. All of this normalized an incredibly abnormal moment in American law and politics.

Their bloodlust may have been good for ratings,[14] but it should be seen as devastating to their credibility. Maddow, who is not a lawyer, for example, and constantly warns her audience about the perceived rise of fascism, stoked demand for Trump to be jailed. You could watch 10,000 hours of MSNBC programming, and no one will ever point out that fairly obvious irony in her coverage.

Our establishment media has played a significant role in the destruction of our legal system. Corporate journalism as we know it is a disgrace, and it must die.

The Masters of the Universe, that is, the leaders of the world's biggest tech and social media companies, also are part of the problem. They hate freedom of speech, which is enshrined in our Constitution under the First Amendment. Facebook cofounder Mark Zuckerberg admitted in 2025, after Trump had won the election, that the Biden administration "had pushed us super hard to take down things that, honestly, were true." Zuckerberg caved to Biden, of course, instead of standing his ground, as is his First Amendment right. He came to regret not being outspoken at the time, but only after Trump won in 2024.[15] He allowed lawfare to triumph at the expense of truth and freedom. Not good!

The 65 Project and Similar Groups: One of the biggest nuisances to the conservative movement since I have been a part of it has been Media Matters for America (MMFA). It's a well-funded nonprofit organization that polices the institutional right, tries to humiliate us, discourage us, silence us, and even bankrupt us. It also was a regular sparring partner for Andrew Breitbart. The founder of MMFA is a man named David Brock, who started his career as a conservative journalist before joining the Clintons as one of their henchmen.

He became the darling of moneyed Democrats; if his name was on it, someone would fund it. In 2022, he started the 65 Project. Its explicit goal was to "disbar and discredit" any attorney who helped Donald Trump in his challenges to the veracity of the 2020 election. He used "dark money" to establish his group, which means his donors remain mysterious.

The "65" in Project 65 is ostensibly in the name because they were targeting sixty-five attorneys who, in their eyes, tried to overthrow democracy with Trump. Not all sixty-five attorneys have been publicly named, so maybe the number is entirely arbitrary. The board consists of assorted leftists both familiar and unfamiliar, as well as establishment Republicans.

The purpose of the group is a new front in lawfare. It was assumed until this point that even the guilty are entitled to competent legal representation. Now if you represent certain types of people (such as Donald Trump) in certain types of cases (such as cases involving Donald Trump), then you might not only lose in the courtroom, but you could lose your law license outright.

Their methodology is simple and devious: Launch bar complaints about Trump-aligned attorneys, then inform simpatico members of the establishment media and watch the circus begin. Maybe the complaint gets thrown out, maybe not, but the reputation of whomever they target will be damaged and they'll have endured personal anguish.

This is the politics of personal destruction, the exact brand of activism Brock pioneered at Media Matters. It's all defamatory by design. The operation ought to be investigated, and perhaps bar complaints ought to be filed against the attorneys behind this lawfare. Fight fire with fire.

Project 65 has had some success already. A court recommended that John Eastman, an attorney and former law school dean, be disbarred over legal advice he gave to Trump that I described earlier. His law license is suspended as of the time this book was completed.

Brock is one of the online left's original warriors. He is highly aggressive, well capitalized, and willing to do whatever is necessary to achieve victory. In other words, he and anything he runs are dangerous.

The Donor Class: The warriors of lawfare can essentially be broken into three categories: the foot soldiers, like the DOJ's Deep State; the generals, like the Weissmanns, the Conways, the Braggs, the Monacos, et al.; and the donors. The donor class drives establishment-Democrat politics. It is a godless culture where money matters more than values, dignity, or autonomy. When a donor says jump, you ask, "For how much?" And then you jump. I will name-check several such donors here.

ProPublica and the Sandler Foundation: In recent years, no one has done more to weaponize fake news against conservative jurists than ProPublica.

ProPublica is a nonprofit largely funded by the Sandler Foundation, which was founded by late leftist banking magnate and billionaire Herb Sandler. Sandler was one of the pioneers of using the veneer of philanthropy to fund activist organizations. For years ProPublica has attempted to destabilize the Supreme Court with their exposés.

ProPublica is essentially a glorified opposition-research-gathering entity that finds dirt on the political targets of their ultrawealthy donors. It's activism with journalism characteristics, and it has its sights set on conservative justices.

This is not a bad business model (we on the right should have more publications like this). Just because someone gathered the information specifically to attack a political target, that doesn't mean the information isn't true.

Media reports tend to omit that ProPublica's top donors are on the activist left.[16] George Soros's Foundation to Promote Open Society has given more than $3 million to ProPublica, for example.[17]

As a journalist, I have begrudging respect for ProPublica. The outlet has broken many stories big and small, and unlike with many leftist publications, I can reasonably assume that when I read something there, they are not lying to me. However, it is purely advocacy journalism. I don't object to advocacy journalism; I'm practicing it right now. However, it's important to understand that ProPublica exists for the express purpose of advancing causes associated with modern liberalism and leftism. That means they cherry-pick their targets.

Their investigations into Clarence Thomas and Samuel Alito, for example, have been pure lawfare. They have repeatedly attacked Thomas because he vacations with a wealthy friend who donates to Republicans. There is no evidence Thomas has done anything illegal or altered a single one of his decisions because of his friend.[18] The reporting adds nothing to our cultural consciousness other than to insinuate that Justice Thomas is a bad guy. The stories are then weaponized by Democrats who call for burdensome investigations and even court-packing.

Their series of hit pieces on Thomas suggest a lot but prove nothing of substance—and are among their most highly trafficked content.

It's also noteworthy that ProPublica obsessively publishes hit pieces on UnitedHealth, an insurance company, for allegedly denying care to certain aggrieved people. The CEO of UnitedHealth was assassinated after one of several ProPublica features on the company. The assassin was not even a UnitedHealth customer. Had he seen the ProPublica stories before he committed the acts of vigilantism? ProPublica doesn't care, apparently, as they continued the series on UnitedHealth just days after the murder.[19]

Good journalists, bad people.

The Sandler Foundation deserves its own special recognition. Aside from starting ProPublica and donating tens of millions of dollars to it, it has cut millions in checks to the Campaign Legal Center and the American Constitution Society, both of which have supported referrals for Justice Thomas to the Justice Department for criminal and civil penalties for alleged ethics violations.[20] The Sandler Foundation is also part of the infamous left-wing dark money network Arabella Advisors.

It funds the group that does the journalism, then funds separate groups that publicize, elevate, and weaponize the journalism. See how the superstructure works?

The Sandler Foundation has funded leftist groups like the Center for American Progress, the American Civil Liberties Union (ACLU), Human Rights Watch, and the Sierra Club, among others.

Much of this is funded with anonymous donations.

Though ethically dubious, this is undeniably powerful in the strategic sense.

They also work closely with other leftist megadonors George Soros and Reid Hoffman to form a lawfare hydra.

Reid Hoffman, Laurene Powell Jobs, and George Soros: The super-villains of the Marlow Universe of investigative research are all essential parts of the lawfare superstructure. This network, in concert with the Sandler Foundation, has strategically placed prosecutors throughout the country who are ready, willing, and able to bend and break the rule of law to suit their benefactors' political desires.

George Soros funded the campaigns of many district attorneys who have let our metropolises rot with crime. He and Hoffman have backed the group Indivisible, which bankrolled the E. Jean Carroll suit against Trump. Indivisible has claimed credit for both Trump impeachments as well as other assorted efforts to disqualify him from the presidential ballot.

Soros also funds other elements of the lawfare superstructure that have been profiled in this book, such as Norm Eisen's CREW.

When they weren't writing puff pieces about her best friend, Kamala Harris, Laurene Powell Jobs's media properties have spent the last decade trumpeting one hysterical anti-Trump hoax after the next.

Local Political Machines: Thanks to Soros, there are lawfare battle-fields all over the country. Places like New York, Washington, D.C., and Arizona have a high concentration of well-funded, pugnacious jurists ready to try to implement Soros's political agenda. "Over the past decade, billionaire George Soros has spent at least $50 million to elect scores of 'social justice' prosecutors across the country," according to the Law Enforcement Legal Defense Fund. "These district attorneys, who represent over 70 million people or more than 1 in 5 Americans, often pursue pro-criminal and anti-police policies."[21] There were 25 Soros-linked district attorneys either on the ballot or up for recall in 2024. Thankfully, 12 were defeated, but it would have been better if all 25 went down.[22]

Andrew Weissmann: The efforts to remove President Trump from office in his first impeachment saw new strategies for how law, politics, and media manipulation could be used to tarnish Trump in the court of public opinion. Many of these were pioneered by Andrew Weissmann, known by some as "Mueller's pit bull."

Weissmann, who was a lead prosecutor on the Mueller team, is a modern lawfare visionary (that's not a compliment). He had already built a reputation of destroying people in order to advance his own career. He first gained public notoriety in 2002 when George W. Bush appointed him deputy director of the FBI's Enron task force. Weissmann had argued that accounting firm Arthur Andersen had covered for the disgraced Enron executives. The firm was convicted of obstructing justice and went out of business.

However, years later it came to light that Weissmann had persuaded the judge to instruct the jury that they could convict the firm whether or not its employees had knowingly violated the law. This outlandish act of prosecutorial misconduct was overturned in a unanimous decision by the U.S. Supreme Court; Chief Justice William H. Rehnquist delivered a brutal takedown of Weissman's tactics. Arthur Andersen remained shuttered.

He abused his power, blatantly broke the rules, and hundreds of people lost their jobs because of it.

He showed no remorse, of course, and continued to build a reputation for ruthless tactics.

This makes him a star of lawfare.

He also was adroit at using the media to advance his ends, becoming an MSNBC legal analyst and podcast host for the Peacock network. He often seemed to create the news and then rush to a camera and microphone so he could opine on his own brilliance.

At the time of this writing, Weissmann is being sued by former Trump White House attorney Stefan Passantino for defamation. Weissmann claimed Passantino coached discredited January 6th Committee witness Cassidy Hutchinson to lie on the witness stand, a fact that Hutchinson herself denies.[23]

Weissmann seems to be enjoying the fruits of his lawfare. Former press secretary and current MSNBC host Jen Psaki put together a puffpiece package on Weissmann's life in Manhattan, where he appears to live alone with a dog in an "extremely hip" apartment (Psaki's phraseology), filled with vintage cameras and high-end espresso equipment. Despite his reputation as a legal pit bull, he's constantly smiling while he tries to destroy the lives of people with whom he differs politically.

The look on his face conveys a reality in our 24/7 news/social media/reality TV era: Sometimes the fictions playing out in the pages of the *New York Times* or on-air at MSNBC are their own form of reality. They certainly help Andrew Weissmann maintain an immaculate New York City condo.

"Pencil Neck" and the Impeachment Managers: Then-Representative Adam "Pencil Neck" Schiff, the lead manager for the Democrats, would go on to become a U.S. senator representing California. Representative Hakeem Jefferies, another manager, would go on to become the minority leader of the U.S. House of Representatives. Others involved in the impeachment have amassed large online followings and write bestselling books.

Schiff himself is a pure lawfare agent. For example, he held the impeachment hearings in a Sensitive Compartmented Information Facility (SCIF), an enclosed place for processing classified information. Only, there was no classified information that was relevant. Schiff was trying to control who was a part of the process and what information was leaked to the public. This allowed him to "audition" witnesses to determine who was ready for their fifteen minutes in the public eye. This meant that even members of the House Judiciary Committee could not attend, despite the fact that they were in charge of drafting the articles of impeachment themselves. In October, Republicans dramatically yet appropriately stormed the room and demanded to have the hearing in public.

Dan Goldman was named director of investigations for the House Intelligence Committee, that is, the Democrat impeachers. Goldman's great-grandfather, Walter A. Haas, was president of Levi Strauss. Abraham Haas, his great-great-grandfather, was the founder of Smart & Final grocery stores, and his descendants are heir to the empire. Goldman went to the posh Sidwell Friends school in Washington, D.C., before attending Yale and Stanford. He covered the Olympics as a researcher for NBC before becoming a federal prosecutor.[24] His net worth is thought to be about a quarter of a billion dollars. He did not make that as a researcher or as an assistant U.S. Attorney in New York or through his gig as a legal pundit on MSNBC.

Goldman is a clear example of someone who was born on third base and thinks he hit a triple. The ultimate lawfare nepo-baby.

Goldman didn't reveal anything earth-shattering during the impeachment, but he has been willing to publicly promote the most sensational fantasies that dwell in the recesses of the Democrats' collective psyche, including that Trump (a germophobe) flew to Moscow to receive a golden shower (look it up . . . or don't).[25]

Goldman, who had donated mountains of cash to Democrats, told the House Judiciary Committee that he was "nonpartisan." In fact, donating to Democrats seemed to be the main criterion to become a part of the Democrats' impeachment team.

He would ultimately buy himself a seat in Congress.[26] "He has poured nearly $4 million of his personal fortune—which includes holdings in major banks, military contractors, health insurers, and fossil fuel companies—into his campaign," the far-left periodical *Common Dreams* reported before he won his race.

It was revealed that Goldman had prepped estranged Trump attorney Michael Cohen to testify against Trump in 2023.[27] He also paid more than $157,000 to the political consulting firm of Judge Juan Merchan's daughter, Loren Merchan, according to Federal Election Commission disbursement filings obtained by *Breitbart News*'s Joel Pollak.[28]

Weissmann, Schiff, Goldman, and so many others used their efforts to destroy Donald Trump as a launchpad for their political and media ambitions. They will remain part of the lawfare firmament for the foreseeable future.

Marc Elias: The superlawyer my colleague Peter Schweizer dubbed "the master of political dark arts" presents himself as the keeper of democracy as we know it, but I regard him as the biggest election denier in America. Elias doesn't see a political contest as lost until he has tried every legal avenue imaginable to contest an undesired outcome.

No doubt he is one of the most adroit players in the American political game. All of his preferred tactics fall under the broad definition of lawfare.

He famously headed the political law practice at Perkins Coie. From there he arranged via a former MI6 operative for Fusion GPS to produce the fraudulent Steele Dossier, which led to the yearslong Russian-collusion hoax. He did this all to benefit Hillary Clinton's campaign.

However, that wasn't Elias's first effort to use political dark arts to alter the outcome of an election. By aggressively contesting ballots, Elias was able turn a narrow defeat into a narrow victory for Al Franken in a highly contested 2008 Minnesota U.S. Senate race. This was the Democrats' sixtieth seat, giving them a filibuster-proof majority and the ability to pass gargantuan bills like Obamacare without trouble.

In the 2020 presidential election, Elias used the coronavirus pandemic as an excuse to greatly expand mail-in voting, which overwhelmingly favors Democrats. Without this strategy, Joe Biden might not have won, and he certainly wouldn't have gotten 80 million votes.

After the election, he took the lead, fending off dozens of lawsuits brought by Trump and his allies contesting election results across the country, earning him folk-hero status in Democrat circles.

He accomplishes so much because he's utterly shameless. After the Democrats pilloried Republicans for claiming that voting machines were used to rig the 2020 election against Donald Trump, Elias alleged in a court filing that an upstate New York congressional race was swung by "voting tabulation machines misread hundreds if not thousands of valid votes as undervotes" that disproportionately affected his Democrat client, who lost a race by a narrow margin.[29] It should come as no surprise that he was unable to prove that vote machine rigging actually took place.

This is classic election denialism, yet it hardly got any attention in the establishment media.

In his spare time, Elias meddles in redistricting battles, using the court system to try to exert control over the congressional map.[30]

During the 2024 election cycle, Elias drafted a team of hundreds of lawyers and thousands of volunteers who were prepared to "sue until blue" (a term coined by GAI's resident election integrity expert Eric Eggers). They would contest every ballot and every close race in hopes of replicating the results of the 2008 Al Franken Senate race. He ended up focusing on the Pennsylvania Senate race, where he attempted to lawfare a victory for then-Senator Bob Casey over Republican Dave McCormick. Elias and Casey denied the election results until there was no possible path to victory.

As far as I can tell, Marc Elias has only one principle: win. He's tough, clever, and willing to be utterly ruthless. One illustrative example of his ruthlessness is that in 2021, while at Perkins Coie, he was sanctioned by the U.S. Court of Appeals for violating his "duty of candor to the court" for not disclosing that the firm had already submitted a nearly identical motion that had been denied.[31] The motion—an attempt to implement straight-ticket voting in the state of Texas—would have helped Democrats win elections, had it succeeded. Data shows straight-ticket voting heavily favors Democrats, especially on down-ticket races.[32]

He is also one of the reasons Democrats are as powerful as they are in this country.

Big Law: Another obvious group that makes up a powerful portion of the lawfare superstructure is the big law firms that sue the Trump administration. Wilmer Cutler Pickering Hale and Dorr; Hogan Lovells; Jenner & Block; Ropes & Gray; Gibson, Dunn & Crutcher; Perkins Coie; Arnold & Porter Kaye Scholer; and Milbank all represented plaintiffs against the Trump administration within the first forty days of his second term. These cases involve lawyers like Neal Katyal (also a prominent cable news legal pundit), Seth Waxman, and Paul Clement, all from major white-shoe firms, all with Supreme Court experience, all former solicitors general.[33] This list could be a mile long by the time this book hits the shelves.

Trump is well aware of the threat Big Law poses, and he has responded accordingly. In March of 2025, he signed an executive order targeting Perkins Coie LLP, Marc Elias's firm, which had represented Hillary Clinton in 2016 and hired Fusion GPS to produce the bogus Steele Dossier. Trump suspended security clearances of Perkins Coie employees, terminated contracts, and limited their access to federal agencies and officials. Judge Beryl Howell, who was appointed by Barack Obama, issued the inevitable injunction.[34]

In fact, more than five hundred firms signed a court brief denouncing Trump's E.O. That's a remarkable number and is a potent illustration of the fact that America's most prestigious firms are often part of the lawfare superstructure and are thus part of the institutional left. "Law professor Derek Muller has found that in the five most politically controversial Supreme Court cases between 2018 and 2022, elite firms filed 93 friend-of-the-court briefs in favor of the liberal position and only five supporting the conservative one," University of Texas at Austin law professor John Greil wrote in the *Wall Street Journal.*[35] Greil also claimed that even superstar attorneys are routinely jettisoned from white-shoe firms simply for representing conservative clients.

There are many additional names of individuals responsible for the lawfare culture that has become so prevalent and pernicious. They are so numerous I could easily fill this book with mini-profiles of key players at all levels of the lawfare superstructure. Take Norm Eisen, the former

Obama ethics czar turned full-time lawfare guru. He is the cofounder and two-time chairman of Citizens for Ethics Reform in Washington (CREW), which works to couch Democrat efforts to target conservatives as "ethics" issues. He laid the groundwork for the first Trump impeachment and then served as counsel for the Democrats in their effort to oust the president.[36] He has been one of the most vocal advocates for criminally convicting Trump.[37] He recently launched a media outlet with anti-Trump zealot Jennifer Rubin.

Kristen Clarke, the assistant attorney general for the Civil Rights Division of Biden's Justice Department, appears to have been busted for lying under oath to Congress. During her nomination, she was asked, "Have you ever been arrested for or accused of committing a violent crime against any person?" She answered an unequivocal "no," which was not true. As it turns out, she had been arrested during a domestic altercation with her then-husband Reginald Avery in July 2006. She slashed at him with a knife, cutting his finger to the bone, according to Avery.[38] Lying to Congress while under oath is a felony. None of this mattered to Biden and Garland, though. She maintained her post at the DOJ until Biden left office.[39]

She wasn't very good at her job supporting civil rights, either. She, along with her boss, Garland, were notably silent when a wave of antisemitism swept university campuses in the aftermath of the October 7, 2023, Hamas terror attack on Israel.[40]

The lawfare superstructure has its moneyed elites, its generals, and its foot soldiers, but there is one last part vital to its function: normal citizens who enable the lawfare combatants. These are the rank-and-file Democrat voters who have seen their cities crumble; they favor wokeness over readiness for the real challenges a society faces. This is the group of people who are willfully blind to the agendas of the likes of George Soros, Mark Elias, Lisa Monaco, and so many others mentioned in this book. Scarier still, many are aware of the effect lawfare has had on American life yet choose to support those who practice it. They stand idly by, voting for Democrats as if they bear none of the blame.

Not everyone in this final group is a radical. In fact, most are normal citizens, your friends and neighbors, just following the zeitgeist.

Perhaps the most easily exploitable weakness in the Democrats' lawfare superstructure isn't at the top with overzealous prosecutors, belligerent attorneys general, and hysterical "legal analysts." Perhaps the key to dismantling the lawfare superstructure is by exposing what lawfare has wrought on the American people and hope they finally see the light.

Then we let democracy take its course.

CHAPTER 9

THE NEW EXISTENTIAL THREAT

One of the principles that guides my editorial judgment at *Breitbart News* is that while I want our coverage to chronicle the present, I insist on keeping an eye on the future as well. I'm not interested in "weird news" or one-off quirky stories so much as spotting developing trends that will grow to become bigger narratives. This principle drove me to investigate lawfare against Donald Trump and his supporters as the topic of my third book. I saw the robust nature in which the left pursued this avenue of attack during and after his first administration, forcing Trump to defend against attacks on a half dozen fronts at a time.

I knew that lawfare would either take down Trump or propel him to the presidency.

He won, as it turned out. And his victory hobbled his traditional foes. Hollywood was sent reeling, their political power broken. Tinsel Town even began to scale back some of the woke in their content.[1] Establishment media brands either died, radically reduced staff, tried to add nonleftists to their newsrooms, or did some combination thereof. Universities remain bastions of leftism, so President Trump cut their federal funding if they didn't eliminate diversity, equity, and inclusion programs. Even the Democrat Party went into disarray, lacking charismatic leadership, unable to decide if they should double down on advocating for men in women's sports and leaving the border unenforced, or if they should moderate and tack toward the center. At the time I'm completing work on this book, the activist left is engaged in a terror campaign against Tesla vehicles and their owners.

None of this is helping them.

However, there is still one powerful group of people standing athwart history yelling "Stop Trump." That is, of course, the lawfare superstructure. The people who used the court system to try to bankrupt and jail Donald Trump were the natural candidates to lead the "Resistance" against him in his second term. And that's exactly what they have done.

Lawfare has become one of the major story lines of Donald Trump's second administration. As I've demonstrated in this book, the left does not value democracy—it resents genuine governance according to the will of the people—and prioritizes political victory above all else. President Trump's victory broke the political and cultural institutions that had driven Democrat politics throughout the twenty-first century. As it became clear the left was now ineffectual in fighting the culture war in the early days of the second Trump administration, weaponizing the law became their preferred tactic to slow down Trump and his agenda.

After a massive electoral rout and general demoralization among their base, the left couldn't rely on mobilizing crowds of liberals in opposition to Trump—as they did in 2016. They couldn't create the illusion of widespread democratic opposition to the president.

But they had one tool that didn't require a popular insurgency: injunctions. An injunction is a court order that blocks a party from engaging in a specific act. These can be permanent or temporary (such as a Temporary Restraining Order [TRO]) and are legally binding, making it difficult if not impossible to go around them, even if you're the president. TROs effectively give judges veto power over executive branch policy. The President of the United States is then forced to wait for a court of appeals to decide if the veto stands. This is all preposterously anti-Democratic.

In the early days of Donald Trump's second administration, virtually every element of his agenda was subject to lawsuits by Democrat-aligned interest groups. Many of these suits led to federal judges issuing injunctions. The judiciary halted eone executive action after the next, preventing the administration from enacting its agenda.

This method of political opposition was not entirely new. Trump's first term saw 64 nationwide injunctions on high-profile cases. According to a *Harvard Law Review* article, only 127 injunctions have been issued against presidential administrations to that point since 1963. That means fully half were issued against Trump administration policies.[2] Moreover, 59 of those 64 injunctions were issued by judges appointed by Democrats. And that is counting just his first term.

The injunctions had a real effect on President Trump's ability to deliver on his campaign promises. Judges placed holds on his ban on travel into the USA from terror-prone nations, his attempt to withhold federal funds from "sanctuary cities," his attempt to ban the transgendered from the military, and his rescission of the Deferred Action for Childhood Arrivals (DACA) program. In the case of DACA, judges in California, New York, and Washington, D.C., blocked Trump, leading to an appeal process that went all the way to the Supreme Court, where Trump was defeated 5–4, with Chief Justice John Roberts siding with the four dependably liberal justices on the court at the time.[3]

Clarence Thomas warned against national injunctions in 2018. "Injunctions did not emerge until a century and a half after the founding," he wrote in a concurring opinion in the *Trump v. Hawaii* case (which concerned travel bans). "And they appear to be inconsistent with longstanding limits on equitable relief and the power of Article III courts. If their popularity continues, this court must address their legality."

The superstructure must have taken this quote as affirmation that they were on to something. A new strategy had emerged, and the left pursued it with all their remaining resources. They were not being subtle. They did lawfare in plain sight.

This was the exact playbook the lawfare superstructure would deploy at the start of Trump's second administration to limit his power and undermine the ability for the democratically elected president to do his job.

FLOODING THE ZONE

Trump signed over one hundred executive actions during his first hundred days in office, including a record-breaking twenty-six on Inauguration Day 2025. Executive actions are a tool that the president can use to enact portions of his agenda that do not require approval from Congress. These actions are not new laws but work within the existing legal framework to direct the behavior of government.

This was the correct approach for President Trump. During his first administration, it seemed as if whenever he tried to accomplish anything, the media would act as though it was impossible, illegal, or even impeachable. Take, for instance, the thirty-five-day partial government shutdown that occurred at the end of 2018 into early 2019, when the Democrats refused to allocate President Trump a paltry $5 billion of funding for his desired border wall. The Democrats held the line, and Trump eventually relented. The reason he caved, I believe, is that the media pummeled him and his Republican colleagues nonstop, blaming them for the shutdown even though Trump was asking for only partial funding of his signature campaign issue.[4]

It was a classic media tactic. The media loves to isolate a political target and focus all of their attention on it. This creates the impression that millions of people are outraged by a story or oppose a given policy. As a result, it's a fool's errand for a Republican to advance one part of their agenda at a time. The media will kill the baby in the crib. Flooding the zone neutralized the Democrats' strategy because the media simply could not keep up. They could not isolate their target the way they had in the past.

Trump and his team were deliberate. They had dozens of executive orders in the chamber and ready to fire on day one of administration two. The lawfare superstructure was prepared, however, and they were ready to file lawsuit after lawsuit to block Trump. By March 5, 2025, Democrats had filed over one hundred legal challenges against Trump.[5] And many of them were working.

In February alone, courts had issued a stunning fifteen injunctions. Judges had filed thirty total injunctions in Trump's first eight weeks. This blocked crucial parts of his agenda. A Seattle judge blocked Trump's day-one order to end "birthright citizenship." On February 21, the judge in the Southern District of New York stopped Elon Musk's Department of Government Efficiency (DOGE) from accessing data from the Treasury Department, the Education Department, and the Office of Personnel Management. On March 12, a preliminary injunction from the federal court in D.C., Judge Ana Reyes, blocked the Department of Defense from barring transgender service members. On March 18, Judge Julie Rubin in Massachusetts reinstated $600 million in teacher-training grants against Trump's directive to cancel them.

And so on.

Virtually every element of the agenda was encumbered by federal judges, from scaling back diversity, equity, and inclusion (DEI) within the government to immigration enforcement and DOGE's work cutting government excess.

It was a race. Could President Trump outrun the superstructure? Could he implement enough of his agenda before the left could shut it down with lawfare?

One thing was certain: The institutional left planned to challenge Trump everywhere, and lawfare judges would lead the charge.

PRESIDENT BOASBERG

A truly extraordinary sequence of events played out over the weekend of March 15 and 16 that illustrates the extent to which the lawfare superstructure would go to stop Trump from doing . . . anything. The action began in response to Trump invoking the Alien Enemies Act of 1798, which he used to deport hundreds of Venezuelans, many of whom were part of the ultraviolent Tren de Aragua (TdA) gang.

Donald Trump had forged a deal with El Salvador's president, Nayib Bukele, to house some of the deported gang members in El Salvador's Centro de Confinamiento del Terrorismo (CECOT) megaprison in exchange for cash. The deal allowed Bukele to fund his tough-on-crime agenda and got violent gangsters out of the United States.

It was the proverbial 360-win.

TdA had been designated a Foreign Terrorist Organization and boasts ties to organized crime, including human, drug, and weapons trafficking, murders, and narcoterrorism. The Alien Enemies Act allows for the president to remove aliens for invasion or predatory incursion into the United States. Due to TdA's ties to the Venezuela government, the Trump administration argued that their presence in the U.S. amounts to warfare against our country.[6]

Much like the U.S. Constitution itself, the Alien Enemies Act might be old, but it's also timeless. It gave Trump's efforts to deport the TdA members a strong legal foundation.

But apparently the foundation was not strong enough for Chief Judge James Boasberg. At 1:12 a.m. on Saturday, March 15, the ACLU and Soros-linked Democracy Forward, both legal advocacy groups, filed suits on behalf of five Venezuelans destined for deportation.

By 5:45 p.m., two planes loaded with illegal aliens had departed the Harlingen, Texas, airport en route to El Salvador.

At 6:45 p.m., Judge Boasberg verbally issued an order that the aliens were to remain in U.S. custody, stating that "any plane containing these folks that is going to take off or is in the air needs to be returned to the United States."

The following morning, the planes had arrived in El Salvador. President Bukele tweeted a *New York Post* headline saying Boasberg had ordered planes turned around, adding "Oopsie . . . Too late" and a tears-of-joy emoji.

It was Trump-level trolling.

White House staff began to circulate the tweet widely, no doubt satisfied with themselves.

The establishment media lost their minds, suggesting that Trump had defied a court order, thus creating a constitutional crisis, which occurs when one of the coequal branches of government goes rogue and the Constitution's normal system of checks and balances has yet to resolve the breakdown.[7]

It's worth noting that a "constitutional crisis" is a political term, not a legal one, contrary to what the yammering establishment media punditry would have you believe.

Trump hadn't defied anything, though. The Alien Enemies Act exists. TdA seems to fit the terms of the statute. (The Supreme Court suggested it agreed on April 8, 2025, when a majority of the justices sided with the Trump administration.[8]) The deportation flights had already departed for El Salvador well before Boasberg made his injunction.

Still, the central question remains: Is it truly within a district judge's power to order a military plane full of federal personnel outside the country to turn around? This is precisely what Boasberg attempted to do. What's more, he tried to dictate orders to President Trump.

On Monday, March 17, Boasberg accused Trump of "possible defiance" of the court order. Lee Gelernt, an ACLU lawyer representing the plaintiffs, suggested a constitutional crisis was upon us.

Who had the ultimate authority? President Trump or President Boasberg?

Boasberg even threatened to hold Trump officials in contempt of court for not facilitating the return of the illegal alien gang members to the U.S.[9]

Trump fired off a post to Truth Social suggesting Boasberg should be

"IMPEACHED," which earned a rare public rebuke from Chief Justice John Roberts. "For more than two centuries, it has been established that impeachment is not an appropriate response to disagreement concerning a judicial decision," wrote Roberts. "The normal appellate review process exists for that purpose."[10]

I met with the president just a couple of days after the incident, and he was genuinely surprised, even bemused, by the judge's attempt to stop him. "Bring Tren De Aragua back? These people are crazy," he told me in a private dining room off the Oval Office.

President Trump was speaking colloquially, but I don't think *crazy* is the correct word. These judges are highly partisan and skilled in the dark arts of lawfare. They weren't acting crazy. They were implementing a rigidly planned political strategy.

"How about the chief judge going after me?" Trump continued, expressing mild astonishment at John Roberts. "And I'm right," he added. "If you have an Obama judge or a Biden judge, you can't get a win, I don't care how good your case. They won't give you a win. And Republicans want to act like they're above it. So, you could lose one. It's a different mentality."

President Trump's description is fundamentally correct, and his core point is important: It was inevitable that Boasberg would side with the illegal alien gang members over the democratically elected president of the United States. To the lawfare superstructure, Donald Trump is the real criminal, not the Latin American gangsters. Boasberg, a 2010 Obama appointee, was always going to rule against Trump, guaranteed. What's more, Republican-appointed judges and justices like Roberts aren't nearly as predictable when it comes to their perceived politics predicting their judicial actions. In our modern lawfare moment, the same can't be said of Obama- and Biden-appointed judges like Boasberg, who was appointed by Obama in 2010 and is known for left-wing rulings and bias against President Trump.

Here's an example: While presiding over the Foreign Intelligence Surveillance Act (FISA) Court, Judge Boasberg ruled that former FBI attorney Kevin Clinesmith, one of the top conspirators in the Russiagate hoax, shouldn't get prison time. Clinesmith admitted he tampered with evidence to say that Trump campaign adviser Carter Page was "not a source" for the Central Intelligence Agency when Page very much had been. Clinesmith's forgery extended the FBI's unlawful and unethical surveillance of the Trump campaign.[11] Boasberg's decision to let Cline-smith skate is lawfare and Trump Derangement Syndrome at the same time.

The Clinesmith ruling is part of Boasberg's pattern of judicial activism. He had ruled for the release of migrants from detention facilities in Trump's first term,[12] he approved the use of warrantless surveillance against American citizens despite evidence of improper data collection,[13] and he ordered the Trump administration to empty the Dakota Access Pipeline pending an environmental review,[14] among other rulings that favored Democrat causes.

Boasberg took on four "Trump cases" in the early weeks of the second Trump adminisration, blocking and stalling the president's first wave of executive actions.[15] One such case was a high-profile lawsuit alleging Defense Secretary Pete Hegseth, Secretary of State Marco Rubio, National Security Advisor Michael Waltz, and others violated the Federal Records Act by using the encrypted messaging app Signal to discuss military strikes against Houthi terrorists.[16]

So how did one left-wing judge get assigned so many sensitive cases? Part of the answer is the legal tactic known as "judge-shopping." It's a straightforward idea: A politically interested party will bring a case to a court with mostly favorable judges to make it likely they get their desired outcome. For example, some courts have only one judge, so it can be easy to anticipate how a judge will rule if you bring the case to that judge's court. Other powerful courts, such as the D.C. District Court, is composed of mostly of judges who appear to be ideologically on the left. The venue rules for federal cases (28 U.S.C. § 1391) make it so that virtually every case brought against the federal government can be filed in that court since it is often where the defendant resides or where the relevant events occurred.

Though they are not consistent from court to court throughout the country, venue rules theoretically limit where a case can be filed to where the plaintiff resides, where the defendant resides, or where a substantial part of the circumstances that led to the claim played out, but attorneys can work around those limitations by simply adding a defendant or a plaintiff to the filing who resides in a jurisdiction with a favorable court.

Conservatives use this to their advantage as well. It's simply how the game is played.

Peter Schweizer credits Marc Elias, a high priest of lawfare if there ever was one, with popularizing the venue-shopping tactic. According to Schweizer, Elias was able to swing the highly contested 2008 Minnesota Senate race for Democrat Al Franken over Republican Norm Coleman by finding a specific court to legitimize over a thousand ballots that had previously been rejected because they had potentially been cast by convicted felons.[17] The recount and trial lasted six months, the longest recount in American history, and in the end, the former *Saturday Night Live* actor won a narrow victory. According to Schweizer, Elias engineered this feat by venue-shopping for a favorable court. A subsequent study suggested many felons did in fact illegally vote in the race, which may well have tipped the election to Franken.[18] As previously noted, that race gave the Democrats a filibuster-proof sixty-vote majority in a Senate, allowing then-President Obama to pass enormous pieces of legislation such as Obamacare.

Though many courts assign cases to judges at random, some courts are small and more predictable. Others are stacked with judges with similar judicial philosophies, so a smart lawyer keen on venue-shopping can hope to match a simpatico judge to his case. Attorneys will also file similar or identical claims in multiple jurisdictions. For example, when Trump tried to end birthright citizenship, four judges blocked him.[19] Judges in Boston, New Hampshire, Seattle, and Maryland—all deep-blue areas—issued injunctions.

Attorneys also file cases at times when they believe that a specific judge is most likely to get assigned the case. This appears to have happened in the Alien Enemies Act case. Boasberg was the judge who "happened to be available" first thing Saturday morning to take the case, despite the fact that he was "away" that weekend. A charitable view of the court transcripts indicate Boasberg was tipped off that the case was coming.[20] A more cynical take: He may be part of a grand conspiracy to rig cases.

All of this is manipulative, against the spirt of judicial impartiality, and highly effective.

In the early portion of Trump's second administration, the lawfare superstructure made sure that as many cases challenging Trump's agenda as possible were heard in the most favorable courts. If you pay close attention, you'll notice a pattern: Trump keeps getting overturned by the same courts, such as Boasberg's court in D.C.

As of spring 2025, there are 677 U.S. district court judgeships. It began to feel as though Trump would effectually need the unanimous consent of all of them in order to have his agenda go through.

This is, of course, antidemocratic. Each of these judges can't have a veto over everything that President Trump does.

Or maybe they can.

Now the cat is out of the bag. The lawfare superstructure figured out how they can block a president they hate.

It's game on.

HUNDREDS OF PRESIDENTS

Here's another story of how a petty tyrant judge can undermine a duly elected president of the United States:

The U.S. Agency for International Development (USAID) was an early target of Elon Musk and DOGE for funding ideas so absurd it would take a Hollywood writer to dream them up: $20 million for a *Sesame Street*-type show in Iraq, circumcisions in Mozambique, a transgender opera in Colombia, sex changes in Guatemala, diversity, equity, and inclusion in Serbia, an Irish DEI musical, and condoms for seemingly everyone on earth. There simply wasn't an expenditure too absurd for USAID.[21] Things were so bad that Secretary of State Marco Rubio eliminated about 5,200 out of 6,200 USAID programs and 83 percent of its staff during the first two months of Donald Trump's administration. He would go on to take over USAID entirely, shifting the remaining programs to the State Department.

But not so fast.

In mid-March, Judge Theodore Chuang of Maryland ruled that cuts to USAID were likely unconstitutional. He issued a preliminary injunction, ruling that only an act of Congress could dismantle the organization. Chuang was nominated by Barack Obama in 2014. In law school he was the editor of the *Harvard Law Review*, where he used the publication to promote critical race theory. He became a donor to Democratic candidates and vice president of a Maryland County Democratic Club. He was

also a board member of the Coalition of Asian Pacific American Democrats of Maryland. In March 2017, he blocked President Trump's "travel
ban" from terror-prone nations, though the ban was amended and eventually upheld by the Supreme Court.[22]

In February 2025, Judge Brendan A. Hurson of the U.S. District
Court for the District of Maryland, a Biden appointee, single-handedly
stopped Trump's plan to cut federal funding to hospitals that facilitated
sex changes for children.[23]

Even some Republican-appointed judges caused Trump problems.
Judge Royce C. Lamberth of the U.S. District Court for the District of
Columbia, a Reagan appointee, stopped an effort by Trump to move all
biological males to men's prisons.[24] He ordered the administration to
send multiple men back to female detention centers after they had
already been moved.[25]

Judge John Bates of the District of Columbia, a George W. Bush appointee, made Trump restore taxpayer-funded web pages that offered advice on transgender surgeries.[26] If Trump can't even remove a web page
without the approval of Judge John Bates, what can the president even
do? It turns out that Bates, though nominated by a Republican, was married to a woman who founded an international nonprofit that received
USAID funds.[27]

The list of leftist judges blocking the Trump agenda is overwhelming.

In March 2025, Senior Judge Amy Berman Jackson of the U.S. District
Court for the District of Columbia, nominated by President Barack
Obama, temporarily reinstated the fired head of the Office of the Special
Counsel, Hampton Dellinger, a Biden appointee and Democrat donor. Previously Jackson presided over the case that sent Trump's former campaign
chair Paul Manafort to jail and multiple January 6th Capitol riot cases.
Judge Jackson is clearly an egomaniac who built her reputation by grand-
standing during "procedural courtroom check-ins," as one excessively
complimentary CNN profile indicated.[28] The New York Times said Jackson
was "known for her sharp criticism of the Trump administration's moves"
after she sentenced Trump ally Roger Stone to forty months in prison. She
also passed out prison time to J6 defendants with enthusiasm.[29]

Chief Judge John J. McConnell Jr. of the U.S. District Court for the
District of Rhode Island threatened the Trump administration with
criminal charges for freezing federal funds. McConnell was appointed by

Obama and was a committed Democrat donor and activist. "While he was in private practice as an attorney until 2009, McConnell donated hundreds of thousands to Democratic campaigns and political action committees, including 2008 presidential campaigns of Hillary Clinton, Joe Biden and Barack Obama, according to Federal Election Commission records," the *Daily Caller* reported. He worked for the ACLU and was on the board of directors for a branch of Planned Parenthood.[30]

Senior Judge Colleen Kollar-Kotelly, U.S. District Court for the District of Columbia, who was nominated by President Bill Clinton, ordered to prevent DOGE from "obtaining access to certain Treasury Department payment records," which includes an estimated 90 percent of federal payments.[31] Kollar-Kotelly has a cruel streak, having sentenced seven pro-life activists to federal prison. The husband of activist Paula "Paulette" Harlow, seventy-seven, who was among the seven, was thoroughly rebuked by the judge when he emphasized that his wife was dying and pleaded for mercy and leniency. In response, Kollar-Kotelly suggested that Harlow "make every effort to stay alive" as part of the "tenets of your religion."[32] Nasty. She also blocked Trump's trans military ban in 2017.

Judge Paul A. Engelmayer of the U.S. District Court for the Southern District of New York, an Obama appointee, blocked DOGE's access to the Treasury Department payment system. In his ruling, Engelmayer forbade all political appointees, including the Treasury secretary, from accessing department data, implying that Scott Bessent's job is purely ceremonial. Not only were Trump administration lawyers not allowed to argue their case in his court, but they weren't even in the room when he rendered his decision.

Senior Judge George O'Toole Jr., of the U.S. District Court for the District of Massachusetts, who was nominated by President Bill Clinton, tried to buck Trump in two significant ways. First he blocked Trump's federal government employee buyout, even after 65,000 federal workers had already taken the offer, prolonging a pause on the deferred resignation program. He also temporarily blocked the transfer of trans women (aka biological males) to men's prisons and prolonged "trans" prisoners' access to "gender-affirming care" after a Trump executive order revoked the policy.

Biden appointee Judge Angel Kelley of the U.S. District Court for the District of Massachusetts granted a restraining order against National Institutes of Health (NIH) funding cuts. The Trump administration had moved to cap indirect costs, that is, reimbursements for "overhead" expenses on university research, at 15 percent. Judge Kelley stepped in on behalf of the universities to ensure that Trump could not slash the wasteful expense at will.

Kelley has a history of judicial activism that is hardly a secret. Senator Elizabeth Warren (D-MA) said in 2021 that Kelley "has made it a personal mission to bring about change through her role on the bench." This is entirely accurate. For starters, Biden boasted that DEI was a factor in her appointment, highlighting her African American and Asian American ancestry as part of his administration's "push to expand diversity on the federal bench." She openly uses DEI criteria in hiring. Senator Ted Cruz (R-TX) reported that she said, "There is systemic racism in almost all systems, particularly the court system." She also participated in the "China Judicial Exchange," which sends American jurists to the People's Court of China, according to a report. Her judicial record has shown a bias for criminals and against law enforcement.[33]

In April of 2025, Judge Indira Talwani (temporarily) blocked the federal terminations of temporary legal status for hundreds of thousands of Cubans, Haitians, Nicaraguans, and Venezuelans.[34] An Obama appointee, Democrat donor,[35] and volunteer for leftist candidates,[36] Talwani had previously ruled that DHS could not remove a detained foreign student tied to anti-Israel protests.[37]

Talwani has consistently taken the leftist position in high-profile cases. In 2023, she ruled in favor of a school that sent a seventh-grade student home for wearing a T-shirt stating that there are only two genders.[38] In 2019, she blocked ICE from arresting illegal immigrants at courthouses.[39]

Judge Julia Eleanor Kobick, a federal judge in Boston, ordered the Trump administration to issue passports that reflect the self-identified gender of trans people rather than requiring them to list their biological sex.[40] Kobick was nominated by Joe Biden, clerked for Ruth Bader Ginsberg, and worked on the Government Bureau's "Racial Equity Working Group" at the Massachusetts Attorney General's office. She also worked for, volunteered for, or donated to, high-profile Democrats such as Massachusetts Governor Deval Patrick, John Kerry, and Elizabeth Warren.[41] She made numerous donations via the controversial "dark money" ActBlue app.[42]

Judge Charlotte N. Sweeney extended a temporary restraining order barring the Trump administration from deporting illegal migrant criminals using the Alien Enemies Act.[43] Sweeney was nominated by Biden in August 2021[44] and was recommended by Democrat Colorado Senators Bennet and Hickenlooper.[45] She is the first openly gay person to serve as a federal judge in Colorado.[46] She has made a series of donations through the ActBlue platforming, including to Democrat Senators Jon Ossoff and Mark Kelly as well as Biden.[47]

In March 2025, Sweeney ruled that the Elizabeth School District in Colorado must return books involving transgender ideology, sexual orientation and race.[48] Prior to serving as a federal judge, Sweeney ran a law practice focused on male-female pay disparities and "representation of employees with disabilities."[49]

In April 2025, Judge Alvin Hellerstein extended an order blocking the deportation of illegals detained under the Alien Enemies Act, arguing that the Trump administration had acted like a "medieval inquisition" in not affording "due process" to the defendants.[50] He donated heavily to Democrats until the mid-nineties[51] and was nominated by Bill Clinton in 1998. He also has another connection to Trump. In 2020, Hellerstein ordered the release of Michael Cohen from prison to home confinement, finding his imprisonment retributive because Cohen had planned to write a book.[52]

Judge Mary Rosado temporarily barred the opening of an ICE center on Rikers Island despite an agreement to do so forged by NYC Mayor Eric Adams and the Trump administration.[53] She is a registered Democrat in New York and won her 2018 election with approval of the LGBT Bar of NY.[54] She had previously ruled that New York wasn't able to block buses filled with illegal migrants.[55]

Rosado was born on October 30, 1949, and was thus 75 when she blocked the Rikers Island deal. This is noteworthy because she serves on the New York Supreme Court which theoretically has a mandatory retirement age of 70 according to the state constitution.[56] She has taken advantage of nuances and loopholes in the language to remain on the bench. She is expected to be forced to retire in December of 2025 at the age of 76.[57]

U.S. District Court for the District of Columbia Judge Beryl Howell, who blocked Trump's efforts to restrict and restrain Perkins Coie, has a long history with the Democrat Party. She was nominated by Obama, is a registered Democrat herself, has donated to Democrats, and has ruled against Trump in multiple cases. In 2023, Representative Elise Stefanik filed an ethics complaint against Howell for "partisan speech and illegal election meddling"[58] after Howell insinuated that reelecting President Trump would give rise to fascism, according to the congresswoman.[59]

In 2020, Howell blocked a Trump administration effort to reform food stamps.[60] The same year, Howell ruled that then-CEO Michael Pack acted unconstitutionally in investigating "deep-seated bias against President Trump" at the Voice of America and the US Agency for Global Media (formerly the Broadcasting Board of Governors).[61] During his investigation into President Trump, she ruled to allow Jack Smith to compel Trump attorney Evan Corcoran to appear before a grand jury; ABC News said that the decision "pierc[ed] attorney-client privilege."[62] She also endorsed the legality and constitutionality of the Democrats' efforts to impeach Trump over the Zelensky phone call in 2019[63] and ordered Rudy Giuliani to pay an absurd $146 million to Georgia election workers he had defamed.[64]

There will be new lawfare judges who announce themselves between the time I complete work on this book and when it hits the shelves. During the editing process for this book, Judge Howell determined that it was illegal for the Department of Government Efficiency (DOGE) and the Trump administration to gut the U.S. Institute of Peace (USIP), for example. Had you ever heard of the USIP? I hadn't.[65] Apparently, it was created by Ronald Reagan and is so essential that it must exist no matter what. Judge Howell will never stop handing down rulings like this so long as she is on the bench.

In May of 2025, as I neared the end of my work on this book, Judge Jamal Whitehead of the U.S. District Court for the Western District of Washington mandated via court order that President Trump bring roughly 12,000 refugees to the United States.[66] Whitehead, a 2023 Biden appointee, blocked an executive action taken by President Trump to suspend the U.S. Refugee Admissions Program, ruling that Trump did not have the authority to do so.[67] Trump had ended the program much to the chagrin of contractors whose funding relies on resettling refugees in American communities, who sued the administration. Whitehead's order required Trump to resettle the refugees who had been approved under an executive order from Joe Biden.

Whitehead, who happens to be black, was the ultimate DEI hire: The Senate Judiciary Committee described him as "Biden's first judicial nominee identifying as a person with a disability" due to his prosthetic leg. He was hired as part of a series of DEI nominations by Biden, who said at the time that Whitehead and his fellow nominees "represent[ed] the diversity that is one of our best assets as a nation."[68]

Whitehead was a Dean's Diversity Scholar at the Seattle University School of Law and a Democrat donor.[69] His Senate questionnaire revealed that he was a trustee at the ACLU and had participated in radical left panels on racism in the workplace and #MeToo.[70]

And now he's the President, kinda.

There will be dozens, if not hundreds more examples like this by the time Trump retires from political life.

Many, if not all, of these lawfare judges would claim that they were interpreting the law as they understand it. Collectively, they are the most formidable resistance against President Trump's second-term agenda.

Trump is not powerless against them, however. He will appeal many of these cases from partisan judges. Some will get overturned, others will stand. Certain judges who appear to be violating the law themselves will be investigated and potentially disciplined.

Perhaps they'll even be jailed themselves, as was the case with Judge Hannah C. Dugan of the Milwaukee County Circuit Court, who was arrested by the FBI in April 2025 on charges of obstructing immigration agents. Dugan is accused of directing illegal alien Eduardo Flores Ruiz to leave through a side door in her courtroom while agents waited to arrest him. FBI Director Kash Patel said Dugan misdirected federal agents so that Ruiz could evade law enforcement. Ruiz had entered the country illegally multiple times and was facing multiple counts of battery with modifiers for domestic abuse. The allegations include charges of suffocation and strangulation.[71]

The Wisconsin Supreme Court temporarily suspended Dugan while her case moves forward.[72]

The public outcry over the Dugan arrest was relatively muted, even from the activist left. Perhaps this is a sign that Trump can successfully make aggressive moves like this to fight back against obstructionist judges if he does so judiciously.

Yet the pattern remains clear: Political operatives are using the judicial system to interfere with the legitimate functions of the executive branch and block core parts of the Trump agenda. While some of this will get overturned, it does slow down the agenda of the democratically elected president. Though the judges discussed in this chapter are mostly unknown to the general public, they are performing the same function as the Lisa Monacos, Jack Smiths, and Alvin Braggs of the world. They are integral to the lawfare superstructure. And they are bending the law to take down President Trump.

What's more, these rogue judges aren't just blocking executive orders. Take the example of Judge Jesse Furman of the U.S. District Court for the Southern District of New York, who blocked the deportation of Palestinian extremist Mahmoud Khalil.

Khalil was arrested in March 2025 for his role in leading pro-Hamas protests at Columbia University in the wake of the brutal October 7th massacre. The organizers of this protest movement "see the U.S. as 'the belly of the beast,' the beast being colonialism, capitalism and essentially all other forces of oppression," according to an article in *Politico*.[73] Yet Khalil was portrayed in the media as a prototypical doctoral student and soon-to-be father, the ultimate sympathetic victim of President Donald Trump's immigration crackdown. The reality is that Khalil has no right to be in the United States, much less agitate on campus. He is a green card holder, which does not equate to citizenship, and he can be deported for virtually any reason.[74]

He is our guest.

"If you told us that's what you intended to do when you came to America, we would have never let you in," Secretary of State Marco Rubio said when Immigration and Customs Enforcement (ICE) took Khalil into custody.[75]

But Judge Jesse Furman blocked his deportation.[76] Furman is a part of the lawfare superstructure and a card-carrying member of the activist left. According to FEC records, Jesse Furman donated $23,200 to Democrats, including to the DNC, John Kerry, and Hillary Clinton, and maxed out ($4,600) to the Obama's 2008 presidential campaign.[77] He served as the treasurer of the Furman Foundation, which has donated to assorted leftist groups like the Soros-funded Media Matters, an organization that polices conservative media to inflict reputational damage and rally advertiser boycotts.[78] His brother, Jason Furman, was an economic advisor to Obama and the chair of Obama's Council of Economic Advisers.[79]

Furman has been a liberal activist dating back to his college days. As far as we can tell, he has never wavered. While a writer for the *Harvard Crimson*, he wrote a piece titled "Bang, Bang, You're Dead, the NRA Supplied the Lead." Later, as a lawyer, he wrote a brief for the Anti-Defamation League in support of a public school excluding a Christian-based extracurricular club, earning him a rebuke from Senator Jim Inhofe: "In short, Furman encouraged judicial activism against religious expression, because he apparently finds the message of Christianity offensive."[80] As a judge, Furman refused to send a man convicted of possessing fentanyl with the intent to distribute to jail while he awaited sentencing because he didn't believe the conditions of the prison were good enough for the drug dealer.[81]

This is a hyperpartisan individual with deep biases against President Trump who claimed the power to single-handedly stop the deportation of a campus agitator and terrorist sympathizer. This isn't the administration of justice, it's pure politics.

Rest assured, the judiciary's unmitigated assault on the executive branch will continue until the system changes. Leftist justices will issue more injunctions and hamper this administration's ability to implement its agenda. They must be stopped.

SAINT ABREGO

That said, no act of lawfare is more absurd than what Judge Paula Xinis did on April 4, 2025. Xinis, in the District of Maryland (notice how frequently that specific court has appeared in this chapter), ordered the return of Kilmar Abrego Garcia to Maryland. Garcia, who entered the U.S. illegally in 2011, was deported to El Salvador due to an administrative error by the Trump administration. The political left and establishment media immediately tried to capitalize on the mistake, so they attempted to canonize Garcia. The Trump administration was unfazed and regarded the error as insignificant because Garcia had reported ties to the MS-13 gang.

What made Xinis's order to return Garcia to the U.S. so absurd was that Garcia was already in El Salvador at the time, where not even President Trump has jurisdiction, much less a district judge. Adding to the absurdity, Xinis gave El Salvador's president, Nayib Bukele (whom else could she have been addressing with the order?), three days to return the man—who happens to be from El Salvador—back to America, which he was residing in illegally.[82]

The implication of Xinis's order is that she believes that her opinion outweighs not only the president of the United States, but the president of El Salvador as well. The arrogance is breathtaking.

What's more, Garcia is what I can safely call a bad hombre. In 2022, he was pulled over for speeding in Tennessee while traveling from Texas with eight people in his vehicle en route to Maryland. There was no luggage in the vehicle, and all the passengers gave Garcia's address as their home address.[83]

If this isn't clear-cut human trafficking, then I don't know what is. Yet he was released by Joe Biden's government.

Garcia's wife also accused him of beating her.[84]

Still, Democrats went all in to champion Garcia's cause. Senator Chris Van Hollen (D-MD) flew down to El Salvador to meet with him. A delegation of congressional Democrats like Representative Maxwell Frost (D-FL) also went to El Salvador to vacation at a ritzy hotel in order to grandstand on behalf of Garcia.[85]

Back in the States, Democrats claimed that Garcia had been deprived of due process. This claim is deliberately misleading. Illegal aliens are not entitled to "due process" as they are not citizens. Even if we Americans wanted to grant them all some form of due process, it is an impossibility. There are at least 11 million illegal aliens in this country even according to liberal sources.[86] (I would not be surprised if that number is three times as high given that Pew estimated there were 12 million illegals as of 2007.[87] Yes, the establishment media often suggests that there are fewer illegal aliens now than before Barack Obama became president.) If each alien claimed "due process" and thus a right to stay in America and had their claims adjudicated in an immigration court, it would take decades, if not centuries, to get through the backlog.

Impossible.

In fact, the Department of Justice's Executive Office of Immigration

Review was already backed up with more than 3.6 million cases by the time Garcia was deported.[88]

Yet these lawfare judges, and the rest of the superstructure, supported the Saint Abrego farce. In retrospect, their perspective seems strategically idiotic, but they stuck with it throughout the spring of 2025.

They certainly assumed that there would be no consequences for anyone who wanted to put illegal alien gang members above Americans.

In fact, it's unlikely that there will be any consequences for Judge Xinis or any of the aforementioned judges profiled in this chapter. They will be feted as heroes in Democrat legal circles.

This is possible only because the well-funded and heavily organized lawfare superstructure has the ability, the time, and the resources to shop their cases around for the ideal forum to use the law to further their political agenda.

These partisan, activist judges are thoroughly undermining the judicial branch and subverting a duly elected president. If this behavior continues, our courts will lose the public trust and our system of justice will endure reputational damage from which it might not be able to recover.

If the public trust in our judicial system erodes, chaos will follow it.

President Trump has a clear understanding of this phenomenon. "They look around all over the country, they find the worst judge possible," he told me in an exclusive interview. "If you get sued someplace, they look around and find the worst judge in the country." He added that you can have the best lawyers in the world, but it doesn't even matter if you get the wrong judge.

It is clear to me that as of early 2025, he regards a rogue judiciary as the primary threat to his second-term agenda. "Judge-shopping is rampant at levels never seen before," Trump told me. "You know the outcome of a case as soon as the judge is picked."

This statement is as scary as it is true.

"And the radical left is using this, their final weapon, to take down America," the president told me.

Unless we stop them.

CHAPTER 10

THE WAY OUT

If we don't have a justice system, we are a third world country," U.S. Attorney for New Jersey Alina Habba told me just before she left her post in Donald Trump's White House. For those of us who would prefer for America to remain in the first world, it's incumbent upon us to try to rein in the lawfare against President Trump and his supporters.

Andrew Breitbart was fond of the phrase "sunlight is the best disinfectant," and I wholeheartedly agree. The first, most obvious, and biggest thing we can do in this regard is to expose and dismantle the superstructure. I think that process is well underway. Many of the most nefarious characters in the lawfare superstructure appear in this book, and there are wonderful journalists who are working to expose the practitioners of lawfare, their funders, and their true motivations.

Take Matthew Graves, the U.S. attorney for the District of Columbia from 2021 to 2025, for example. Graves was appointed by Joe Biden and went to work prosecuting at least 1,100 January 6 defendants. Journalist Julie Kelly reported that his wife, Fatima Goss Graves, is a far-left activist.[1] Natalie Winters, a White House reporter on Steve Bannon's *War Room* podcast, observed that Fatima Goss Graves was on the board of Indivisible,[2] a Soros-funded astroturf (fake grassroots) group that used lawfare to try to get Donald Trump removed from the 2024 presidential ballot.[3] After Trump won, members of Indivisible were accused of organizing the campaign of violence targeting Tesla Motors and Tesla vehicle owners in early 2025.[4] Fatima Goss Graves's bio was removed from the Indivisible website after this was exposed.

This is the lawfare superstructure on full display, and dogged reporting will make the bad guys famous, which is a good thing.

But that's not nearly enough.

Trump, for his part, is doing what he can with the powers he has to right wrongs. Immediately upon assuming office, he pardoned, commuted the prison sentences, or vowed to dismiss the cases of all of the J6 prisoners—over 1,500 in all.[5] I was initially surprised that he didn't confine the acts of clemency to merely the nonviolent, but I have a theory on why he didn't draw that distinction: He likely thought the lawfare that was practiced against his supporters in the aftermath of J6 was tantamount to prosecutorial misconduct. If that's what he was thinking, I agree with him. Given the broad scope of his ability to grant acts of clemency, it was well within his right to declare a de facto mistrial—or 1,500 of them.

Trump also pardoned twenty-three pro-life activists who were targeted by Joe Biden's DOJ.[6] "Twenty-three people were prosecuted—they should not have been prosecuted. Many of them are elderly people.[7] They should not have been prosecuted. This is a great honor to sign this," he said at the time. Beautiful.

When I met with Trump about eight weeks into his new administration, it was clear to me that the lawfare he had endured in between the two presidencies was still top-of-mind for him. He didn't convey anger or bitterness in his tone, but he was clear that he intended to address the systemic rot that had led to his persecution—and nearly his assassination. "I went through four years of hell with this scum I had to deal with. I spent millions of dollars in legal fees, and I won. It's really hard to say that they shouldn't have to go through it also," Trump told Fox News's Sean Hannity just after his inauguration.[8]

He won't be forgetting what was done to him anytime soon.

So, he went about dismantling parts of the superstructure.

On February 18, Trump fired all of the top prosecutors from Joe Biden's Justice Department. "Over the past four years, the Department of Justice has been politicized like never before. Therefore, I have instructed the termination of ALL remaining 'Biden Era' U.S. Attorneys," Trump Truthed, adding, "We must 'clean house' IMMEDIATELY, and restore confidence. America's Golden Age must have a fair Justice System—THAT BEGINS TODAY!"[9]

He wasn't messing around.

On February 25, 2025, Trump suspended security clearances for employees of the law firm Covington & Burling LLP for providing former Special Counsel Jack Smith with $140,000 in free legal services.[10]

On March 14, 2025, Trump signed an executive order ending government sponsorship of the law firm Paul, Weiss, Rifkind, Wharton & Garrison LLP. "In 2021, a Paul Weiss partner and former leading prosecutor in the office of Special Counsel Robert Mueller brought a pro bono suit against individuals alleged to have participated in the events that occurred at or near the United States Capitol on January 6, 2021, on behalf of the District of Columbia Attorney General," according to a memorandum accompanying the presidential action.[11] More importantly, though, lawfare engineer Mark Pomerantz had a decades-long history with the firm. Pomerantz was hired as a partner at Paul Weiss in 2000 and maintained a connection to the firm until he left for the Manhattan district attorney's office in February 2021 specifically to take down Trump. Recall that he thought Alvin Bragg was not pursuing Trump intensely enough. Pomerantz left the Manhattan DA office and returned to Paul Weiss.

Paul Weiss chairman Brad S. Karp has been a vocal critic of Trump and a major Democrat fundraiser.[12] Karen Dunn, a top litigator at the firm, helped Kamala Harris prep for her lone presidential debate.[13] Roberta Kaplan, who was the lead attorney representing E. Jean Carroll in "the woman" case against Trump, was a partner at Paul Weiss for nearly two decades, overlapping with Pomerantz for seventeen years.

I know from personal experience that not everyone in the firm is a bad person, but this is quite the roster of anti-Trump judicial activists on their staff.

Trump's dramatic action against Paul Weiss worked almost instantly. Karp bent the knee, pledging $40 million in pro bono legal work on issues important to President Trump, such as combating antisemitism as well as an agreement to end DEI policies at the company.[14] By succumbing to Trump, Karp likely saved Paul Weiss, which does billions in revenue a year, but also positioned Trump to be able to get certain allowances from other firms.[15]

The Art of the Deal bested lawfare this time around.

Trump had devised a genius way to combat liberal culture in America's white-shoe firms. Perhaps the necessity to work with Trump on mutually agreeable initiatives will facilitate and encourage our biggest law firms in the country to not be so woke.

Trump wasn't done righting wrongs. He continued to attempt to exact a price from law firms associated with people who sought to fine or jail him between his administrations. Some have yielded large concessions; others have pushed back against Trump with lawsuits.[16]

In May of 2025, CBS's *60 Minutes*—in a segment clearly designed to attack Trump, favorably featuring Marc Elias—reported that nine firms had cut deals with President Trump. Nine firms in total had pledged nearly $1 billion "to causes that the firms and Trump support."[17]

Trump remains undeterred and will certainly continue to salt the earth—that is, unless firms are willing to play ball.

On March 22, 2025, he revoked the security clearances and access to classified information from some of the stars of my *Breaking* series (especially the book you're reading now): Lisa Monaco, Norman Eisen, Letitia James, Alvin Bragg, Andrew Weissmann, Hillary Clinton, Elizabeth Cheney, Kamala Harris, Antony Blinken, Jacob Sullivan, Adam Kinzinger, Alexander Vindman, Joseph R. Biden Jr., other members of Joseph R. Biden Jr.'s family, among a few others.[18] This move was more symbolic and punitive than practical, but I delighted in it. It is absolutely essential to bring whatever consequences you can to those who weaponized government against our republic, which is exactly what these individuals had done.

We need to use whatever legal means necessary to resist the lawfare superstructure. And when legal means are not adequate, we need to consider public shaming and ridicule, but also changes to the law itself.

For example, it's imperative we move to end judge- and forum-shopping immediately. The damage a politicized judge can do goes beyond injunctions and TROs. These judges decide the rules of the court, who and what goes in and out, what decisions juries can and can't make, etc. As was the case in Judge Merchan's courtroom, the jury instructions and other peculiarities of a particular judge's courtroom can determine the outcome of the case.

When litigation is clearly funded by politically interested donors—think anything connected to Marc Elias—the judge selected must have an incredibly high level of trust. They must have no perceptible political biases or they should not preside over such a case. We can accept nothing less.

Republicans have discussed breaking up the U.S. Court of Appeals for the Ninth Circuit since the early days of Trump's first administration, if not longer. It's time to finally do that. Trump has said that any case that goes through that circuit yields "an automatic loss" for his policies and values. He's not wrong, and that is incredibly unjust.

There are many reasons beyond politics that justify splitting up the court. It is by far the largest district by all measures: population, judges, sheer geographic area, and the number of opinions published. The latter is relevant because lawyers and district judges are tasked with keeping up with all these opinions, which is an impossible task. The Ninth Circuit has also proven to be particularly inefficient, meaning that cases are backlogged and take far longer than other courts to come to final judgment or last opinion.[19]

The Fifth Circuit Court of Appeals was divided into two circuits, the Fifth and the Eleventh in 1981.[20] There is no reason we can't do something with the Ninth Circuit now. In fact, the Ninth Circuit's vast output suggests subdividing twice, giving us two new districts.

Juries are also extremely problematic in areas with deep political division. Take the New York cases against Donald Trump. They assembled a bunch of jurors who essentially functioned as Democratic operatives. The fact that the Stormy Daniels case, arguably the weakest of the case studies I profiled in this book, was the only one that yielded a criminal conviction, gives away the game. As Trump told me, the outcome of that case was already decided when the jury was empaneled. That is a direct affront to the principles of due process and equal protection under the law.

Law schools pose another set of problems to those who oppose the politicization of the legal system. Currently, the federal government subsidizes juris doctorate programs to groom the next generation of lawfare attorneys and lawyers; they do this via expansive student aid programs, grants, and loan forgiveness programs. The federal government also provides money directly to the institutions that house the law schools, which are almost all incubators for leftism. That has to be curtailed. The federal government should not be funding law schools at all, but if they must, there must be an exceedingly high bar for ethics that must be hit. The schools must focus on mastery of laws, procedures, history, and judicial ethics, not using the law to shape policy to oppose Donald Trump and his movement.

If any university is deemed to discriminate against conservatives, then they should become ineligible for federal funding.

Some of the issues with the law schools can be traced to the

American Bar Association. The ABA wields its power because it is the government-recognized accrediting organization for law schools. The ABA's leadership skews left (i.e., it's woke) and this is reflected in their priorities, which align closely with the modern Democratic Party on issues like DEI, abortion, and guns. Through their Model Rules, the ABA sets the standard for how modern law is practiced. In an America where every legal issue increasingly appears to be political, this discrepancy is problematic. Either conservatives need to endeavor to make reforms to the ABA or we must start our own alternative. The Trump administration ought to immediately review the ABA's accreditation process and demand reform as necessary.

Until recently, the ABA also had special access to judicial nominees, and the ABA would supply supposedly neutral vetting in return. The nominees would grant the ABA information, answer questionnaires, and sit for interviews with their personnel. The association was even given waivers so it could access non-public information. That is, until Attorney General Pam Bondi shut that down in 2025, writing, "the ABA no longer functions as a fair arbiter of nominees' qualifications, and its ratings invariably and demonstrably favor nominees put forth by Democratic administrations."

This is a good start. Conservatives have come to regard the ABA as an activist organization hostile to conservatives. To continue to allow the ABA special privileges is to indulge the lawfare superstructure.[21]

There are other problems at some state bars, which are part of the state supreme courts (not to be confused with the American Bar Association, which is entirely different). "They intimidate you at the bar to make sure you represent [Donald Trump]," Alina Habba told me. "Letters are written so that the bar can investigate you. They do this to deter people from representing him." That is corruption, and it cannot be tolerated. Conservatives must do what they can to become part of executive leadership and sit on boards of governors/trustees of every state bar to exert influence and ensure that leftists are neutralized.

The left has also built a massive network of law firms willing to do pro bono work for political causes. Conservatives have these as well, but not as many. We must be able to fight fire with fire.

One thing I don't recommend to fix lawfare is to defy orders of district judges. Trump has intentionally avoided this as of the time I completed work on this book. The dispute over whether he defied Judge Boasberg's orders with regard to the Alien Enemies Act deportation flights is the exception that proves the rule. The left could not find one example where he clearly defied an order, so they obsessed over one where he *nearly* did. There may be a day that there is no alternative but to choose to not abide by the decision of a rogue judge looking to subvert the law and democracy itself, but we ought to avoid that if at all possible.

Yet nationwide injunctions unilaterally declared by a hyperpartisan district judge must end. These judges who have blocked portions of Trump's agenda are unelected trial judges who are at the lowest level in our system. They are often "district" judges who are operating as if their district is the entirety of the county. It is outrageous on its face. Now consider that Chuck Schumer bragged about putting 235 "progressive judges" on the bench,[22] giving away that they were chosen not for their brilliant legal minds, but because of their opposition to Donald Trump and his movement.

If we for some reason cannot block judicial tyranny from rogue district judges, they need to be subject to immediate review from higher courts.

When an executive action does get blocked, the approval process also needs to accelerate. As Deputy Chief of Staff Stephen Miller said, "[T]he most important commodity in the executive branch is time,"[23] and blocking an executive order for political reasons could tie up part of the presidential agenda for years awaiting appeal. There must be a way to fast-track review of executive actions through the appeals process and up to the Supreme Court if necessary so the lawfare superstructure does not drain the time of the executive branch.

When a court issues an injunction against executive actions, the appeals process typically takes between six months and two years. (Theoretically it can take less than two months, though that is rare.) There ought to be an expedited review process for these types of cases. We might find that these cases are overwhelming the Supreme Court, which is why a special panel might be necessary to review these specific cases before it is determined whether the Supreme Court should take the case. The forming of this panel would be contentious, but it seems to me that it could be necessary one day soon. That said, even with this new panel in place, the president could still potentially be blocked by rogue judges for months at a time. I believe this would be a good start, but it is far from a panacea.

We conservatives also cannot rely on the U.S. Supreme Court to bail us out. Not only did John Roberts surprisingly rebuke Trump at the height of the lawfare against him, but it was revealed that he has a cozy relationship with CREW founder Norm Eisen, literally. In a 2024 podcast, Eisen said, "I know the Chief Justice well. He stayed, when I was ambassador [to the Czech Republic], stayed under my roof, came and spent a week with us. We worked on American and European rule of law issues together." Recall that Trump told me, "[T]he only thing CREW ever did is sue me."

CREW and other Soros-funded groups have raised ethics concerns regarding disclosures about travel from Justices Clarence Thomas and Samuel Alito. They are understandably less interested in where the chief justice stays when he's abroad.

The current makeup of the Supreme Court is certainly "conservative" overall, but there are several justices who are unreliable votes, particularly Amy Coney Barret. Republican presidents have routinely nominated justices who have defected from conservatism; in my lifetime, John Paul Stevens, Sandra Day O'Connor, Anthony Kennedy, and David Souter all were nominated by Republicans but had the records of moderates or liberals. I fear Barret may soon officially join this list.

In order to ensure that an inconsistent justice like Barret is never again nominated by a Republican, conservative presidents must change the way they evaluate potential nominees. There is only one criterion that matters: how confident we can be that their judicial decisions will be in line with originalism and conservatism. How to do this is simple: Do not nominate anyone without long-term bona fides as a conservative. The only people to consider are those who have taken stands and fought for conservative values throughout their lives, especially if they have come at a personal or political cost.

In order to find these individuals, we need to look beyond judges who have consistently let us down. We need to include U.S. senators (and perhaps congressmen, governors, or generals) who have also had legal careers.

If Donald Trump gets to nominate more Supreme Court Justices, it should come from this group. His next two picks ought to be Senators Mike Lee (R-UT) and Ted Cruz (R-TX). Both men have brilliant legal minds and hail from states where Republican governors would choose their replacements. Lee clerked for Justice Samuel Alito and Cruz for Chief Justice William Rehnquist, so they have the requisite experience. They are both in their fifties, which means that they are old enough to have a long-term track record of consistent conservativism but are young enough to (hopefully) optimize the lifetime appointment. Most important, of course, is that they are rock-ribbed conservatives—and proud of it.

If somehow Trump gets a third pick, he ought to consider Senator Josh Hawley (R-MO), who attended Yale Law School and clerked for Chief Justice John Roberts before becoming the attorney general of Missouri.

Conservative warriors who represent red states in the Senate. This is where to find the next generation of Supreme Court justices.

If it wasn't already clear to you by this point in the book, we cannot rely on the left to come back around to the realm of sanity any time soon. Take, for example, a March 2025 executive action requiring people to prove they are U.S. citizens when they register to vote in federal elections. The Democrats and liberal nonprofits brought suits against it.[24] Their argument against the order was that it falls outside the scope of presidential powers, but the subtext is clear: They do not want a citizenship requirement for voting. That is irreconcilable with anyone remotely "conservative," and we are not going to have a similar interpretation of the law to people who hold a view like this in the foreseeable future.

We know this to be true: If it had been any person other than Donald Trump who had signed these executive actions, the vast majority of them would have gone unchallenged.

It is imperative to recognize this, and to have a spine. We cannot nominate or vote for judges who do not see lawfare as an existential threat. Trump and the voters who elected him need warriors who understand this fundamental fact. This principle cannot be overemphasized.

We regard the lawfare against President Trump to be election interference, an effort to undo the result of the 2024 election. It is as bad as the Russiagate hoax. Maybe worse. The superstructure is attempting to disenfranchise 77 million voters who chose Donald J. Trump as the president of the United States.

Trump was forced to win a presidential campaign "from a courthouse," Trump attorney and U.S. Attorney for the District of New Jersey Alina Habba told me in an interview in 2025. "He would rally, go to bed at one a.m., then get up and go to the courthouse," she said. The amount of money and time Donald Trump spent fighting for his own freedom is immeasurable. Lawfare effectually shortened the length of his first term and severely curtailed his ability to fight for a second. He kept on winning despite it all.

And now that he's in office, he ought to be able to carry out his agenda without the permission of every single lower-court judge who was never elected by anyone.

To use lawfare to block him is judicial supremacy.

It is tyranny.

And it must stop.

What those in the lawfare firmament might not understand now is that the reforms I recommend above might actually help them in the long term. The courts' only power is based on perception. They are without a military or a treasury to enforce their rulings. Thus they must maintain credibility. We, the people, grant the court its legitimacy because, until now, we have believed in the integrity of the system.

But that trust has been eroded.

Now reforms must be made, or else the whole edifice could topple.

Yet even if all the changes I recommend are adopted, there is truly only one way out of the chaos that lawfare has wrought: conservatives winning elections.

The problems identified in this book are, more often than not, easy to identify but hard to fix. There are certain parts of our system that must be overhauled or curtailed, such as nationwide injunction rules and judge-shopping, but don't count on new ordinances or laws to magically remove the threat imposed by the superstructure. And if we create any new panels of judges or attempt to enforce stricter ethical standards, count on the left to find a way to weaponize them for their own benefit.

They always do.

The problem with the American judicial system is as simple as it is vast: there are too many liberals on the bench. The only way to fix that is to vet, nominate, and elect good judges.

And the only way to do that is to build the strongest conservative movement possible.

CONCLUSION

You cannot run a country without the rule of law. When you don't have a set of regulations and norms to which we collectively adhere, you have anarchy. The law is an antidote to chaos. Equal justice under the law isn't merely our birthright; it is the foundation upon which everything else rests. When any aspect of our legal system fails—from cops on the beat to the highest echelons of our federal courts and Justice Department—trust erodes. We become less safe, less unified, less patriotic, less happy. No good comes from a broken legal system aside from one party's short-term political gain.

And, as demonstrated throughout the course of this book, we've seen that not even that is a given.

The Democrats mangled the rule of law to defeat Donald Trump, but he got the last laugh. He won a second nonconsecutive term. In the four intervening years between his two administrations, he learned how to do many of the things he failed to do in his first administration.

He arguably accomplished as much in his first two weeks on the job the second go-round as he did in his entire first four years. He entered his administration with a completely different energy. He understood the forces that were trying to defeat him weren't only trying to beat him at the polls. They wanted to bankrupt him, jail him, even kill him. They wanted to break Donald Trump.

All his opponents did for eight years and counting is break *the law*.

They broke literal laws, of course. Take Jack Smith's unconstitutional appointment, where he was allowed to harass the Trump family round-the-clock for a year and a half until it finally dawned on people that his entire position was illegal.

But it goes deeper than that: The lawfare activists of the Democrat Party *broke the law*, as in our entire system of justice.

Laws that were on the books were not applied to criminals in our cities or illegal aliens invading our country, while laws that didn't really exist were imposed on Trump and his supporters. And when judgments came down against the MAGA faithful, the practitioners of lawfare inflicted cruel and unusual punishments. These punishments were designed to ruin their lives, not restore order in our society.

Meanwhile, Joe Biden was so convinced of his family members' own criminality that he gave blanket pardons to six of them. While his DOJ looked into a single crime committed by Hunter Biden, they ignored suspicious foreign business deals by James, Frank, and Hunter himself. Hunter was never charged with being an unregistered foreign agent despite mountains of evidence in the Laptop from Hell. Of course, they didn't charge him with these crimes, because it's a guarantee that if they were investigated to the fullest extent, it would implicate Joe Biden himself.

Hunter Biden's blatant influence-peddling with his art sales also didn't raise the ire of the Department of Justice—which was controlled by his own father. The one instance when the DOJ pursued Hunter over his gun offense, there was internal discussion within the DOJ about whether to kill the case entirely. Ultimately, the little justice that was served came by way of the people in the form of a jury.

The lawfare left has operated as if the goal is not an independent judiciary, but one that simply complies with their political will. They have always harbored these opinions, dating back to Franklin Delano Roosevelt and especially since Joe Biden took over the Senate Judiciary Committee, but it has accelerated in recent years. Barack Obama made it a habit to publicly rebuke the courts when he didn't get his way. The most famous example is during the 2010 State of the Union address, when he called out members of the Supreme Court to their faces; they had no recourse to respond.

This impulse among leftist jurists continues to this day. The very week I completed work on the first draft of this book, Judge Tanya Chutkan felt compelled to weigh in on President Trump's dismissal of the January 6th cases, saying he "cannot whitewash the blood, feces, and terror that the mob left in its wake." This is a masturbatory comment, totally inconsequential other than as a talking point for news media liberals to parrot. She is powerless to do anything about the hearings. It would have been unorthodox had she conveyed this sentiment in an opinion editorial, but to voice it from the bench, as she did, is entirely inappropriate and born of the left's worst instincts.

Judicial activism on social and political issues undermines the courts' legitimacy among Americans. In fact, it's scary. All of this is.

The extent of the institutional rot is overwhelming. Consider E. Jean Carroll's unprovable allegations that were riddled with inconsistencies and remained a secret until the exact worst moment for Trump. Stormy Daniels's case was the weakest of any of the major cases I profiled, yet it was the only one that got a conviction thanks entirely to the fact that it was prosecuted in a venue where there were nothing but Democrats. Fani Willis, Alvin Bragg, and Tish James all blatantly denied President Trump due process by verbally committing to destroying him before they even got power. And finally, Jack Smith and those who backed his appointment ought to be remembered as historical lawfare supervillains for reasons specified herein.

We are in the midst of an ideological civil war in America. There is a fundamental disagreement about the role the legal system ought to play in our lives. Conservatives and constitutional originalists believe judges must apply the law to the facts before them, and we are bound within those limits. We might want the law changed, but we don't do it ourselves. We regard judicial powers as limited in scope.

The left sees the law as a creative-writing exercise. They torture words to get what they want. They stretch until things like abortion are deemed constitutional rights even though they never appear in our founding documents; they strain until the right to bear arms is not guaranteed despite it appearing in multiple places.

They are compelled at a cultural level to change the law to suit modern politics. This attitude is fostered in our law schools, in law firms large and boutique, and throughout the American government. Though this is all legally questionable, there have thus far been no consequences for turning the bench into a quasi-legislature.

They use the law to punish people not necessarily for violating the law, but for being politically disagreeable.

And we are politically disagreeable. Thus the lawfare will continue.

Consider that in the immediate aftermath of Donald Trump's victory in the 2024 presidential election, Gavin Newsom, the California governor and likely 2028 presidential candidate, convened the California Legislature to appropriate $25 million for an anti-Trump lawsuit.

California sued the Trump administration 123 times in his first term on issues such as environment rules, immigration, and health care.[2] The Golden State sued him another 15 times in the first 100 days of his second term.[3] There is nothing to suggest that this tactic won't continue in perpetuity.

The left views these tactics as win-win propositions. Worst-case scenario: They tie up their political opponents, costing them time and money while discouraging others from joining or emulating them. Consider Miguel Estrada, whose 2001 appointment to become the first Latino to serve on the U.S. Court of Appeals to the D.C. circuit was held up for blatantly political (and racist) purposes. According to the *The Washington Times*, poweful Democrat Sen. Dick Durbin believed Estrada to be "especially dangerous" because "he is Latino."[4] He also had a clear path to the Supreme Court. He was put on the sidelines while his confirmation process dragged on. This meant that his employer couldn't put him on cases in fear he would have to depart for the bench mid-case. While he waited in limbo, he was bleeding his law firm partners dry financially while he made little money himself. This situation is untenable for normal people; he eventually withdrew his nomination.

This example proved to be a harbinger of lawfare yet to come.[5]

Consider the story of the FBI raid on Mar-a-Lago over suspected classified documents. The *Washington Post* reported that some FBI field agents wanted to shut down the probe entirely, but Justice Department operatives pushed ahead. Not only did the probe remain open, but they got the surprise underwear-drawer raid of their dreams. Some of the names who advocated for the highly aggressive tactics were Democrat donor Jay Bratt,[6] the prosecutor in charge of counterespionage, Assistant Attorney General Matt Olsen, and DOJ counterintelligence official George Toscas. All deserve to be called out, and there are countless more like them.

Attorneys like Kevin Clinesmith, a former FBI lawyer, abound throughout the Deep State. Clinesmith falsified an email that was used to obtain a wiretap on a Trump campaign adviser. He pleaded guilty but avoided prison thanks to Judge Boasberg and, most relevant, was reinstated by the D.C. bar.[7] That means he's free to practice law and engage in lawfare.

The reason U.S. Attorney for the District of Columbia Matthew Graves is not a household name is that there are simply too many others like him. He released 56 percent of those arrested by the D.C. Metropolitan Police Department in 2023 back onto the streets.[8]

Why do we tolerate this? First of all, the media is comfortable with it. They support it, even, creating a culture where enforcing the laws on the books can get you branded as a racist or worse. But most importantly, the superstructure supports it. The lawfare arsonist George Soros, Reid Hoffman, Marc Elias, David Brock, the 65 Project, Andrew Weissmann, Matthew Colangelo, Lisa Monaco, and so many others have acquired immense amounts of power in this country by breaking the judicial process.

"Sue until blue," as the saying goes.

Donald Trump was gritty enough, determined enough, ambitious enough, and, frankly, wealthy enough to survive everything that was thrown at him. But he cannot take on the lawfare superstructure alone. He needs Americans to assume a warrior mentality and join him in this fight. It's not enough to have gun-for-hire consiglieres who are part of the conservative economy but aren't fully bought into the notion that this is a war and the country is at stake if we lose. We don't have time for passive participation right now.

We need combatants.

Luckily, there are some people who have taken it upon themselves to join the fight for equal protection under the law. Here are some important ones:

- Trump's legal team, especially Alina Habba, Emil Bove, Todd Blanche, John Sauer, John Lauro, and myriad assistants. Boris Epshteyn is Trump's eyes and ears on all things lawfare. He is a tireless, happy warrior for the president and was also exceedingly helpful to me while compiling this book.

- Leonard Leo: Chairman of the Federalist Society, Leo developed the farm team of conservative legal talent. He laid the groundwork for the single largest insurgence of originalist federal appeals judges we've ever seen (during Trump's first administration). He also has built infrastructure for conservative organizations to make sure our movement can rival the left's vast and well-funded networks.

- Citizens United and David Bossie: Citizens United gained international notoriety with the landmark SCOTUS case *Citizens United v. FEC* (2010). It is the biggest political free-speech victory at the Supreme Court in modern history. They also backed Ken Klukowski's legal brief arguing that Jack Smith's special counsel office was unconstitutional. Bossie, Citizens United's president and chairman, is a veteran of the conservative movement and one of the earliest supporters of President Trump's political rise.

- Former Attorneys General Ed Meese and Michael Mukasey joined amicus briefs that legitimized Ken Klukowski's argument that led to Jack Smith's ouster.

- Stephen Miller's America First Legal litigates and funds strategic litigation to advance a MAGA agenda in the courts that typical white-shoe law firms would never touch. It is essential work, and he has built a terrific team, including his top legal brain, Gene Hamilton.

- Will Scharf is another of Trump's attorneys. He has an elite attorney and is every bit a Trumpian populist. A hard-charging MAGA warrior, he not only helped Trump get elected, but he immediately went to work executing Trump's historic barrage of executive orders signed immediately after inauguration. Since assuming office, Trump has hired attorneys who are also bona fide conservative warriors, like Harmeet Dhillon, Ed Martin, and Judge Jeanine Pirro. This is precisely the correct approach.

- Mark Paoletta is a battle-tested general of the America First movement in our nation's capital. He is our fiercest legal combatant in national politics.

- Judicial Watch: Tom Fitton and his team are the best in U.S. history at using FOIA to force into the public information the government is desperate to keep secret.

- Mike Davis and his Article III Project are at the cutting edge of fighting leftist lawfare fire with fire. Mike and Article III Project attorneys like Will Chamberlain lead the fight against lawfare on social media.

- America First Policy Institute: The research nonprofit engaged in many of the big fights to advance or defend America First causes in court during Joe Biden's administration. They notched a lot of successes.

- Kash Patel: He could prove to be our Elliot Ness. If there is one man in America who can perform a deep cleansing of the federal law enforcement system, it's Kash.

- Republican state attorneys general such as the mighty Ken Paxton of Texas, U.S. Attorney General Pam Bondi (formerly Florida AG), Jonathan Skrmetti of Tennessee, Kris Kobach of Kansas, and Jason Miyares of Virginia.

- Legal-minded Republican senators, especially Mike Lee of Utah, Ted Cruz of Texas, Josh Hawley and Eric Schmitt of Missouri, Tom Cotton of Arkansas, and Marsha Blackburn of Tennessee. Many attorneys in the House of Representatives deserve mention, especially Jim Jordan of Ohio.

- Attorneys who are quality communicators on television and radio arm the rest of us with the information and facts we need to win over friends and family, especially Mark Levin, Jonathan Turley, Alan Dershowitz, and John Yoo.

- Journalists Joel Pollak of *Breitbart*, Mollie Hemingway and Margot Cleveland (herself a highly accomplished attorney) of the *Federalist*, Julie Kelly, and X ace Mike Cernovich report and explain lawfare news to vast audiences.

- Ken Blackwell is so ubiquitous in conservative and Republican causes that if he isn't on your board of directors, it raises questions about the legitimacy of your organization. Another happy warrior if there ever was one.

- Finally, Justices Clarence Thomas and Samuel Alito: I could not begin to pay homage to their contributions to this country in a list like this one. They are our standard-bearers. They are the U.S. Constitution's two greatest living defenders. There is no one else close.

No list like this can be definitive; there are certainly others who deserve to be included in this group that I will have regretfully left out. Everyone named above deserves more attention than I am paying them here. I'm sincerely grateful for all they do for this country.

However, our bench is not deep enough. If you, dear reader, are inclined to support any of these people or groups, you must. They are the tip of the spear in this war to restore equal protection under the law, and they need your help.

To this point we have been entirely too tolerant of corruption in our system. There is nothing legitimate about the political persecutions that have filled this text; those responsible for them need to be held to account. Fortunately, We the People seem to understand that, as is, this house cannot stand. Still, we must make sure that the November 2024 election marks the beginning of a new era. It is now time to hold those accountable who broke the law. The investigations must proceed. Every stone must be turned over. We must run up the score.

Our task is to persuade and convert people to our side while making it untenable to be a political operative while also being a part of America's system of law and order.

If we fail and the left is allowed to wield lawfare as it has in recent years, there will never be a free or fair election again, legal harassment will become the norm, and they will eventually criminalize conservatism itself.

Among the millions of words I've heard Donald Trump speak over the last decade, there is one phrase that stands alone as his most important: "In the end, they're not coming after me. They're coming after you—and I'm just standing in their way."[8]

It is often a mistake to take Donald Trump literally, but in this instance, you should.

They aren't attacking Trump merely because they hate him personally. After all, he was a Democrat most of his life, a beloved television personality, and is an incredibly personable individual. They never really believed he was a fascist or a criminal or anything of the sort. What they did believe—what they knew, actually—is that he is a singular threat to the permanent political class of which they are a part.

He isn't a threat to democracy. Quite the opposite. He wants to replace the American oligarchy with a real honest-to-God republic where the power resides with the people and not a select elite.

The superstructure regards that as intolerable. Thus, he must be stopped. That's where lawfare comes in.

I'm not an attorney, yet I felt it important to dedicate more than a year of my life to writing this book and delivering this warning. A key reason that I took on this project is that lawfare isn't as much about the law as much as it's about electioneering.

The left takes a *politics über alles* approach to the world. That means that politics is above truth, justice, law, order, their relationships, their communities, their families, even God himself. The best thing for society, in their view, is to achieve total political victory by any means necessary.

Yes, lawfare, at its core, is election interference.

They knocked him down so many times, but like the Phoenix, Donald Trump rose again and mounted the greatest political comeback in American history on November 5, 2024.

The left hoped to make Trump and his movement a blip or a hiccup in world history. Now it is the most powerful political groundswell in modern history, with worldwide converts from every background.

This is progress, but it's not good enough. The lawfare superstructure remains incredibly capitalized. They still dominate our judiciary and legal bureaucracy. Their generals remain highly active, motivated to achieve victory.

In other words, we may have won some major battles, but we certainly have not yet won the war.

Trump won't be here forever, so we must fortify our position. We must defeat lawfare and *unbreak* the law. Today.

We cannot fail.

After all, they aren't just coming after him. They are coming after you.

ACKNOWLEDGMENTS

'm blessed to have a full life that keeps me occupied with satisfying, meaningful work. Of those meaningful pursuits, I consider writing books to be the tallest mountain that I climb with any regularity. Perhaps even more so than my first two books, I feel as though *Breaking the Law* needed to be written. These are the people who helped me do it:

The cornerstone of my life is my wife, Mrs. Dr. Marlow. Everything I do is for her, yet she is the one who sacrifices the most when I take on a book project. I owe her everything. Our babies, Master Marlow, Master Marlow Jr., Duchess Marlow, and Duchess Marlow Jr., motivate me beyond words—and are often my only source of joy when I'm coming up on a deadline.

My father, Robert, mother, Wynn, and sister, Molly, are the most supportive family members imaginable and helped take care of the aforementioned babies on the occasional night or weekend when I needed to lock in (i.e., write). Also thank you to my parents-in-law, Lauren Wilson and Francesco Federico.

I have one of the best research teams in all of publishing: Jacob MacLeod. That's it. That's the team. Jacob has been with me for every book in the *Breaking* series and hopefully will be with me for many more.

I had two aces up my sleeve that supplemented the information that Jacob and I uncovered: Ken Klukowski and Joel Pollak. These are two of the most brilliant people I've ever met and also two of the most patriotic. These gentlemen are wonderful friends who are truly generous with their time and brainpower. They are great lawyers and better Americans.

The team at Simon & Schuster provided terrific support, as they have throughout the *Breaking* series. My editor, Natasha Simons, has the best eye in the publishing world, and her right-hand at Threshold Editions, Young Master Paul Choix, lent me his ample talents and made this book immeasurably better. My agent, Tom Flannery, is a consummate professional, as is his boss, Super-Agent David Vigliano.

Larry Solov, Elizabeth Moore, Jon Kahn, Wynton Hall, and the rest of the Breitbart News news room change the world every day and I'm forever grateful that they believe in me.

Thank you to Dean Reuter of the Federalist Society, Alina Habba, and Boris Epshteyn for their insight and guidance.

Thank you to President Donald J. Trump for the interviews, the endorsement, and most importantly, the inspiration. He is a testament to the human spirit and I am in awe of him every day.

And to Andrew Breitbart, for still, somehow, showing me the way, even after all these years.

NOTES

PREFACE

1. Bezos, Jeff. "The Hard Truth: Americans Don't Trust the News Media." *The Washington Post*, October 28, 2024. https://www.washingtonpost.com/opinions/2024/10/28/jeff-bezos-washington-post-trust/.
2. Fry, Richard, Dana Braga and Kim Parker. "Is College Worth It?" *Pew Research Center*, May 23, 2024. https://www.pewresearch.org/social-trends/2024/05/23/is-college-worth-it-2/.
3. "Taylor Swift and Her World." Harvard University, Department of English. Accessed April 28, 2025. https://english.fas.harvard.edu/english-183ts-taylor-swift-and-her-world.
4. Liberty Daily. "Peter Navarro Speaks from Prison, Discusses Biden's Lawfare." *YouTube*, June 4, 2024. https://www.youtube.com/watch?v=2nimBA71nYk.

INTRODUCTION

1. Hawkins, AWR. "Operation Choke Point: Feds Pressure Credit Union to Close Wisconsin Gun Dealer's Bank Account." *Breitbart*, January 14, 2015. https://www.breitbart.com/politics/2015/01/14/operation-choke-point-feds-pressure-credit-union-to-close-wisconsin-gun-dealers-bank-account/.
2. Hall, Wynton. "Obama Administration's 'Operation Choke Point' on Mission to Destroy Key Sectors of Private Lending Industry." *Breitbart*, January 8, 2014. https://www.breitbart.com/politics/2014/01/08/obama-administration-s-operation-choke-point-on-mission-to-destroy-key-sectors-of-private-lending-industry/.
3. Boyle, Matthew. "Exclusive—Sen. Tim Scott: 'Disgusting' Biden Weaponized Financial Markets to Debank Conservatives, Trump Family." *Breitbart*, January 28, 2025. https://www.breitbart.com/politics/2025/01/28/exclusive-sen-tim-scott-disgusting-biden-weaponized-financial-markets-to-debank-conservatives-trump-family/.
4. Office for Victims of Crime. "Hate Crimes." *U.S. Department of Justice*. Accessed April 28, 2025. https://ovc.ojp.gov/topics/hate-crimes#:~:text=A%20hate%20crime%20is%20defined,%2C%20sexual%20orientation%2C%20or%20ethnicity.

5. Ohanian, Lee E. "Why Shoplifting Is Now De Facto Legal in California." *Hoover Institution*, September 19, 2023. https://www.hoover.org/research /why-shoplifting-now-de-facto-legal-california.

6. Lehman, Charles Fain. "Comparing Crime Rates to 2019 Shows Just How Dangerous Reforms Have Been." *New York Post*, December 13, 2023. https:// nypost.com/2023/12/13/opinion/comparing-crime-rates-to-2019-show-just -how-dangerous-reforms-have-been/.

7. New York City Criminal Justice Agency. "People Prosecuted." https://www .nycja.org/people-prosecuted.

8. Lee, Ella. "Jan. 6 Rioters Who Were Passive Can Be Convicted of Disorderly Conduct, Court Rules." *The Hill*, February 7, 2024. https://thehill.com/home news/4392449-jan-6-rioters-who-were-passive-can-be-convicted-of-disor derly-conduct-court-rules/.

9. Bruggeman, Lucien, and Alexander Mallin. "3 Years After Jan. 6: By the Numbers—Over 1,200 Charged, 460 Sentenced." *ABC News*, January 5, 2024. https://abcnews.go.com/Politics/3-years-jan-6-numbers-1200-charged-460 /story?id=106140326.

10. Bergengruen, Vera. "The Capitol Rioters Are Still Being Sentenced. Here's What We Know." *Time*, January 6, 2022. https://time.com/6133336/jan-6-cap itol-riot-arrests-sentences/.

11. Dixon-Hamilton, Jordan. "Proud Boys' Enrique Tarrio Receives Record 22-Year Prison Sentence for Capitol Riots." *Breitbart*, September 5, 2023. https://www.breitbart.com/politics/2023/09/05/proud-boys-enrique-tarrio -receives-record-22-year-prison-sentence-for-capitol-riots/.

12. Van Laar, Jennifer. "RedState Columnist and LA County GOP 1st Vice Chair Siaka Massaquoi Arrested for Protesting on J6." *RedState*, December 4, 2023. https://redstate.com/jenvanlaar/2023/12/04/redstate-columnist-and-la -county-gop-1st-vice-chair-siaka-massaquoi-arrested-for-protesting-on -j6-n2167133.

13. Rasmussen Reports. *49% Favor J6 Riot Pardons on Case-by-Case Basis*. December 3, 2024. https://www.rasmussenreports.com/public_content/politics /biden_administration/49_favor_j6_riot_pardons_on_case_by_case_basis.

14. Broadwater, Luke. "The Committee Hired a TV Executive to Produce the Hearings for Maximum Impact." *The New York Times*, June 9, 2022. https:// www.nytimes.com/2022/06/09/us/the-committee-hired-a-tv-executive-to -produce-the-hearings-for-maximum-impact.html.

15. Hamilton, Katherine. "Election Denier Jamie Raskin Announces 4 Criminal Referrals of Trump to DOJ." *Breitbart*, December 19, 2022. https://www.bre itbart.com/politics/2022/12/19/election-denier-jamie-raskin-announces-4 -criminal-referrals-of-trump-to-doj/.

16. Pollak, Joel B. "January 6 Committee Destroyed Records, Videos— Trump Rights Violated." *Breitbart*, August 9, 2023. https://www.breitbart .com/politics/2023/08/09/january-6-committee-destroyed-records-videos -trump-rights-violated/.

17. Haberman, Maggie, and Luke Broadwater. "Cassidy Hutchinson Said Trump Tried to Grab Steering Wheel of Limo on Jan. 6." *The New York Times*, June 28, 2022. https://www.nytimes.com/2022/06/28/us/cassidy-hutchin son-trump-jan-6.html.

18. Spiering, Charlie. "Donald Trump Mocks Allegation He Tried to Grab Steering Wheel of the Presidential Limo on January 6." *Breitbart*, June 28, 2022. https://www.breitbart.com/politics/2022/06/28/not-possible-donald-trump -mocks-allegation-he-tried-to-grab-steering-wheel-of-the-presidential-limo -on-january-6/.

19. Poor, Jeff. "Trump: If Pelosi Had Not Turned Down Soldiers/National Guard on January 6, 'You Would Not Have Had Any Problem.'" *Breitbart*, January 21, 2022. https://www.breitbart.com/clips/2022/01/21/trump-if-pelosi-had-not -turned-down-soldiers-national-guard-on-january-6-you-would-not-have -had-any-problem/.

20. Pollak, Joel B. "Watch: Unaired Video Shows Nancy Pelosi Admitting Responsibility for Not Having National Guard at Capitol." *Breitbart*, June 10, 2024. https://www.breitbart.com/politics/2024/06/10/watch-unaired-video-shows-nan cy-pelosi-admitting-responsibility-for-not-having-national-guard-at-capitol/.

21. Hamilton, Katherine. "Justice Department Reveals 26 FBI Informants Attended January 6 Protests." *Breitbart*, December 12, 2024. https://www .breitbart.com/politics/2024/12/12/justice-department-reveals-26-fbi-infor mants-attended-january-6-protests/.

22. Hamilton, Katherine. "Report: FBI Interviewed Priest, Choir Director as Part of Investigation Targeting Catholics." *Breitbart*, December 5, 2023. https://www .breitbart.com/politics/2023/12/05/report-fbi-interviewed-priest-choir-di rector-part-investigation-targeting-catholics/.

23. Singman, Brooke. "FBI Targeted Parents via Terrorism Tools, Despite Garland Testimony." *Fox News*, October 6, 2022. https://www.foxnews.com/poli tics/fbi-targeted-parents-via-terrorism-tools-despite-garland-testimony.

24. Jaye, Bradley. "Report: 5,000 FBI Employees Worked on January 6 Cases While Crime Skyrocketed." *Breitbart*, February 4, 2025. https://www.breitbart.com/pol itics/2025/02/04/report-5000-fbi-employees-worked-on-january-6-cases -while-crime-skyrocketed/.

25. Galston, William A., and Elaine Kamarck. "Polls Show Americans Are Divided on the Significance of January 6." *Brookings Institution*, January 5, 2024. https://www.brookings.edu/articles/polls-show-americans-are-divided -on-the-significance-of-january-6/.

26. Skelley, Geoffrey. "Americans Are Moving On From Jan. 6, Even If Congress Hasn't." *FiveThirtyEight*, January 6, 2023. https://fivethirtyeight.com/features /americans-are-moving-on-from-jan-6-even-if-congress-hasnt/.

27. Boyle, Matthew. "Exclusive—Peter Navarro Speaks from Behind Bars: Joe Biden Prison Warns 'Unrestrained Lawfare' Designed to Interfere with Election." *Breitbart*, June 5, 2024. https://www.breitbart.com/politics/2024/06/05 /exclusive-peter-navarro-speaks-from-behind-bars-joe-biden-prison-warns -unrestrained-lawfare-designed-interfere-election/.

CHAPTER 1: BROKEN SCALES

1. Spiering, Charlie. "$200K Payment to President Biden from Brother James Appears Linked to Family Business." *Breitbart*, October 20, 2023. https://www .breitbart.com/politics/2023/10/20/200k-payment-president-biden-brother -james-appears-linked-family-business/.

2. Mazemoore. "$200K Check to Joe Biden from His Brother James Biden from Americore Scam." *X* (formerly Twitter) April 24, 2025. https://x.com /mazemoore/status/1881334756304118234.

3. Passel, Jeffrey S., D'Vera Cohn, and Anna Brown. "What We Know about Unauthorized Immigrants Living in the U.S." *Pew Research Center*, July 22, 2024. https://www.pewresearch.org/short-reads/2024/07/22/what-we-know -about-unauthorized-immigrants-living-in-the-us.

4. Binder, John. "Five Years of Chain Migration Adds More People to U.S. than One Year of American Births." *Breitbart*, December 18, 2017. https://www .breitbart.com/politics/2017/12/18/five-years-of-chain-migration-adds -more-people-to-u-s-than-one-year-of-american-births/.

5. Binder, John. "Fact Check: Obama, Biden Used 'Cages' for Border Crossers." *Breitbart*, October 22, 2020. https://www.breitbart.com/politics/2020/10/22 /fact-check-obama-biden-used-so-called-cages-border-crossers/.

6. Lopez, German. "Hatemonger Paints Trump Advisor Stephen Miller as a Case Study in Radicalization." *NPR*, August 24, 2020. https://www .npr.org/2020/08/24/905403716/hatemonger-paints-trump-advisor-ste phen-miller-as-a-case-study-in-radicalization.

7. Ohanian, Lee. "Why Shoplifting Is Now De Facto Legal in California." *Hoover Institution*. https://www.hoover.org/research/why-shoplifting-now-de-facto -legal-california.

8. Movement for Family Power. "Cash Bail: Racist, Wealth-Based, Unfair." *MFF Action*. https://www.mffaction.org/the-issues/cash-bail-racist-wealth-based-unfair.

9. Hains, Tim. "Fact Check: Trump Says Kamala Harris Raised Money for 2020 Minnesota Rioters." *Breitbart*, September 10, 2024. https://www.breitbart .com/politics/2024/09/10/fact-check-trump-says-kamala-harris-raised -money-for-2020-minnesota-rioters,

10. Editorial Board. "Kamala Harris and Trump on Crime: Who Has the Better Record?" *New York Times*, August 22, 2024. https://www.nytimes .com/2024/08/22/opinion/kamala-harris-trump-crime.htmll

11. Colton, Emma. "FBI Quietly Updates Crime Data to Show Big Jump in Violence under Biden-Harris Admin: 'Shocking.' " *Fox News*. https://www.foxnews .com/politics/fbi-quietly-updates-crime-data-show-big-jump-violence-un der-biden-harris-admin-shocking.

12. Ropac, René and Michael Rempel. "Does New York's Bail Reform Law Impact Recidivism? A Quasi-Experimental Test in New York City." *Data Collaborative for Justice*. March 2023. https://datacollaborativeforjustice.org/wp-con tent/uploads/2023/03/RecidivismReport-1.pdf.

13. Binder, John. "New York Bail Law Freed Illegal Alien Wanted by Feds, Accused of Rape." *Breitbart*, August 17, 2023. https://www.breitbart.com /politics/2023/08/17/new-york-bail-law-freed-illegal-alien-wanted-feds-ac cused-rape/

14. Binder, John "Watch: Migrants Brutally Attack NYC Cops, Get Freed from Jail without Bail." *Breitbart*, January 31, 2024. https://www.breitbart.com/pol itics/2024/01/31/watch-migrants-brutally-attack-nyc-cops-get-freed-from -jail-without-bail/

15. Binder, John "Sanctuary Church Helps Free from Jail Illegal Alien Charged with Migrant Mob Attack on NYPD Officers." *Breitbart*, February 15, 2024.

https://www.breitbart.com/politics/2024/02/15/sanctuary-church-helps
-free-from-jail-illegal-alien-charged-with-migrant-mob-attack-on-nypd-of
ficers/

16. Nolte, John. "New York: Five Illegal Migrants Escape after Being Released on
Bail Following Jewelry Store Theft." *Breitbart*, November 15, 2024. https://
www.breitbart.com/politics/2024/11/15/new-york-five-illegal-migrants-es
cape-after-being-released-on-bail-following-jewelry-store-theft

17. https://www.breitbart.com/crime/2025/04/29/california-democrat-lawmaker
-wants-to-decriminalize-welfare-fraud-under-25000/

18. https://www.breitbart.com/crime/2025/04/29/california-democrat-lawmaker
-wants-to-decriminalize-welfare-fraud-under-25000/

19. Law Enforcement Legal Defense Fund. *Justice for Sale*. Scribd. Accessed
April 28, 2025. https://www.scribd.com/document/577278421/Justice-for
-Sale-LELDF-Report

20. Law Enforcement Legal Defense Fund. *Justice for Sale*. Scribd. Accessed
April 28, 2025. https://www.scribd.com/document/577278421/Justice-for
-Sale-LELDF-Report

21. Blau, Reuven. "Kathy Boudin, Weather Underground Radical in Fatal 1981
Heist, Dies." *The Journal News*, May 2, 2022. https://www.lohud.com/story
/news/local/rockland/2022/05/02/kathy-boudin-weather-underground-fa
tal-1981-nyack-brinks-heist-dies/9616467002

22. Pollak, Joel B. "Andrew Cuomo Grants Clemency to Former Weather Underground Militant, Father of San Francisco DA." *Breitbart*, August 24, 2021.
https://www.breitbart.com/crime/2021/08/24/andrew-cuomo-grants-clem
ency-to-former-weather-underground-militant-father-of-san-francisco-da

23. Bromwich, Jonah E. "David Gilbert, Brink's Heist Figure, Has Sentence
Commuted." *The New York Times*, August 23, 2021. https://www.nytimes
.com/2021/08/23/nyregion/david-gilbert-brinks-sentence-commuted.html

24. Chesa Boudin Campaign Website (Archived). "Issues." *Chesa Boudin for
District Attorney*. Archived November 11, 2019. https://web.archive.org
/web/20191111133839/https://www.chesaboudin.com/issues.

25. Neilson, Susie, and Abhinanda Bhattacharyya. "These Charts Show What
Makes Chesa Boudin Different from Past District Attorneys." *San Francisco
Chronicle*, March 25, 2022. https://www.sfchronicle.com/projects/2022/chesa
-boudin-charts/.

26. Furr, Amy. "Report: George Soros-Backed District Attorney Pamela Price's
Laptop Stolen in Crime-Ridden Oakland." *Breitbart*, October 30, 2023.
https://www.breitbart.com/crime/2023/10/30/report-george-soros-backed
-district-attorney-pamela-prices-laptop-stolen-in-crime-ridden-oakland/.

27. Pollak, Joel B. "Report: U.S. Has 75 'Soros-Backed' Radical Prosecutors." *Breitbart*, June 8, 2022. https://www.breitbart.com/politics/2022/06/08/report-u
-s-has-75-soros-backed-radical-prosecutors/.

28. Queally, James. "How Jackie Lacey's and George Gascón's Visions Shape D.A.'s
Race." *Los Angeles Times*, February 18, 2020. https://www.latimes.com/cali
fornia/story/2020-02-18/district-attorney-election-jackie-lacey-george-gas
con-race.

29. Melugin, Bill (@BillMelugin_). "EXCLUSIVE/THREAD: LAPD arrested a
man for stabbing the neck of a construction worker, nearly killing him . . ."

X (formerly Twitter), June 1, 2023. https://x.com/BillMelugin_/status/1663553
226963292163.

30. Leonard, Eric. "Murders Are Dropping Across the Country—But Not in
L.A." *NBC Los Angeles*. Accessed April 28, 2025. https://www.nbclosange
les.com/investigations/murders-are-dropping-across-the-country-but-not
-in-la/3386783/.

31. "Homicide and Auto Theft Surge in Los Angeles County." *ABC7 News*.
Accessed April 28, 2025. https://abc7.com/homicide-auto-theft-los-ange
les-county-villanueva/11463877/.

32. "George Gascón's No-Bail Policies and Rising Crime Rates." *ABC7 News*. Accessed April 28, 2025. https://abc7.com/district-attorney-george-gascon-no
-bail-criminal-justice-reform-los-angeles-crime/11314247/

33. "George Gascón's No-Bail Policies and Rising Crime Rates." *ABC7 News*.
Accessed April 28, 2025. https://abc7.com/district-attorney-george-gascon
-no-bail-criminal-justice-reform-los-angeles-crime/11314247/; "District Attorney George Gascón Issues Statement on Money Bail." *Los Angeles County
District Attorney's Office*. https://da.lacounty.gov/media/news/district-attor
ney-george-gascon-issues-statement-money-bail.

34. "Woke L.A. District Attorney George Gascón Has 10K-Case Backlog." *New
York Post*, May 24, 2023. https://nypost.com/2023/05/24/woke-la-district-at
torney-george-gascon-has-10k-case-backlog/

35. "Gas-Gone: Soros-Backed L.A. District Attorney Gascón Loses in Land-
slide." *Breitbart*, November 6, 2024. https://www.breitbart.com/law-and
-order/2024/11/06/gas-gone-soros-backed-l-a-district-attorney-gascon-loses
-in-landslide/.

36. "Alvin Bragg, Soros-Linked District Attorney Behind Trump Charges, Builds
Record Refusing to Prosecute Felonies." *Breitbart*, April 3, 2023. https://www
.breitbart.com/politics/2023/04/03/alvin-bragg-soros-linked-district-attor
ney-behind-trump-charges-builds-record-refusing-to-prosecute-felonies/.

37. "Alvin Bragg, Soros-Linked District Attorney Behind Trump Charges, Builds
Record Refusing to Prosecute Felonies." *Breitbart*, April 3, 2023. https://www
.breitbart.com/politics/2023/04/03/alvin-bragg-soros-linked-district-attor
ney-behind-trump-charges-builds-record-refusing-to-prosecute-felonies/.

38. "Bragg Defends No-Bail Decision for Alleged Cop Beaters." *PIX11*, Accessed
April 28, 2025. https://pix11.com/news/local-news/they-should-be-sitting
-in-rikers-bragg-defends-no-bail-decision-set-for-alleged-cop-beaters/

39. McCarthy, Craig. "NYC Bodega Worker Jose Alba Sues DA Alvin Bragg and
NYPD." *New York Post*, September 30, 2023. https://nypost.com/2023/09/30
/nyc-bodega-worker-jose-alba-sues-da-alvin-bragg-nypd/.

40. Oliveira, Alex. "Psychiatrist: Daniel Penny Feared for His Life During Jordan Neely Encounter." *Daily Mail*, 2024. https://www.dailymail.co.uk/news
/article-14105693/Daniel-Penny-Jordan-Neely-psychiatrist-testimony-court
.html.

41. Sabes, Adam. "Cook County State's Attorney Kim Foxx's Office Dismissed Over 25,000 Felony Cases, 35% Higher Than Predecessor." *Fox
News*, Accessed April 28, 2025. https://www.foxnews.com/us/cook-county
-state-attorney-kim-foxxs-office-has-dismissed-more-than-25000-felony-cas
es-more-than-35-higher-than-her-predecessor.

42. "Federal Prosecutors Charge Gang Members in Chicago Veteran's Murder After Kim Foxx Refused." *Breitbart*, June 9, 2024. https://www.breitbart.com /crime/2024/06/09/federal-prosecutors-charge-gang-members-in-chicago -veterans-murder-after-kim-foxx-refused/.

43. Ng, David. "Jussie Smollett Hate Crime Hoax Goes to Trial Years After Soros- Backed D.A. Kim Foxx Dropped Charges." *Breitbart*, November 29, 2021. https://www.breitbart.com/entertainment/2021/11/29/jussie-smollett-hate -crime-hoax-goes-to-trial-years-after-soros-backed-d-a-kim-foxx-dropped -charges/.

44. Ng, David. "Cook County Prosecutor Kim Foxx Gloats Over Jussie Smollett Conviction Reversal But Acknowledges His Guilt." *Breitbart*, November 22, 2024. https://www.breitbart.com/entertainment/2024/11/22/cook-county -prosecutor-kim-foxx-gloats-over-jussie-smollett-reversal-but-acknowledges -his-guilt/.

45. Lussenhop, Jessica. "Mark and Patricia McCloskey: What Really Went on in St Louis That Day?" *BBC News*, August 25, 2020. https://www.bbc.com/news /election-us-2020-53891184.

46. Lussenhop, Jessica. "Mark and Patricia McCloskey: What Really Went on in St Louis That Day?" *BBC News*, August 25, 2020. https://www.bbc.com/news /election-us-2020-53891184.

47. LeBlanc, Paul, and Keith Allen. "Missouri Governor Pardons St. Louis Cou- ple Who Pointed Guns at Protesters." CNN, August 3, 2021. https://www .cnn.com/2021/08/03/politics/mark-mccloskey-patricia-mccloskey-pardon /index.html

48. Sanders, Sam, and Kenya Young. "A Black Mother Reflects on Giving Her 3 Sons 'The Talk' . . . Again and Again." *NPR*, June 28, 2020. https://www.npr .org/2020/06/28/882383372/a-black-mother-reflects-on-giving-her-3-sons -the-talk-again-and-again.

49. Mac Donald, Heather. "The Ferguson Effect Lives On." *City Journal*, Decem- ber 23, 2016. https://www.city-journal.org/article/the-ferguson-effect-lives-on.

50. Price, Bob. "Ferguson Effect Is Real, Police Survey Finds." *Breitbart*, Jan- uary 17, 2017. https://www.breitbart.com/border/2017/01/17/ferguson-ef fect-real-police-survey-finds/.

51. Thompson, Christie. "The Obama Justice Department Had a Plan to Hold Po- lice Accountable for Abuses. The Trump DOJ Has Undermined It." *ProPublica*, March 5, 2018. https://www.propublica.org/article/the-obama-justice-de partment-had-a-plan-to-hold-police-accountable-for-abuses-the-trump -doj-has-undermined-it.

52. MacFarquhar, Neil. "Police Forces Face a Reckoning as Retirements and De- partures Surge." *The New York Times*, June 11, 2021. https://www.nytimes .com/2021/06/11/us/police-retirements-resignations-recruits.html.

53. Campanile, Carl. "NYPD Headcount Faces Record Lows—200 NYC Cops Leave Per Month: Data." *New York Post*, May 18, 2024. https://nypost .com/2024/05/18/us-news/nypd-headcount-faces-record-lows-200-nyc -cops-leave-per-month-data/.

54. Moselle, Aaron. "Police Officer Hiring Increases in 2023 After Historic Lows." *WHYY*, March 13, 2023. https://whyy.org/articles/police-officer-hiring-in crease-2023/

55. Schleifer, Theodore. "The Lost Gospel of SBF." *Puck News*, Accessed May 16, 2025. https://puck.news/the-lost-gospel-of-sbf/

56. "Countries with the Most Prisoners per 100,000 Inhabitants." *Statista*, Accessed May 16, 2025. https://www.statista.com/statistics/262962/countries-with-the-most-prisoners-per-100-000-inhabitants/.

57. Ng, David. "California Passes Anti-Crime Proposition 36, Which Kamala Harris Refused to Back." *Breitbart*, November 5, 2024. https://www.breitbart.com/politics/2024/11/05/california-passes-anti-crime-proposition-36-which-kamala-harris-refused-to-back/.

58. Ng, David. "Kamala Harris Repeatedly Refuses to Take Stance on California Proposition to Toughen Crime Penalties." *Breitbart*, October 25, 2024. https://www.breitbart.com/crime/2024/10/25/kamala-harris-repeatedly-refuses-take-stance-california-proposition-toughen-crime-penalties/.

59. "Soros-Backed DAs Suffer 12 Big Defeats; Billionaire's Agenda Faces Uncertain Future." *Fox News*, Accessed May 16, 2025. https://www.foxnews.com/politics/soros-das-suffer-12-big-defeats-billionaires-agenda-faces-uncertain-future.

60. "City Council Votes to Establish Los Angeles as a Sanctuary City." *City of Los Angeles*, Accessed May 16, 2025. https://cd4.lacity.gov/press-releases/city-council-votes-to-establish-los-angeles-as-a-sanctuary-city/. Rosenhall, Laurel. "California Democrats Reconsider Sanctuary Policies Amid Immigration Debate." *CalMatters*, February 2025. https://calmatters.org/politics/2025/02/california-sanctuary-immigrants-democrats/.

61. Rosenhall, Laurel. "California Democrats Reconsider Sanctuary Policies Amid Immigration Debate." *CalMatters*, February 2025. https://calmatters.org/politics/2025/02/california-sanctuary-immigrants-democrats/.

CHAPTER 2: THE TRIAL THAT NEVER SHOULD HAVE HAPPENED

1. Broder, John M. "Obama to Open Offshore Areas to Oil Drilling for First Time." *The New York Times*, June 25, 2010. https://www.nytimes.com/2010/06/25/us/politics/25caribou.html.

2. "The White House Guest List: Who's In and Who's Out." *HuffPost*, March 31, 2011. https://www.huffpost.com/entry/the-white-house-guess-lis_b_839232.

3. United States District Court, Southern District of New York. "Citizens for Responsibility and Ethics in Washington et al. v. Donald J. Trump." Case No. 17 Civ. 458 (GBD), December 21, 2017. https://www.politico.com/f/?id=00000160-7b12-dcd4-a96b-7f3bae5a0000.?

4. Caplan, Joshua. "Flashback: Trump on Charlottesville: Neo-Nazis 'Should Be Condemned Totally.'" *Breitbart*, August 8, 2019. https://www.breitbart.com/politics/2019/08/08/flashback-trump-on-charlottesville-neo-nazis-should-be-condemned-totally/

5. Collinson, Stephen. "Mueller Investigation Witnesses: Who Has Been Interviewed?" *CNN*, January 3, 2020. https://www.cnn.com/2020/01/03/politics/mueller-investigation-witnesses-interviewed-list/index.html

6. "Hush Money Trial: Here Is What Stormy Daniels Testified Happened Between Her and Trump." *AP News*, May 7, 2024. https://apnews.com/article/stormy-daniels-donald-trump-trial-takeaways-f34f094124fc7ec455d6a73cbb6eec21

7. "Trump Trial Resumes; Prosecutors Indicate Hush Money Testimony Halfway Done." *NBC News*, April 30, 2024. https://www.nbcnews.com/politics/donald-trump/trump-trial-resumes-prosecutors-indicate-hush-money-testimony-halfway-rcna150950

8. Gregorian, Dareh, Adam Reiss, and Lisa Rubin. "Trump Trial Resumes as Prosecutors Indicate Hush Money Testimony Is Halfway Done." *NBC News*, May 6, 2024. https://www.nbcnews.com/politics/donald-trump/trump-trial-resumes-prosecutors-indicate-hush-money-testimony-halfway-rcna150950.

9. Rutenberg, Jim, and Rebecca Ballhaus. "National Enquirer Shielded Donald Trump from Playboy Model's Affair Allegation." *The Wall Street Journal*, November 4, 2016. https://www.wsj.com/articles/national-enquirer-shielded-donald-trump-from-playboy-models-affair-allegation-1478309380

10. Haberman, Maggie, and Jim Rutenberg. "Trump Lawyer Says He Paid Stormy Daniels Out of His Own Pocket." *The New York Times*, February 13, 2018. https://www.nytimes.com/2018/02/13/us/politics/stormy-daniels-michael-cohen-trump.html

11. "Trump Calls Raid on His Lawyer Michael Cohen's Office a 'Disgrace' and a 'Witch Hunt.'" *CBS News*, April 9, 2018. https://www.cbsnews.com/news/trump-calls-raid-on-his-lawyers-office-a-disgraceful-situation-and-a-witch-hunt/

12. Winter, Tom, and Jonathan Dienst. "Feds Tapped Trump Lawyer Michael Cohen's Phones." *NBC News*, May 3, 2018. https://www.nbcnews.com/politics/donald-trump/feds-tapped-trump-lawyer-michael-cohen-s-phones-n871011

13. "Cohen Pleads Guilty, Implicates Trump in Hush-Money Scheme." *AP News*, August 21, 2018. https://apnews.com/article/north-america-donald-trump-us-news-ap-top-news-michael-cohen-74aaf72511d64fceb1d64529207bde64

14. Trump, Donald J. "A total WITCH HUNT with massive conflicts of interest!" *X* (formerly Twitter), July 24, 2018. https://x.com/realDonaldTrump/status/1022097879253635072

15. Tribe, Laurence H. "The rule of law is under siege." *X* (formerly Twitter), August 13, 2018. https://web.archive.org/web/20210514173300/https://twitter.com/tribelaw/status/1028646970561359872

16. Pollak, Joel B. "Soros-Backed Group Helped Elect D.A. Allegedly Planning Trump Arrest." *Breitbart*, March 18, 2023. https://www.breitbart.com/politics/2023/03/18/soros-backed-group-helped-elect-d-a-allegedly-planning-trump-arrest

17. Rutenberg, Jim. "Alvin Bragg and the Trump Trial: The Manhattan D.A.'s Moment." *The New York Times Magazine*, April 9, 2024. https://www.nytimes.com/2024/04/09/magazine/alvin-bragg-donald-trump-trial.html

18. Goodman, Ryan. "Why Did Federal Prosecutors Drop Trump's Hush Money Case?" *Lawfare*, April 14, 2024. https://www.lawfaremedia.org/article/why-did-federal-prosecutors-drop-trump's-hush-money-case

19. Swan, Jonathan. "Alvin Bragg Prosecutor in Trump Trial Reflects on Case's Impact." *Politico*, June 1, 2024. https://www.politico.com/news/2024/06/01/alvin-bragg-prosecutor-trump-trial-impact-00161112

20. Goldman, Adam. "Mark Pomerantz Resignation Letter: Why He Left the Trump Investigation." *The New York Times*, March 23, 2022. https://www.nytimes.com/2022/03/23/nyregion/mark-pomerantz-resignation-letter.html

21. Rutenberg, Jim. "Alvin Bragg and the Trump Trial: The Manhattan D.A.'s Moment." *The New York Times Magazine*, April 9, 2024. https://www.nytimes.com/2024/04/09/magazine/alvin-bragg-donald-trump-trial.html

22. Honig, Elie. "Trump Was Convicted—But Prosecutors Contorted the Law." *New York Magazine*, May 31, 2024. https://nymag.com/intelligencer/article/trump-was-convicted-but-prosecutors-contorted-the-law.html

23. Hutzler, Alexandra. "How the Trump Hush Money Case Compares to the John Edwards Indictment." *ABC News*, March 24, 2023. https://abcnews.go.com/Politics/trump-hush-money-case-compared-democrat-john-edwards/story?id=98053273

25. "Michael Avenatti Pleads Guilty to Federal Fraud and Tax Charges That Allege He Stole Millions of Dollars from Clients." *United States Department of Justice*, June 16, 2022. https://www.justice.gov/usao-cdca/pr/michael-avenatti-pleads-guilty-federal-fraud-and-tax-charges-allege-he-stole-millions

26. "Michael Avenatti Sentenced to 14 Years in Prison for Stealing Millions from Clients." *CNN*, December 5, 2022. https://www.cnn.com/2022/12/05/politics/michael-avenatti-prison-sentence-client-embezzlement/index.html.

27. "Judge in Trump Case Donated to Biden Campaign." *CNN*, April 6, 2023. https://www.cnn.com/2023/04/06/politics/judge-merchan-trump-biden-contribution/index.html

28. Kates, Graham. "New York Judge Says He Will Bar Selective Prosecution Claim in Trump Organization Criminal Trial." *CBS News*, September 12, 2022. https://www.cbsnews.com/news/trump-organization-trial-new-york-judge-bar-selective-prosecution-claim/

29. Campanile, Carl. "Dem Clients of Daughter of NY Judge in Trump Hush-Money Trial Raised $93M off the Case." *New York Post*, March 30, 2024. https://nypost.com/2024/03/30/us-news/dem-clients-of-daughter-of-judge-in-trump-trial-raised-90m-off-case

30. Campanile, Carl. "Dem Clients of Daughter of NY Judge in Trump Hush-Money Trial Raised $93M off the Case." *New York Post*, March 30, 2024. https://nypost.com/2024/03/30/us-news/dem-clients-of-daughter-of-judge-in-trump-trial-raised-90m-off-case

31. "Vendor/Recipient Profile: Authentic Campaigns." *OpenSecrets*, 2024. https://www.opensecrets.org/campaign-expenditures/vendor?cycle=2024&vendor=Authentic+Campaigns.

32. Pollak, Joel B. "Rep. Dan Goldman, Client of Judge Merchan's Daughter, Says He Prepped Michael Cohen for Trump Trial." *Breitbart*, May 15, 2024. https://www.breitbart.com/2024-election/2024/05/15/rep-dan-goldman-client-judge-merchans-daughter-says-he-prepped-michael-cohen-trump-trial

33. "Vendor/Recipient Profile: Authentic Campaigns." *OpenSecrets*, 2024. https://www.opensecrets.org/campaign-expenditures/vendor?cycle=2024&vendor=Authentic+Campaigns.

34. "Donald Trump Campaign Speech Canceled After Judge Decides to Start Trial Early Monday." *Breitbart*, May 20, 2024. https://www.breitbart.com/2024-election/2024/05/20/donald-trump-campaign-speech-canceled-after-judge-decides-start-trial-early-monday/

35. Trump, Donald J. "I Should Be Out Campaigning – Election Interference!" *Truth Social*, May 15, 2024. https://truthsocial.com/@realDonaldTrump/posts/112225363872196974

36. Cohen, Marshall. "Judge Holds Trump in Contempt for Violating Gag Order." *CNN*, May 6, 2024. https://www.cnn.com/2024/05/06/politics/merchan-trump-gag-order-contempt/index.html

37. Pollak, Joel B. "Donald Trump Starts 4th Week of Trial: 'I Should Be Out Campaigning—Election Interference!'" *Breitbart*, May 13, 2024. https://www.breitbart.com/2024-election/2024/05/13/donald-trump-starts-4th-week-of-trial-i-should-be-out-campaigning-election-interference

38. "Hush Money Trial: Here Is What Stormy Daniels Testified Happened Between Her and Trump." *AP News*, May 7, 2024. https://apnews.com/article/stormy-daniels-donald-trump-trial-takeaways-f34f094124fc7ec455d6a73cbb6eec21

39. Maher, Bill. "Bad Witness: Bill Maher Digs Up Old Stormy Daniels Interview to Slam Her Testimony in Trump Trial." *Toronto Sun*, May 7, 2024. https://torontosun.com/news/world/bad-witness-bill-maher-digs-up-old-stormy-daniels-interview-to-slam-her-testimony-in-trump-trial

40. Pollak, Joel B. "CNN's Paula Reid Cross-Examination of Stormy Daniels Was 'Devastating, Eviscerating.'" *Breitbart*, May 7, 2024. https://www.breitbart.com/politics/2024/05/07/cnns-paula-reid-cross-examination-of-stormy-daniels-was-devastating-eviscerating

41. Breuninger, Kevin. "Trump Probe: Porn Star Stormy Daniels Will 'Dance' if He Is Jailed." *CNBC*, March 21, 2023. https://www.cnbc.com/2023/03/21/trump-probe-porn-star-stormy-daniels-will-dance-if-he-is-jailed.html

42. "Stormy Daniels Testifies About Alleged Sex with Trump." *The Spokesman-Review*, May 7, 2024. https://www.spokesman.com/stories/2024/may/07/stormy-daniels-testifies-about-alleged-sex-with-tr

43. Enten, Harry. "After all the testimony in Trump's hush money case, the effect on the public has been zero. Voters simply just don't care that much. They are far more tuned into news about inflation, immigration, etc. than Trump's trials. Unsurprisingly, Trump small lead over Biden is holding." *X* (formerly Twitter), May 29, 2024. https://x.com/ForecasterEnten/status/1795814140272873982

44. Enten, Harry. "Poll: Most Predict Trump Conviction 'on Some Charges' in Business Records Trial, Plurality Says It Has Been Unfair." *Breitbart*, May 7, 2024. https://www.breitbart.com/politics/2024/05/07/poll-most-predict-trump-conviction-on-some-charges-in-business-records-trial-plurality-says-it-has-been-unfair

45. Key, Pam. "'He Is Such a Great Judge': MSNBC's Weissmann Says He Has a 'Man Crush' on Judge Merchan." *Breitbart*, May 30, 2024. https://www.breitbart.com/clips/2024/05/30/he-is-such-a-great-judge-msnbcs-weissmann-says-he-has-a-man-crush-on-judge-merchan

46. Poor, Jeff. "Michael Cohen: Judge Merchan 'Absolute Gentleman,' 'Judicial Perfection'—'To See Him on that Stand Is to See Poetry.'" *Breitbart*, May 30, 2024. https://www.breitbart.com/clips/2024/05/30/michael-cohen-judge-merchan-absolute-gentleman-judicial-perfection-to-see-him-on-that-stand-is-to-see-poetry

47. Pollak, Joel B. "Trump Campaign Announces $53 Million Raised in 24 Hours After Trump Conviction." *Breitbart*, May 31, 2024. https://www.bre itbart.com/politics/2024/05/31/trump-campaign-announces-53-million -raised-24-hours-trump-conviction

48. Pollak, Joel B. "Blue State Blues: The Trump Verdict and the Collapse of the Rule of Law." *Breitbart*, May 31, 2024. https://www.breitbart.com/pol itics/2024/05/31/blue-state-blues-the-trump-verdict-and-the-collapse-of -the-rule-of-law, ForecasterEnten. "Poll: Most Predict Trump Conviction 'on Some Charges' in Business Records Trial, Plurality Says It Has Been Un- fair." *X* (formerly Twitter), May 29, 2024. https://x.com/ForecasterEnten/sta tus/1795814140272873982

CHAPTER 3: THE WOMAN CASE

1. "Submitted Complaint – E. Jean Carroll v. Donald J. Trump." *Document- Cloud*, November 4, 2019. https://s3.documentcloud.org/documents/6538 591/2019-11-4-Submitted-Complaint-9-2-1-2.pdf

2. "E. Jean Carroll – Testimony Clip." *YouTube*. https://www.youtube.com /watch?v=RumPGMUSw2A

3. Campanile, Carl. "Trump Lawyer Asks E. Jean Carroll About 'Law & Order: SVU' Episode at Trial." *New York Post*, May 1, 2023. https://nypost.com/2023/05/01 /trump-lawyer-asks-e-jean-carroll-about-svu-episode-at-trial

4. law of ruby (@lawofruby). "Tweet." *X* (formerly Twitter), May 2, 2023. https://x.com/lawofruby/status/1653122887790764033

5. Gregorian, Dareh. "Trump's Defense Grills E. Jean Carroll Over Old Social Media Posts in Civil Rape Trial." *NBC News*, May 1, 2023. https://www.nbc news.com/politics/donald-trump/trumps-defense-grills-e-jean-carroll-old -social-media-posts-trial-rape-rcna82254

6. E. Jean Carroll (@ejeancarroll). "Tweet." *X* (formerly Twitter), May 4, 2010. https://x.com/ejeancarroll/status/13566108254

7. Multiple Authors. "E. Jean Carroll Joked About Sex in Bergdorf's Department Store Years Before Alleged Trump Rape." *Breitbart*, June 28, 2019. https:// www.breitbart.com/politics/2019/06/28/e-jean-carroll-joked-about-sex-in -bergdorfs-department-store-years-before-alleged-trump-rape/

8. Levine, Daniel. "E. Jean Carroll vs Trump: What Happened at Trial So Far." *The Guardian*, May 2, 2023. https://www.theguardian.com/us-news/2023 /may/02/e-jean-carroll-trump-rape-trial-case-latest

9. E. Jean Carroll (@ejeancarroll). "Tweet." *X* (formerly Twitter), February 20, 2010. https://x.com/ejeancarroll/status/1363271665606656002

10. E. Jean Carroll (@ejeancarroll1). "Instagram Post." *Instagram*. https://www .instagram.com/ejeancarroll1/p/CAL5ianpq91/?hl=en

11. Rupar, Aaron (@atrupar). "Tweet." *X* (formerly Twitter), May 9, 2023. https://x .com/atrupar/status/1656455585913503747

12. "Stormy Daniels Cross-Examination: Courtroom Clip." *YouTube*. https:// www.youtube.com/watch?v=ldP8YNAPlTw

13. Levine, Daniel. "Trump Rape Trial: Kellyanne Conway's Husband Targeted by Trump Allies." *The Guardian*, May 1, 2023. https://www.theguardian.com/us -news/2023/may/01/e-jean-carroll-trump-rape-trial-kellyanne-conway-husband

14. Neumeister, Larry. "George Conway Knocks CNN Trump Trial Coverage." *The Hill*, May 10, 2024. https://thehill.com/homenews/media/4700777 -george-conway-knocks-cnn-trump-trial-coverage/mlite/

15. Singal, Jesse. "George Conway: Anti-Trump Lawyer Behind New Ad Campaign." *AlterNet*, Accessed May 16, 2025. https://www.alternet.org /george-conway-ad

16. Multiple Authors. "George Conway Denies Close Ties to Lincoln Project Co-Founder John Weaver—Penned Op-Ed Together." *Breitbart*, February 1, 2021. https://www.breitbart.com/politics/2021/02/01/george-conway-denies-close -ties-lincoln-project-co-founder-john-weaver-penned-op-ed-together/

17. Conway, George. "Juanita Broaddrick's Claims Against Bill Clinton Are Credible." *The Washington Post*, June 22, 2019. https://www.washingtonpost.com /opinions/2019/06/22/george-conway-juanita-broaddricks-claims-against -bill-clinton-are-credible-latest-accusations-against-trump/

18. "Nonprofits Want Foreigners to Boycott Chinese Internet Summit." *The Hill*. Accessed May 16, 2025. https://thehill.com/policy/cybersecurity /263112-nonprofits-want-foreigners-to-boycott-chinese-internet-summit/.?

19. "Project Birmingham (Disinformation Campaign)." *Wikipedia*. Accessed May 16, 2025. https://en.wikipedia.org/wiki/Project_Birmingham_(disinfor mation_campaign)

20. Marlow, Alex. "LinkedIn Billionaire Reid Hoffman's Dark Money Behind Clandestine Good Information Foundation Group Accused of Election Meddling." *Breitbart*, October 5, 2022. https://www.breitbart.com/politics/2022 /10/05/marlow-linkedin-billionaire-reid-hoffmans-dark-money-behind -clandestine-good-information-foundation-group-accused-of-election -meddling

21. Confessore, Nicholas. "Reid Hoffman Apologizes for Deceptive Facebook Page Tied to Alabama Senate Race." *The New York Times*, December 26, 2018. https://www.nytimes.com/2018/12/26/us/reid-hoffman-alabama-elec tion-disinformation.html

22. Marlow, Alex. "LinkedIn Billionaire Reid Hoffman's Dark Money Behind Clandestine Good Information Foundation Group Accused of Election Meddling." *Breitbart*, October 5, 2022. https://www.breitbart.com/politics/2022 /10/05/marlow-linkedin-billionaire-reid-hoffmans-dark-money-behind -clandestine-good-information-foundation-group-accused-of-election -meddling/

23. Knudsen, Hannah. "Biden Mega-Donor Reid Hoffman Admits to Visiting Jeffrey Epstein's Island." *Breitbart*, May 3, 2023. https://www.breitbart.com /politics/2023/05/03/biden-mega-donor-reid-hoffman-admits-to-visit ing-jeffrey-epsteins-island

24. Knudsen, Hannah. "Trump Accuser E. Jean Carroll Backed by Known Democrat Party Activists, Mega-Donor Reid Hoffman Who Backs Haley." *Breitbart*, January 17, 2024. https://www.breitbart.com/politics/2024/01/17/trump-ac cuser-e-jean-carroll-backed-by-known-democrat-party-activists-mega-do nor-reid-hoffman-who-backs-haley

25. Moran, Sean. "Top Adviser to Democrat Megadonor Reid Hoffman Pushed Reporters to Consider Trump Shooting Staged." *Breitbart*, July 14, 2024. https://www.breitbart.com/politics/2024/07/14/top-adviser-democrat

-megadonor-reid-hoffman-pushed-reporters-consider-trump-shooting
-staged/

26. "Hoffman, Mehlhorn, and Biden: A Complicated Relationship." *The Washington Post*, July 19, 2024. https://www.washingtonpost.com/politics/2024/07/19/hoffman-mehlhorn-biden-trump

27. Kantor, Jodi, and Michael Gold. "Roberta Kaplan, Who Aided Cuomo, Resigns from Time's Up." *The New York Times*, August 9, 2021. https://www.nytimes.com/2021/08/09/nyregion/roberta-kaplan-times-up-cuomo.html

28. "Clients, Staffers Slam Hollywood Time's Up After Co-Founder Helped Advise Andrew Cuomo." *Breitbart*, August 12, 2021. https://www.breitbart.com/entertainment/2021/08/12/clients-staffers-slam-hollywood-times-up-after-co-founder-helped-advise-andrew-cuomo/.

29. "Trump Lawyer Confronts Trump Accuser E. Jean Carroll: Rape Allegations Similar to 'Law & Order: SVU' Episode." *Breitbart*, May 2, 2023. https://www.breitbart.com/politics/2023/05/02/trump-lawyer-confronts-trump-accuser-e-jean-carroll-rape-allegations-similar-to-law-order-svu-episode/.

30. "E. Jean Carroll v. Donald Trump 11/24/22." *DocumentCloud*. https://www.documentcloud.org/documents/23317687-e-jean-carroll-v-donald-trump-112422

31. Breuninger, Kevin. "Trump Suffers Big Loss in E. Jean Carroll Defamation Case; Judge Says He's Liable." *CNBC*, September 6, 2023. https://www.cnbc.com/2023/09/06/trump-suffers-big-loss-in-e-jean-carroll-defamation-case-judge-says-hes-liable.html

32. Live: Trump Appeals E. Jean Carroll Verdict." *BBC News*. https://www.bbc.co.uk/news/live/world-us-canada-68109585

33. "Trump's Appeal in E. Jean Carroll Case Rejected." *Axios*, April 25, 2024. https://www.axios.com/2024/04/25/trumps-appeal-e-jean-carroll-rejected

34. "Trump's Appeal in E. Jean Carroll Case Denied." *The New York Times*, December 30, 2024. https://www.nytimes.com/2024/12/30/nyregion/trump-carroll-appeal-denied.html

35. Pollak, Joel B. "Fact Check: George Stephanopoulos Lies About Trump and 'Rape.'" *Breitbart*, March 10, 2024. https://www.breitbart.com/the-media/2024/03/10/fact-check-george-stephanopoulos-lies-about-trump-and-rape

CHAPTER 4: A VICTIMLESS CRIME

1. @TrumpWarRoom. "Letitia James: 'The number one issue in this country is defeating Donald Trump. Nothing else matters.'" *X* (formerly Twitter), September 21, 2022. https://x.com/TrumpWarRoom/status/1572613244170240001

2. "For Tish James, a Steady Ascent Through New York Politics." *NY1*, October 30, 2021. https://ny1.com/nyc/all-boroughs/news/2021/10/30/for-tish-james—a-steady-ascent-through-new-york-politics.

3. "New Yorker's Choice for AG Boils Down to Litigation-Minded Public Advocate or Big Law Partner." *New York Law Journal*, September 14, 2018. https://www.law.com/newyorklawjournal/2018/09/14/new-yorkers-choice-for-ag-boils-down-to-litigation-minded-public-advocate-or-big-law-partner/.

4. "New Yorker's Choice for AG Boils Down to Litigation-Minded Public Advocate or Big Law Partner." *New York Law Journal*, September 14, 2018. https://www.law.com/newyorklawjournal/2018/09/14/new-yorkers-choice-for-ag-boils-down-to-litigation-minded-public-advocate-or-big-law-partner/.

5. Edelman, Adam. "Incoming New York Attorney General Plans Wide-Ranging Investigations into Trump." *NBC News*, December 12, 2018. https://www.nbcnews.com/politics/donald-trump/incoming-new-york-attorney-general-plans-wide-ranging-investigations-trump-n946706

6. Caplan, Joshua. "Letitia James Backs NYC Vaccine Mandate—and Wants a Statewide Mask Requirement." *Breitbart*, December 6, 2021. https://www.breitbart.com/politics/2021/12/06/letitia-james-backs-nyc-vaccine-mandate-and-wants-a-statewide-mask-requirement

7. "Letitia James Pushes NYPD Reforms." *The New York Times*, July 8, 2020. https://www.nytimes.com/2020/07/08/nyregion/letitia-james-nypd-reforms.html

8. "Letitia 'Tish' James on Becoming New York's Next Attorney General." *Ebony*, November 6, 2018. https://www.ebony.com/letitia-tish-james-on-becoming-new-yorks-next-attorney-general/

9. Knudsen, Hannah. "New York Attorney General Letitia James Hosts and Celebrates 'Drag Story Hour Read-a-Thon.'" *Breitbart*, March 20, 2023. https://www.breitbart.com/politics/2023/03/20/new-york-attorney-general-letitia-james-hosts-celebrates-drag-story-hour-read-a-thon/

10. Alafriz, Olivia. "As War Broke Out, Trump Focused on Tish James, N.Y. Fraud Trial." *Politico*, October 7, 2023. https://www.politico.com/news/2023/10/07/as-war-broke-out-trump-focused-on-letitia-james-n-y-fraud-trial-00120486

11. "Who Is Arthur Engoron? Judge Weighing Future of Donald Trump Empire Is Ivy League-Educated Ex-Cabbie." *AP News*, October 2, 2023. https://apnews.com/article/trump-engoron-letitia-james-fraud-new-york-9bd42690d327f6f63c9eb31c046f8426

12. Wallace, Danielle. "Judge Presiding over Trump's Manhattan Civil Trial Donated to Democrats." *Fox News*, October 3, 2023. https://www.foxnews.com/politics/judge-presiding-trumps-manhattan-civil-trial-donated-democrats

13. Knudsen, Hannah. "Angry Arthur Disrobed: Trump New York Trial Judge Posts Nude Bonus Torso Photo on HS Alumni Blog He Edits." *Breitbart*, November 9, 2023. https://www.breitbart.com/politics/2023/11/09/angry-arthur-disrobed-trump-new-york-trial-judge-posts-nude-bonus-torso-photo-on-hs-alumni-blog-he-edits/

14. Raw Story. "Judge in Trump Case Spotted Shirtless at Gym, Sparking Online Buzz." Accessed May 16, 2025. https://www.rawstory.com/arthur-engoron-shirtless

15. "Judge Rules Donald Trump Defrauded Banks, Insurers as He Built Real Estate Empire." *Breitbart*, September 26, 2023. https://www.breitbart.com/news/judge-rules-donald-trump-defrauded-banks-insurers-as-he-built-real-estate-empire/

16. "Trump Inflated His Total Assets When It Served His Purposes, Cohen Alleges in His Hearing, Citing Financial Documents." *The Washington Post*, February 27, 2019. https://www.washingtonpost.com/politics/trump

-inflated-his-total-assets-when-it-served-his-purposes-cohen-alleges-in-his
-hearing-citing-financial-documents/2019/02/27/4c41d4e2-3ab3-11e9
-a2cd-307b06d0257b_story.html

17. "Michael Cohen Sentenced to Jail." *Breitbart*, December 12, 2018. https://
www.breitbart.com/politics/2018/12/12/michael-cohen-sentenced-jail

18. "Donald Trump's Mar-a-Lago Is Worth Much More Than $18 Million, Real
Estate Experts Say." *The Wall Street Journal*, September 28, 2023. https://
www.wsj.com/real-estate/luxury-homes/donald-trump-mar-a-lago-worth
-71c278a1

19. "History of Mar-a-Lago." *The Mar-a-Lago Club*. Accessed May 16, 2025.
https://www.maralagoclub.com/history

20. "The Fascinating History of Mar-a-Lago." *Elle Decor*, October 2, 2023. https://
www.elledecor.com/celebrity-style/celebrity-homes/a63548843/mar-a-lago
-history

21. Associated Press. "Is Mar-a-Lago Worth $1 Billion? Trump's Winter Home
Valuations Are at the Core of His Fraud Trial." *NY1*, October 9, 2023.
https://ny1.com/nyc/all-boroughs/news/2023/10/09/is-mar-a-lago-worth—
1-billion—trump-s-winter-home-valuations-are-at-the-core-of-his-fraud
-trial.

22. Dixon-Hamilton, Jordan. "Donald Trump Called Democrat Operative Judge
in New York Fraud Case 'Disbarred.'" *Breitbart*, October 2, 2023. https://www
.breitbart.com/politics/2023/10/02/donald-trump-called-democrat-opera
tive-judge-new-york-fraud-case-disbarred/

23. Mordowanec, Nick. "Donald Trump Bankruptcy: Michael Cohen Fraud
Lawsuit." *Newsweek*, October 3, 2023. https://www.newsweek.com/donald
-trump-bankruptcy-michael-cohen-fraud-lawsuit-1830207

24. Dixon-Hamilton, Jordan. "Cohen: NY AG James Giving Trump 'Corporate Death Penalty.'" *Breitbart*, October 2, 2023. https://www.breitbart.com
/clips/2023/10/02/cohen-ny-ag-james-giving-trump-corporate-death-pen
alty/

25. Campanile, Carl. "Judge Muzzles Trump After Social Media Post About
Court Clerk." *New York Post*, October 3, 2023. https://nypost.com/2023/10/03
/judge-muzzles-trump-after-social-media-post-about-court-clerk/

26. Dixon-Hamilton, Jordan. "Complaint Calls for Trump New York Trial
Judge's Clerk to Be Disbarred for Excessive Political Donations." *Breitbart*,
November 2, 2023. https://www.breitbart.com/politics/2023/11/02/com
plaint-calls-for-trump-new-york-trial-judges-clerk-to-be-disbarred-for-ex
cessive-political-donations/

27. Tolan, Casey. "Facts First: What to Know About Closing Arguments in Trump's
Civil Fraud Trial." *CNN*, January 11, 2024. https://www.cnn.com/2024/01/11
/politics/facts-first-donald-trump-civil-trial-closing-arguments/index.html

28. Mordowanec, Nick. "Judge Engoron's Wife's Alleged Anti-Trump Posts Go
Viral." *Newsweek*, January 12, 2024. https://www.newsweek.com/donald
-trump-judge-engoron-wife-attacks-1848282

29. Klasfeld, Adam (@KlasfeldReports). "Engoron says he never saw the meme
at the heart of the controversy and attributes it to a 'conspiracy theory.'" *X*
(formerly Twitter), November 6, 2023. https://x.com/KlasfeldReports/status
/1721556796186255604

30. Peltz, Jennifer. "Deutsche Bank Was Keen to Land a 'Whale' of a Client in Trump, Documents at Civil Fraud Trial Show." *PBS NewsHour*, January 11, 2024. https://www.pbs.org/newshour/politics/deutsche-bank-was-keen-to -land-a-whale-of-a-client-in-trump-documents-at-civil-fraud-trial-show

31. Protess, Ben and Jonah E. Bromwich. "Trump Fraud Trial Hinges on Century-Old New York Law." *The New York Times*, February 16, 2024. https://www .nytimes.com/2024/02/16/nyregion/trump-fraud-trial-ny-law.html

32. Worldometer. "GDP by Country." Accessed May 16, 2025. https://www.world ometers.info/gdp/gdp-by-country/.

33. Gregorian, Dareh. "NY AG Calls for $370 Million Fine, Trump Lifetime Ban from Real Estate Industry." *NBC News*, February 16, 2024. https://www.nbc news.com/politics/donald-trump/ny-ag-calls-370-million-fine-trump-life time-ban-real-estate-industry-rcna132540

34. Protess, Ben and Jonah E. Bromwich. "Trump Civil Fraud Trial: Judge Issues Ruling." *The New York Times*, February 16, 2024. https://www.nytimes .com/2024/02/16/nyregion/trump-civil-fraud-trial-ruling.html

35. Mordowanec, Nick. "Letitia James's Courtroom Smile Compared to Donald Trump Jr. Goes Viral." *Newsweek*, February 16, 2024. https://www.newsweek .com/letitia-james-courtroom-smile-compared-donald-trump-jr-goes-viral -1843283

36. Turley, Jonathan. "Turley on Trump Civil Trial: 'At Some Point, New Yorkers Have to Wonder, Is This What We Want from a Legal System?'" *RealClearPolitics*, February 16, 2024. https://www.realclearpolitics.com/video/2024/02/16 /turley_on_trump_civil_trial_at_some_point_new_yorkers_have_to_won der_is_this_what_we_want_from_a_legal_system.html.

37. Dixon-Hamilton, Jordan. "NY Attorney General Letitia James Gloats after Fining Trump $354.8M." *Breitbart*, February 27, 2024. https://www.breitbart .com/politics/2024/02/27/ny-attorney-general-letitia-james-gloats-fining -trump-354-8m/

38. Dixon-Hamilton, Jordan. "Letitia James Says She'll Seize Trump's Assets If He Can't Pay $354M Fine." *Breitbart*, February 21, 2024. https://www.breitbart .com/politics/2024/02/21/letitia-james-says-shell-seize-trumps-assets-if-he -cant-pay-354m-fine/.

39. Dixon-Hamilton, Jordan. "Trump Must Pay Half a Billion Dollars Before He Can Appeal New York Decision." *Breitbart*, February 19, 2024. https://www .breitbart.com/politics/2024/02/19/trump-must-pay-half-a-billion-dollars -before-he-can-appeal-new-york-decision/

40. Dixon-Hamilton, Jordan. "Media: Trump Wins Crucial, Unexpected Victory in Bond Ruling." *Breitbart*, March 25, 2024. https://www.breitbart.com/pol itics/2024/03/25/media-trump-wins-crucial-unexpected-victory-bond-rul ing/

41. Katersky, Aaron and Peter Charalambous. "New York AG to Continue to Pursue $454 Million Civil Judgment Against Trump." *ABC News*, March 25, 2024. https://abcnews.go.com/US/new-york-ag-continue-pursue-454-mil lion-civil/story?id=116639628

42. Klukowski, Ken. "Donald Trump Should Appeal Unconstitutional Civil Fraud Fine All the Way to U.S. Supreme Court." *Breitbart*, March 25, 2024. https://www.breitbart.com/politics/2024/03/25/klukowski-donald-trump

-should-appeal-unconstitutional-civil-fraud-fine-all-the-way-to-u-s-supreme
-court/

43. Nelson, David. "Trump Administration Refers NY AG Tish James for Prosecution." *New York Post*, April 15, 2025. https://nypost.com/2025/04/15/us
-news/trump-administration-refers-ny-ag-tish-james-for-prosecution/

44. Nelson, David. "Trump Administration Refers NY AG Tish James for Prosecution." *New York Post*, April 15, 2025. https://nypost.com/2025/04/15/us
-news/trump-administration-refers-ny-ag-tish-james-for-prosecution/

45. Weiser, Benjamin. "Read the Letter from NY AG Letitia James to AG Ashley
Moody." *New York Times*, April 24, 2025. https://www.nytimes.com/interac
tive/2025/04/24/us/nyag-james-letter-to-ag-bondi.html

46. Nelson, David. "Trump Administration Refers NY AG Tish James for Prosecution." *New York Post*, April 15, 2025. https://nypost.com/2025/04/15/us
-news/trump-administration-refers-ny-ag-tish-james-for-prosecution/

CHAPTER 5: THE CONSPIRACY TO PROVE A CONSPIRACY

1. Collinson, Stephen. "Transcript: Trump Pressured Georgia Secretary of State
to 'Find' Votes." *CNN*, January 3, 2021. https://www.cnn.com/2021/01/03
/politics/trump-brad-raffensperger-phone-call-transcript/index.html

2. Nolte, John. "Washington Post Admits Trump's 'Find the Fraud' Quote Was
Fake News." *Breitbart*, March 15, 2021. https://www.breitbart.com/the-me
dia/2021/03/15/washington-post-admits-trumps-find-the-fraud-quote-was
-fake-news/

3. Giaritelli, Anna. "Media Misquoted Trump in Notorious Phone Call with
Georgia Investigator." *Washington Examiner*, March 15, 2021. https://www
.washingtonexaminer.com/news/1919792/media-misquoted-trump-in-no
torious-phone-call-with-georgia-investigator/

4. Scanlan, Quinn. "Trump Demands Georgia Secretary of State 'Find' Votes by
Hand." *ABC News*, January 4, 2021. https://abcnews.go.com/Politics/trump
-demands-georgia-secretary-state-find-votes-hand/story?id=75027350.

5. Halpert, Madeline. "Donald Trump: Georgia Prosecutors Interview Witnesses
in Criminal Probe." *BBC*, August 9, 2023. https://www.bbc.com/news/world-us
-canada-66443921

6. Bluestein, Greg. "Who Is John Clifford Floyd III, Father of DA Fani Willis?"
Atlanta Journal-Constitution, August 15, 2023. https://www.ajc.com/politics
/who-is-john-clifford-floyd-iii-father-of-da-fani-willis/JPLLXJFEHRH7B
K42AVD35V2YUQ/

7. Snead, Jason. "Connecting the Dots Between Fani Willis and Unrepentant
Communists." *The Heritage Foundation*, February 21, 2024. https://www.heri
tage.org/progressivism/commentary/connecting-the-dots-between-fani-wil
lis-and-unrepentant-communists

8. Peltz, Jennifer. "Fani Willis's Father Testifies: Didn't Know About Her Relationship with Prosecutor." *PBS NewsHour*, February 16, 2024. https://www
.pbs.org/newshour/politics/fani-willis-father-testifies-he-didnt-know-until
-recently-about-her-relationship-with-prosecutor

9. Redmon, Jeremy. "Trump, 18 Others Indicted for Trying to Overthrow
2020 Georgia Election." *Atlanta Journal-Constitution*, August 14, 2023.

https://www.ajc.com/politics/trump-18-others-indicted-for-trying-to-over throw-2020-georgia-election/PQ3N2YBIDRDJFLJGFLEBZUWM6I/

10. Boyle, Matthew. "Georgia Grand Jury Returns 10 Indictments in Trump 2020 Election Investigation." *Breitbart*, August 14, 2023. https://www.bre itbart.com/politics/2023/08/14/georgia-grand-jury-returns-10-indict ments-in-trump-2020-election-investigation/

11. Price, Greg (@greg_price11). "BREAKING: Trump and 18 Others In- dicted in Georgia." *X* (formerly Twitter), August 14, 2023. https://x.com/greg _price11/status/1691255739719835649

12. Mitchell, Ian. "Mitchell: On Fani Willis—A Strong Black Woman Standing Up to Donald Trump Is Something to Behold." *Breitbart*, August 15, 2023. https://www.breitbart.com/clips/2023/08/15/mitchell-on-fani-willis-strong -black-woman-standing-up-to-donald-trump-is-something-to-behold/

13. McCaskill, Claire. "McCaskill: We Finally Have Rudy Giuliani Indicted—'Woo Hoo!' " *Breitbart*, August 15, 2023. https://www.breitbart.com/clips/2023/08/15 /mccaskill-we-finally-have-rudy-giuliani-indicted-woo-hoo/

14. Jansa, Cameron. "Radical Georgia D.A. Fani Willis Launched Reelection Fundraising Site Days Before Trump Indictment." *Breitbart*, August 15, 2023. https://www.breitbart.com/2024-election/2023/08/15/radical-georgia-d-a -fani-willis-launched-reelection-fundraising-site-days-before-trump-indict ment/

15. Boyle, Matthew. "Trump Attorneys: Georgia Indictment 'As Flawed and Un- constitutional as This Entire Process.'" *Breitbart*, August 14, 2023. https:// www.breitbart.com/politics/2023/08/14/trump-attorneys-georgia-indict ment-as-flawed-and-unconstitutional-as-this-entire-process/

16. Montellaro, Zach. "Trump's Mug Shot Fuels a Fundraising Bonanza." *Politico*, August 26, 2023. https://www.politico.com/news/2023/08/26/trump-mug shot-fundraising-00113118

17. Dorman, Sam. "Trump: Georgia Booking Was 'Terrible Experience,' It's Elec- tion Interference." *Breitbart*, August 24, 2023. https://www.breitbart.com /clips/2023/08/24/trump-georgia-booking-was-terrible-experience-its-elec tion-interference/.

18. Gillespie, Nick. "Trump and 18 Others Charged with Election-Related Crimes in Georgia." *Reason*, August 15, 2023. https://reason.com/2023/08/15/trump -and-18-others-charged-with-election-related-crimes-in-georgia/

19. Marlow, Alex. *Breaking the News: Exposing The Establishment Media's Hidden Deals and Secret Corruption.* (Simon & Schuster, 2021). Chapter 8.

20. Cheney, Kyle. "See the 1960 Electoral College certificates that the false Trump electors say justify their gambit." *Politico*, February 7, 2022. https://www.po litico.com/news/2022/02/07/1960-electoral-college-certificates-false-trump -electors-00006186.

21. Cheney, Kyle. "Trump Allies Handed Fake Electoral Certificates to National Archives in December 2020." *Politico*, February 7, 2022. https://www.politico .com/news/2022/02/07/1960-electoral-college-certificates-false-trump-elec tors-00006186

22. Murray, Sara. "John Eastman Disbarment Trial Ends as Judge Weighs Fate of Trump Ally." *CNN*, May 2, 2024. https://www.cnn.com/2024/05/02/politics /john-eastman-law-license/index.html

23. Breitbart. "Biden, Democrats Assemble 600 Lawyers to Fight Election 'Chicanery.'" *Breitbart*, July 2, 2020. https://www.breitbart.com/2020-election/2020/07/02/biden-democrats-assemble-600-lawyers-to-fight-election-chicanery.

24. Lynch, Timothy. "RICO and the Man." *Reason*, March 1, 1990. https://reason.com/1990/03/01/rico-and-the-man/

25. Charalambous, Peter. "In charging Trump with RICO crimes, Georgia prosecutors reach for a familiar tool." *ABC News*, August 14, 2023.

26. Mallin, Alexander. "Charging Trump with RICO Crimes: Georgia Prosecutors Reach for Familiar Tool." *ABC News*, August 15, 2023. https://abcnews.go.com/Politics/charging-trump-rico-crimes-georgia-prosecutors-reach-familiar/story?id=102105196

27. Boyle, Matthew. "Embattled Special Prosecutor in Trump Case Nathan Wade Allegedly Billed Fani Willis's Office $6K for 24 Hours of Work in 1 Day." *Breitbart*, January 12, 2024. https://www.breitbart.com/2024-election/2024/01/12/embattled-special-prosecutor-in-trump-case-nathan-wade-allegedly-billed-fani-williss-office-6k-for-24-hours-of-work-in-1-day/; Boyle, Matthew. " 'Sugar Mama': Fani Willis Paid Inexperienced Alleged Lover More Than Top Lawyer in Trump Prosecution." *Breitbart*, January 16, 2024. https://www.breitbart.com/politics/2024/01/16/sugar-mama-fani-willis-paid-inexperienced-alleged-lover-more-than-top-lawyer-in-trump-prosecution/.

28. Bluestein, Greg. "Filing Alleges Improper Relationship Between Fulton DA and Top Trump Prosecutor." *Atlanta Journal-Constitution*, January 8, 2024. https://www.ajc.com/politics/breaking-filing-alleges-improper-relationship-between-fulton-da-top-trump-prosecutor/A2N2OWCM7FFWJBQH2ORAK2BKMQ/

29. State of Georgia. *Filing in Georgia v. Trump: Motion to Dismiss Based on Improper Relationship Between District Attorney and Special Prosecutor.* January 2024. https://static01.nyt.com/newsgraphics/documenttools/41940dd55b533f11/20adae2b-full.pdf

30. Sneed, Tierney. "How Georgia Prosecutors Built a Case Against Trump over the 2020 Election." *Politico*, January 10, 2024. https://www.politico.com/news/2024/01/10/jan-6-georgia-trump-probe-00134941

31. Boyle, Matthew. "Report: Fani Willis Visited White House for Five-Hour Meeting with Kamala Harris before Indicting Donald Trump." *Breitbart*, January 10, 2024. https://www.breitbart.com/politics/2024/01/10/report-fani-willis-visited-white-house-for-five-hour-meeting-with-kamala-harris-before-indicting-donald-trump/.

32. Boyle, Matthew. "Exclusive: Partner of Fani Willis's Deputy Jeff DiSantis Works with Biden 2024 Campaign." *Breitbart*, March 3, 2024. https://www.breitbart.com/politics/2024/03/03/exclusive-partner-of-fani-williss-deputy-jeff-disantis-works-with-biden-2024-campaign/; Boyle, Matthew. "Exclusive: Former Biden Aide Paid Fani Willis's Deputy Jeff DiSantis $131K in 2023." *Breitbart*, February 29, 2024. https://www.breitbart.com/politics/2024/02/29/exclusive-former-biden-aide-paid-fani-williss-deputy-jeff-disantis-131k-2023

33. Jansa, Cameron. "Exclusive: Biden Admin Planted Operative Jeff DiSantis in Fani Willis's Office to Target Trump, Sources Say." *Breitbart*, February 26, 2024. https://www.breitbart.com/2024-election/2024/02/26/exclusive-biden

-admin-planted-operative-jeff-disantis-fani-willis-office-target-trump
-sources-say/

34. Fulton County Government. "Jeff DiSantis – Media Relations Division." *FultonCountyGA.gov*. Accessed May 16, 2025. https://www.fultoncountyga.gov
/inside-fulton-county/fulton-county-departments/district-attorney/da-exec
utive-team/media-relations-division/jeff-disantis

35. State of Georgia. *Georgia v. Trump: Order on Special Demurrers*. March 2024.
https://www.documentcloud.org/documents/24478989-georgia-v-trump
-order-on-special-demurrers/

36. Gregorian, Dareh. "Georgia Judge Allows Most Charges in Trump Election
Case to Stand." *NBC News*, March 15, 2024. https://www.nbcnews.com/poli
tics/donald-trump/fani-willis-trump-georgia-rcna139810

37. Weissmann, Andrew. "Weissmann: GA Ruling a 'Huge Body Blow' to Fani
Willis, 'She Should Recuse Herself'." *Breitbart*, March 15, 2024. https://www
.breitbart.com/clips/2024/03/15/weissmann-ga-ruling-huge-body-blow-to
-fani-willis-she-should-recuse-herself/

38. Toobin, Jeffrey. "CNN's Toobin: 'Good Day for Trump,' Fani Willis Case Is
'Going Nowhere'." *Breitbart*, March 15, 2024. https://www.breitbart.com
/clips/2024/03/15/cnns-toobin-good-day-for-trump-fani-willis-case-is-go
ing-nowhere

39. Watson, David. "How Can You Not Hit That? Nathan Wade Discusses Fani
Willis Relationship in Bizarre Daily Show Interview." *Breitbart*, June 20, 2024.
https://www.breitbart.com/entertainment/2024/06/20/how-can-you-not-hit
-that-nathan-wade-discusses-fani-willis-relationship-in-bizarre-daily
-show-interview/

40. Georgia Court of Appeals. *State of Georgia v. Donald J. Trump: Appellate
Filing—Bond Ruling*. Filed March 2024. https://efast.gaappeals.us/down
load?filingId=39918e55-241a-4fd9-802d-7c4fb9f7921a

CHAPTER 6: DEPARTMENT OF INJUSTICE

1. Dawsey, Josh. "Biden's Lonely Battle to Sell American Democracy." *Washington Post*, December 28, 2024. https://www.washingtonpost.com/poli
tics/2024/12/28/bidens-lonely-battle-to-sell-american-democracy/

2. Stancil, Kenny. "Biden Revolvers: Lisa Monaco." *Revolving Door Project*. Accessed May 16, 2025. https://therevolvingdoorproject.org/biden
-revolvers-lisa-monaco/

3. Boyle, Matthew. "Exclusive: Donald Trump Deputy Attorney General
Lisa Monaco Is 'Really Running' the Justice Department." *Breitbart*, January 10, 2024. https://www.breitbart.com/politics/2024/01/10/exclusive-don
ald-trump-deputy-attorney-general-lisa-monaco-is-really-running-the
-justice-department/.

4. Neidig, Harper. "Biden DOJ Nominee Apologizes for Harsh Rhetoric amid
GOP Criticism." *The Hill*, March 9, 2021. https://thehill.com/regulation
/administration/542342-biden-doj-nominee-apologizes-for-harsh-rhetoric
-amid-gop-criticism/

5. Multiple authors. "Six Pro-Life Activists Found Guilty, Face 11 Years in Prison
for Peaceful Protest." *Breitbart*, January 30, 2024. https://www.breitbart.com

/politics/2024/01/30/six-pro-life-activists-found-guilty-face-11-years-in
-prison-for-peaceful-protest/

6. Multiple authors. "More Pro-Life Activists Sentenced to Years Behind Bars, Including Veteran, Elderly Women." *Breitbart*, May 15, 2024. https://www .breitbart.com/politics/2024/05/15/more-pro-life-activists-sentenced-years -behind-bars-including-veteran-elderly-women/

7. Levine, Rachel. "Abortion Arson Attack in Wisconsin Claimed by 'Jane's Revenge'." *The Guardian*, May 10, 2022. https://www.theguardian.com/us -news/2022/may/10/abortion-arson-attack-wisconsin-pro-choice-janes-re venge

8. Multiple authors. "Summer of Rage, Part VI: Biden Administration Ignores Systematic Attack on Religious Communities in Wake of Dobbs Leak." *Breit- bart*, August 20, 2022. https://www.breitbart.com/politics/2022/08/20 /summer-of-rage-part-vi-biden-administration-ignores-systematic-attack -on-religious-communities-in-wake-of-dobbs-leak/

9. Multiple authors. "Summer of Rage, Part I: Militant Pro-Abortion Radicals Flourish in Madison, Wisconsin, Violence Memed on Twitter." *Breitbart*, July 24, 2022. https://www.breitbart.com/politics/2022/07/24/summer-of -rage-part-i-militant-pro-abortion-radicals-flourish-in-madison-wisconsin -violence-memed-on-twitter/.

10. Boyle, Matthew. "Exclusive: Donald Trump Deputy Attorney General Lisa Monaco Is 'Really Running' the Justice Department." *Breitbart*, Janu- ary 10, 2024. https://www.breitbart.com/politics/2024/01/10/exclusive-don ald-trump-deputy-attorney-general-lisa-monaco-is-really-running-the -justice-department/

11. Multiple authors. "FBI Raids Former President Donald Trump's Home." *Breit- bart*, August 8, 2022. https://www.breitbart.com/politics/2022/08/08/fbi -raids-former-president-donald-trumps-home

12. Multiple authors. "Exclusive: Jordan Blasts Blinken's Response on Letter Un- dermining Hunter Biden Story: 'He Continues to Deflect'." *Breitbart*, June 27, 2023. https://www.breitbart.com/politics/2023/06/27/exclusive-jordan-blasts -blinkens-response-on-letter-undermining-hunter-biden-story-he-contin ues-to-deflect/

13. U.S. House Judiciary Committee. "New Testimony Reveals Secretary Blinken and Biden Campaign Behind Infamous Intel Letter." *House.gov*, May 2023. https://judiciary.house.gov/media/press-releases/new-testimony-reveals-sec retary-blinken-and-biden-campaign-behind-infamous

14. Brown, Julie K. "Deflecting blame, Acosta pointed finger at others. Why they may have some explaining to do." *Miami Herald*, July 14, 2019. https://www .miamiherald.com/news/state/florida/article232595847.html

15. Rohrer, Gray. "Judge Who Approved FBI Raid on Mar-a-Lago Once Linked to Jeffrey Epstein." *New York Post*, August 9, 2022. https://nypost .com/2022/08/09/judge-who-approved-fbi-raid-on-mar-a-lago-once-linked -to-jeffrey-epstein/

16. Trump, Melania. *Melania Trump Responds to FBI Search of Wardrobe*. You- Tube, uploaded by Sky News Australia, August 2022. https://www.youtube .com/watch?v=Vzf-Clwf7XM.

17. Radar Online Staff. "Melania Trump Buys New Underwear After FBI Raid." *Radar Online*, August 10, 2022. https://radaronline.com/p/melania-trump-new-underwear-fbi-search

18. Multiple authors. "FBI Blasted for 'Staged' Photo of Documents Seized in Mar-a-Lago Raid." *Breitbart*, August 31, 2022. https://www.breitbart.com/politics/2022/08/31/fbi-blasted-for-staged-photo-of-documents-seized-in-mar-a-lago-raid/

19. Multiple authors. "FBI Agents Were Authorized to Use Deadly Force at Mar-a-Lago When Seizing Documents." *Breitbart*, May 22, 2024. https://www.breitbart.com/politics/2024/05/22/fbi-agents-were-authorized-use-deadly-force-mar-a-lago-when-seizing-documents/

20. Multiple authors. "FBI Found Secret Documents at Trump's Mar-a-Lago Residence." *NewsNation*, May 2024. https://www.newsnationnow.com/trump-investigation/secret-documents-donald-trump/.

21. Goodreads. "In Politics, Nothing Happens by Accident. If It Happens, You Can Bet It Was Planned That Way." Accessed May 16, 2025. https://www.goodreads.com/quotes/6030617-in-politics-nothing-happens-by-accident-if-it-happens-you.

22. White House. "Remarks by President Biden in Press Conference." *WhiteHouse.gov*, November 9, 2022. https://www.whitehouse.gov/briefing-room/speeches-remarks/2022/11/09/remarks-by-president-biden-in-press-conference-8

23. Dawsey, Josh. "Biden's Lonely Battle to Sell American Democracy." *Washington Post*, December 28, 2024. https://www.washingtonpost.com/politics/2024/12/28/bidens-lonely-battle-to-sell-american-democracy

24. Multiple authors. "Jim Jordan: Special Counsel Jack Smith Tried to Target Conservatives During Obama IRS Scandal." *Breitbart*, November 21, 2022. https://www.breitbart.com/politics/2022/11/21/jim-jordan-special-counsel-jack-smith-tried-to-find-ways-to-target-conservatives-during-obama-irs-scandal/

25. Multiple authors. "Supreme Court Throws Out McDonnell's Federal Conviction." *Breitbart*, June 27, 2016. https://www.breitbart.com/politics/2016/06/27/supreme-court-throws-out-mcdonnells-federal-conviction//

26. Hume, Tim. "Ex-Virginia Gov Who Saw Conviction by Jack Smith Thrown out Says He'd Rather Win than Get It Right." *Fox News*, June 2023. https://www.foxnews.com/media/ex-virginia-gov-who-saw-conviction-by-jack-smith-thrown-out-says-hed-rather-win-than-get-it-right

27. Feuer, Alan. "How Jack Smith's View of the Presidency Could Shape the Trump Trials." *New York Times*, January 14, 2025. https://www.nytimes.com/2025/01/14/us/politics/jack-smith-trump-presidents.html

28. Multiple authors. "US Sanctions ICC Chief Prosecutor over Israel Investigations." *Breitbart*, May 2024. https://www.breitbart.com/news/us-sanctions-icc-chief-prosecutor-over-israel-investigations/

29. Multiple authors. "Israel Calls on All Civilized Nations to Oppose 'Outrageous' ICC Warrants." *Breitbart*, May 21, 2024. https://www.breitbart.com/middle-east/2024/05/21/israel-calls-on-all-civilized-nations-to-oppose-outrageous-icc-warrants/

30. Savage, Charlie. "Jack Smith, Special Counsel for Trump Inquiries, Has Long Career Prosecuting Public Corruption." *New York Times*, November 19, 2022.

https://www.nytimes.com/2022/11/19/us/politics/jack-smith-trump-special
-counsel.html

31. Wolfe, Kristina Cooke. " 'Fearless' Special Counsel Jack Smith Arrives in Washington to Lead Trump Probes." *Reuters*, January 4, 2023. https://www.reuters.com/world/us/fearless-special-counsel-jack-smith-arrives-washington-lead-trump-probes-2023-01-04/

32. Multiple authors. "49-Page Indictment of Donald Trump Unsealed." *Breitbart*, June 9, 2023. https://www.breitbart.com/politics/2023/06/09/49-page-indictment-of-donald-trump-unsealed/

33. Multiple authors. "Trump Could Face 400 Years in Prison If Convicted on All Federal Charges." *Breitbart*, June 9, 2023. https://www.breitbart.com/politics/2023/06/09/trump-could-face-400-years-in-prison-if-convicted-on-all-federal-charges/

34. Breuninger, Kevin. "Third Defendant Added to Trump Classified Documents Case." *CNBC*, July 27, 2023. https://www.cnbc.com/2023/07/27/third-defendant-added-to-trump-classified-documents-case.html

35. Breuninger, Kevin. "Third Defendant Added to Trump Classified Documents Case." *CNBC*, July 27, 2023. https://www.cnbc.com/2023/07/27/third-defendant-added-to-trump-classified-documents-case.html

36. Post Millennial. "Video Commentary on Trump Charges." *X* (formerly Twitter), June 2023. https://x.com/TPostMillennial/status/1668789917298688000

37. Multiple authors. "Gaetz Demands Answers: Trump Prosecutor Karen Gilbert Donated to Obama, Biden, Democrats." *Breitbart*, June 13, 2023. https://www.breitbart.com/podcast/2023/06/13/gaetz-demands-answers-trump-prosecutor-karen-gilbert-donated-to-obama-biden-democrats/

38. Visser, Nick. "Justice Department Prosecutor for Trump Cases Donated Thousands to Biden, Democrats." *Washington Examiner*, June 2023. https://www.washingtonexaminer.com/news/128788/justice-department-prosecutor-for-trump-cases-donated-thousands-to-biden-democrats

39. Multiple authors. "Wife of Special Counsel in Trump Probe Contributed to Campaigns of Joe Biden, Rashida Tlaib." *Breitbart*, November 21, 2022. https://www.breitbart.com/politics/2022/11/21/wife-special-counsel-trump-probe-contributed-campaigns-joe-biden-rashida-tlaib/

40. Multiple authors. "Trump Trashes Special Counsel Jack Smith's Wife's Michelle Obama Netflix Documentary: 'The Reviews Are Even Worse.'" *Breitbart*, June 14, 2023. https://www.breitbart.com/entertainment/2023/06/14/trump-trashes-special-counsel-jack-smiths-wifes-michelle-obama-netflix-documentary-the-reviews-are-even-worse/

41. Campanile, Carl. "Biden Staffers Met with Special Counsel Jack Smith's Aides before Trump Indictment." *New York Post*, August 26, 2023. https://nypost.com/2023/08/26/biden-staffers-met-with-special-counsel-jack-smiths-aides-before-trump-indictment/

42. Trump Legal Team. *Trump Request for Recusal of Judge Chutkan*, filed August 2023. https://s3.documentcloud.org/documents/23963171/trump-request-for-recusal-of-judge-chutkan.pdf

43. Kelly, Julie. "Judge Tanya Chutkan's Anti-Trump Sentencing Exposed." *X* (formerly Twitter), August 29, 2023. https://x.com/julie_kelly2/status/1696350705357824172

44. Multiple authors. "Donald Trump Shares Revealing Quote from Judge Overseeing January 6 Case: 'She Obviously Wants Me behind Bars.'" *Breitbart*, August 14, 2023. https://www.breitbart.com/politics/2023/08/14/donald-trump-shares-revealing-quote-from-judge-overseeing-january-6-case-she-obviously-wants-me-behind-bars/

45. Multiple authors. "Judge Tanya Chutkan Refuses to Recuse Herself from Donald Trump's January 6 Case." *Breitbart*, September 27, 2023. https://www.breitbart.com/politics/2023/09/27/judge-tanya-chutkan-refuses-recuse-herself-donald-trumps-january-6-case/

46. Multiple authors. "Trump's 25% 2005 Tax Rate Much Higher Than Normal—Even for the Wealthy." *Breitbart*, March 15, 2017. https://www.breitbart.com/politics/2017/03/15/trumps-25-2005-tax-rate-much-higher-normal-even-wealthy/

47. Multiple authors. "Court Blocks Release of Trump Tax Returns amid Latest Appeal." *Breitbart*, September 1, 2020. https://www.breitbart.com/politics/2020/09/01/court-blocks-release-of-trump-tax-returns-amid-latest-appeal/

48. Multiple authors. "Supreme Court (7–2): House Cannot Force Trump to Provide Tax Returns." *Breitbart*, July 9, 2020. https://www.breitbart.com/politics/2020/07/09/supreme-court-7-2-house-cannot-force-trump-to-provide-tax-returns/

49. Multiple authors. "8 Cases Where Mishandling of Classified Information Went Unpunished." *Breitbart*, June 24, 2023. https://www.breitbart.com/politics/2023/06/24/8-cases-where-mishandling-of-classified-information-went-unpunished/

50. Mallin, Alexander. "Hillary Clinton Jokes about Wiping Email Server: 'Like with a Cloth?'" *ABC News*, August 18, 2015. https://abcnews.go.com/Politics/hillary-clinton-jokes-wiping-email-server-cloth/story?id=33165517

51. Multiple authors. "8 Cases Where Mishandling of Classified Information Went Unpunished." *Breitbart*, June 24, 2023. https://www.breitbart.com/politics/2023/06/24/8-cases-where-mishandling-of-classified-information-went-unpunished/

52. Multiple authors. "University Housing Biden's Think Tank Recently Experienced a Surge of Chinese Donations, Records Show." *Fox News*, January 2023. https://www.foxnews.com/politics/university-housing-bidens-think-tank-recently-experienced-a-surge-of-chinese-donations-records-show

53. Multiple authors. "America First Legal: Obama Foundation Likely Stored Classified Docs Illegally." *Breitbart*, May 5, 2023. https://www.breitbart.com/politics/2023/05/05/america-first-legal-obama-foundation-likely-stored-classified-docs-illegally/

54. Jost, Kenneth. "Obama Administration Plugs Leaks, Prosecutes Leakers." *Reporters Committee for Freedom of the Press*, Fall 2011. https://www.rcfp.org/journals/obama-administration-plugs/

55. Associated Press. "Democratic Sen. Feinstein Suggests Some Leaked Info Came from the White House." *Fox News*, June 2013. https://www.foxnews.com/politics/democratic-sen-feinstein-suggests-some-leaked-info-came-from-the-white-house

56. Gerstein, Josh. "DOJ Watchdog Finds Comey Violated Policies with Private Memos about Trump." *Politico*, August 29, 2019. https://www.politico.com

/story/2019/08/29/doj-watchdog-finds-comey-violated-policies-with-pri vate-memos-about-trump-1477698

57. Gregorian, Dareh. "DOJ Closes Pence Classified Documents Investigation, No Charges." *NBC News*, June 2, 2023. https://www.nbcnews.com/politics /doj-closes-pence-classified-documents-investigation-no-charges-rcna87396

58. McNeal, Gregory. "Leon Panetta Revealed Top Secret Information about Bin Laden Raid." *Forbes*, December 11, 2013. https://www.forbes.com/sites /gregorymcneal/2013/12/11/leon-panetta-revealed-top-secret-information -about-bin-laden-raid/

59. Wilson, Joseph C. "The Politics of Truth." *The Spectacle*, August 2004. https:// www.spectacle.org/0804/wilson.html

60. U.S. House of Representatives. *Report on Sandy Berger's Unauthorized Removal of Classified Documents*. 2007. https://irp.fas.org/congress/2007_rpt /berger.pdf

61. Multiple authors. "Why Was This Posted? FBI Seizure of Classified Docs from Trump Has Precedent in LBJ's Secret Files." *Free Republic*, July 2004. https:// freerepublic.com/focus/f-news/1176125/posts

62. Grim, Ryan. "Trump's FBI Mar-a-Lago Search Echoes Another President's Secrets." *The Intercept*, August 11, 2022. https://theintercept.com/2022/08/11 /trump-fbi-mar-a-lago-classified-documents-lbj/

63. Miller Center. "Johnsons' Secret White House Recordings: Collection Specifications." *Miller Center of Public Affairs, University of Virginia*. https://miller center.org/johnson-secret-white-house-recordings-collection-specifications

64. Barr, Luke. "Trump Heard on Audio Recording Discussing Secret Information and Declassifying Documents." *ABC News*, June 2023. https://abcnews .go.com/US/secret-information-trump-audio-recording-talks-declassify ing-documents/story?id=99960824

65. Gerstein, Josh. "Legal Experts Dissect Mueller Report." *Politico Magazine*, April 19, 2019. https://www.politico.com/magazine/story/2019/04/19/muel ler-report-analysis-legal-experts-226662/

66. United States v. Curtiss-Wright Export Corp., 299 U.S. 304 (1936). *Justia US Supreme Court Center*. https://supreme.justia.com/cases/federal/us/283/25/

67. Multiple authors. "Jack Smith's Special Counsel Appointment Is Unconstitutional, Former Attorney General Tells Supreme Court." *Breitbart*, December 20, 2023. Multiple authors. "Hearing Scheduled in Trump's Classified Documents Case Could Invalidate Jack Smith's Appointment." *Breitbart*, June 5, 2024. https://www.breitbart.com/politics/2023/12/20/jack -smiths-special-counsel-appointment-is-unconstitutional-former-attor ney-general-tells-supreme-court/

68. Multiple authors. "NBC Legal Analyst Tells Liberals to File Complaints against Judge Cannon." *Breitbart*, June 4, 2024. https://www.breitbart.com /the-media/2024/06/04/watch-nbc-legal-analyst-glenn-kirschner-tells-liber als-to-file-complaints-against-judge-cannon/

69. Multiple authors. "NBC Legal Analyst Tells Liberals to File Complaints against Judge Cannon." *Breitbart*, June 4, 2024. https://www.breitbart.com /the-media/2024/06/04/watch-nbc-legal-analyst-glenn-kirschner-tells-liber als-to-file-complaints-against-judge-cannon/

70. Multiple authors. "Supreme Court: Government Cannot Abuse 'Enron Law' to Prosecute Jan. 6 Defendants, Including Trump." *Breitbart*, June 28, 2024. https://www.breitbart.com/politics/2024/06/28/supreme-court-says-govern ment-cannot-abuse-enron-law-to-prosecute-jan-6-defendants-including -trump/

71. Multiple authors. "Justice Thomas Questions Legality of Jack Smith's Appointment in Potential Roadmap for Judge Cannon." *Breitbart*, July 1, 2024. https://www.breitbart.com/politics/2024/07/01/justice-thomas-questions-le gality-of-jack-smiths-appointment-in-potential-roadmap-for-judge-cannon/

72. Balsamo, Michael. "Trump's Classified Documents Case Grows as Special Counsel Jack Smith Presses Ahead." *Associated Press*, September 2024. https:// apnews.com/article/trump-classified-documents-smith-c66d5ffb7ba86c1b 991f95e89bdeba0c

73. Turley, Jonathan (@JonathanTurley), "The dismissal of the classified documents case is a seismic development. From the beginning of all of these cases, I have said that the Mar-a-Lago case was the greatest threat to the former president. It is now dismissed," *X* (formerly Twitter), July 15, 2024, https://x .com/JonathanTurley/status/1812850437948657898.

74. Campanile, Carl. "Judge Grants Special Counsel Jack Smith's Motion to File an Oversized Brief on Presidential Immunity in Trump 2020 Election Interference Case." *New York Post*, September 24, 2024. https://nypost .com/2024/09/24/us-news/judge-grants-special-counsel-jack-smiths-mo tion-to-file-an-oversized-brief-on-presidential-immunity-in-trump-2020 -election-interference-case/

75. Vladeck, Steve. "The Justice Department's Policy Against Election Interference Is Open to Abuse." *Lawfare*, September 6, 2023. https://www .lawfaremedia.org/article/justice-departments-policy-against-election-inter ference-open-abuse

76. Mallin, Alexander. "DOJ's 60-Day Rule Could Play a Key Role in Trump's Trial Timeline." *ABC News*, May 28, 2024. https://abcnews.go.com/Politics /dojs-60-day-rule-role-play-trump-trial/story?id=107789927

77. Multiple authors. "In Triumph for President-Elect." *Breitbart*, November 25, 2024. https://www.breitbart.com/2024-election/2024/11/25/in-triumph-for -president-elect/

78. Brown, Joseph. " 'Their Days Are Numbered': Federal Bureaucrats Are Panicking over Trump Win—Especially at the DOJ and FBI." *The Blaze*, December 1, 2024. https://www.theblaze.com/news/their-days-are-numbered-federal-bu reaucrats-are-panicking-over-trump-win-especially-at-the-doj-and-fbi

CHAPTER 7: THE LEFT HATES DEMOCRACY

1. Palmieri, Jennifer. "Clinton, Brazile, and the Hacks: Inside Hillary's Secret Takeover of the DNC." *Politico Magazine*, November 2, 2017. https://www.po litico.com/magazine/story/2017/11/02/clinton-brazile-hacks-2016-215774/

2. @neontaster. "This was the second image in that tweet, with the DNC– Clinton agreement excerpt." *X* (formerly Twitter), November 3, 2017. https://x.com/neontaster/status/926438725009199104/photo/2

3. "Donna Brazile: I Found Evidence Hillary Clinton Rigged the 2016 Primary." *BBC News*, November 3, 2017. https://www.bbc.com/news/world-us-can ada-41850798

4. "Donna Brazile: I Found Evidence Hillary Clinton Rigged the 2016 Primary." *BBC News*, November 3, 2017. https://www.bbc.com/news/world-us-can ada-41850798

5. Multiple authors. "ABC, CBS, NBC Fail to Cover Brazile's Claim DNC Rigged Primary for Clinton." *Breitbart*, November 4, 2017. https://www.breitbart .com/the-media/2017/11/04/abc-cbs-nbc-fail-cover-braziles-claim-dnc -rigged-primary-clinton/

6. Multiple authors. "DNC Chair Donna Brazile's Allegation Hillary Rigged 2016 Primary 'Moving Forward'." *Breitbart*, November 2, 2017. https://www .breitbart.com/clips/2017/11/02/dnc-chair-donna-braziles-allegation-hil lary-rigged-2016-primary-moving-forward/

7. @neontaster. "Excerpt from Donna Brazile's book showing the joint fundrais ing agreement between the DNC and Clinton campaign." *X* (formerly Twitter), November 3, 2017. https://x.com/neontaster/status/926438725009199104 /photo/1

8. Singman, Brooke. "Court Admits DNC and Debbie Wasserman Schultz Rigged Primaries Against Sanders." *Observer*, August 2017. https://observer .com/2017/08/court-admits-dnc-and-debbie-wasserman-schulz-rigged-pri maries-against-sanders/

9. YouTube. "Donna Brazile on the DNC and Clinton Primary Agreement – Full Interview." *YouTube*, uploaded November 2017. https://www.youtube.com /watch?v=VRoKgfoqmFQ

10. Sherman, Amy. "Fact-Check: Was the 2016 Primary Rigged against Bernie Sanders?" *Austin American-Statesman*, October 10, 2022. https://www.states man.com/story/news/politics/politifact/2022/10/10/2016-election-fact -check-democrats-hillary-clinton-bernie-sanders/69548196007/

11. Rucker, Philip. "Jimmy Carter Says Trump Wouldn't Be President without Help from Russia." *Washington Post*, June 28, 2019. https://www.washingtonpost .com/politics/jimmy-carter-says-trump-wouldnt-be-president-without -help-from-russia/2019/06/28/deef1ef0-99b6-11e9-8d0a-5edd7e2025b1 _story.html

12. Seitz-Wald, Alex. "John Lewis: Trump Won't Be Legitimate President." *NBC News*, January 14, 2017. https://www.nbcnews.com/storyline/meet-the-press -70-years/john-lewis-trump-won-t-be-legitimate-president-n706676

13. Multiple authors. "Congresswoman Maxine Waters Booed after Objection to Electoral College Count." *CBS News Los Angeles*, January 6, 2017. https://www .cbsnews.com/losangeles/news/congresswoman-maxine-waters-booed-af ter-objection-to-electoral-college-count/

14. Concha, Joe. "Adam Schiff Insists His Russia Collusion Claim Wasn't an Overstatement." *Fox News*, May 17, 2023. https://www.foxnews.com/media /adam-schiff-insists-his-russia-collusion-claim-wasnt-overstatement

15. Multiple authors. "No Remorse: Democrats Stick to Trump-Russia Collusion Claims." *Washington Times*, May 16, 2023. https://www.washingtontimes .com/news/2023/may/16/no-remorse-democrats-stick-trump-russia-collu sion-/

16. Benen, Steve. "GOP Uses Durham Report to Pretend Russia Scandal Wasn't Real." *MSNBC*, May 17, 2023. https://www.msnbc.com/rachel-mad dow-show/maddowblog/gop-uses-durham-report-pretend-russia-scandal -wasnt-real-rcna84903

17. Koebler, Jason. "Russia's Disinformation Campaign Is Already Targeting the 2024 Election." *Wired*, January 2024. https://www.wired.com/story/rus sia-election-disinformation-2024-election-day/

18. Allen, Jonathan. "Trump Acknowledges He Lost 2020 Election 'by a Whisker'." *NBC News*, February 2024. https://www.nbcnews.com/politics/2024-elec tion/trump-acknowledges-lost-2020-election-whisker-rcna169526

19. Marcus, Ruth. "The Democratic Party Rigs the Primaries." *Wall Street Journal*, February 2, 2024.https://www.wsj.com/articles/the-democratic-party -rigs-the-primaries-candidate-election-voter-new-hampshire-georgia-dnc -kennedy-nominee-326c63d6

20. Harsanyi, David. "Democrats Rigged the Primary for Biden. His Resignation Sticks Them with Harris." *Washington Examiner*, January 30, 2024. https:// www.washingtonexaminer.com/opinion/3092746/democrats-rigged-the-pri mary-for-biden-his-resignation-sticks-them-with-harris

21. Epstein, Reid J. "Biden's Democratic Challengers Hit Ballot Access Roadblocks." *ABC News*, March 6, 2024. https://abcnews.go.com/Politics/bidens-demo cratic-challengers-hit-ballot-access-roadblocks/story?id=105882807

22. Multiple authors. "Special Counsel Hur: Biden's Poor Memory a Key Factor in Not Charging Him." *Breitbart*, March 12, 2024.https://www.breitbart.com /politics/2024/03/12/special-counsel-hur-bidens-poor-memory-key-factor -not-charging-him/

23. YouTube. "Hur Report on Biden Memory." *YouTube Video*, uploaded by ABC News, March 2024. https://www.youtube.com/watch?v=vV_WDBqE8VI

24. Karni, Annie, and Carl Hulse. "Schumer Privately Urged Biden to Consider Future, Then Publicly Backed Him." *New York Times*, January 17, 2025. https://www.nytimes.com/2025/01/17/us/politics/schumer-biden-2024-elec tion.html

25. Blow, Charles M. "Joe Biden Should Not Be the Democratic Nominee." *New York Times*, July 10, 2024. https://www.nytimes.com/2024/07/10/opinion /joe-biden-democratic-nominee.html

26. Campanile, Carl. "Biden Camp Suggests Prez Quickly Endorsed Harris to Defy Obama." *New York Post*, July 26, 2024. https://nypost.com/2024/07/26 /us-news/biden-camp-suggests-prez-quickly-endorsed-harris-to-defy -obama/

27. Smith, Kathryn Watson. "Kamala Harris Fundraising for 2024: Campaign Appeals Surge." *CBS News*, July 2024. https://www.cbsnews.com/news/kamala -harris-fundraising-campaign-appeals/

28. Multiple authors. "NBC Exit Poll: Majority of Americans List Democracy, Economy as Top Issues." *Breitbart*, November 5, 2024. https://www.breitbart .com/politics/2024/11/05/nbc-exit-poll-majority-americans-list-democracy -economy-top-issues/

29. Illing, Sean. "Democrats Say Trump Is an Existential Threat to Democracy. Do They Mean It?" *Vox*, July 2024. https://www.vox.com/today-explained-news letter/358061/democrats-biden-trump-existential-threat-democracy-debate

30. Paul, Kelley. "Since the Attack on My Husband, I've Learned Some Horrible Truths." *CNN Opinion*, November 22, 2017. https://www.cnn.com/2017/11/22/opinions/kelley-paul-since-the-attack-opinion/index.html

31. Nolte, John. "Rap Sheet: Acts of Media-Approved Violence and Harassment Against Trump Supporters." *Breitbart*, July 5, 2018. https://www.breitbart.com/the-media/2018/07/05/rap-sheet-acts-of-media-approved-violence-and-harassment-against-trump-supporters/

32. Multiple authors. "New York Times Publishes Fantasy About Trump Getting Assassinated." *Breitbart*, October 25, 2018. https://www.breitbart.com/the-media/2018/10/25/new-york-times-publishes-fantasy-about-trump-getting-assassinated/

33. Multiple authors. "Paul Schrader Ponders Assignment About Killing President Trump." *Breitbart*, January 15, 2020. https://www.breitbart.com/entertainment/2020/01/15/paul-schrader-ponders-assignment-about-killing-president-trump/

34. Multiple authors. "Flashback: Bennie Thompson, Pelosi's J6 Chair, Once Called for Stripping Trump's Secret Service Protection." *Breitbart*, July 13, 2024. https://www.breitbart.com/politics/2024/07/13/flashback-bennie-thompson-top-dem-pelosis-j6-committee-called-stripping-trumps-secret-service-protection/

35. Multiple authors. "RFK Jr. on Secret Service Pulling Protection: 'I'm Technically Still Running for President.'" *Breitbart*, August 27, 2024. https://www.breitbart.com/politics/2024/08/27/rfk-jr-on-secret-service-pulling-protection-im-technically-still-running-for-president/

36. Crane, Emily. "Secret Service Boss Kimberly Cheatle Says 'The Buck Stops with Me,' Calls Trump Rally Shooting Response 'Unacceptable'—But Still Won't Resign." *New York Post*, July 16, 2024. https://nypost.com/2024/07/16/us-news/secret-service-boss-kimberly-cheatle-says-the-buck-stops-with-me-calls-trump-rally-shooting-response-unacceptable-but-still-wont-resign/

37. Multiple authors. "Exclusive: Donald Trump Unveils Dramatic Details of Assassination Attempt—Moment It Happened, Who's to Blame, Why He Got Up and Yelled 'Fight! Fight! Fight!'" *Breitbart*, August 25, 2024. https://www.breitbart.com/politics/2024/08/25/exclusive-donald-trump-unveils-dramatic-details-assassination-attempt-moment-happened-whos-blame-why-he-got-up-yelled-fight-fight-fight/

38. @Timodc. "Biden's inner circle, knowing they were losing control of the narrative . . ." *X* (formerly Twitter), July 29, 2024. https://x.com/Timodc/status/1819856970108584314

CHAPTER 8: MAPPING THE SUPERSTRUCTURE

1. Thrush, Glenn, and Michael S. Schmidt. "I.R.S. Official Says Justice Dept. Intervened in Hunter Biden Case." *New York Times*, June 27, 2023. https://www.nytimes.com/2023/06/27/us/politics/irs-official-justice-dept-hunter-biden.html

2. Multiple authors. "House Oversight Committee Releases Official Timeline of Biden Influence Peddling." *Breitbart*, July 18, 2023. https://www.breitbart

.com/politics/2023/07/18/house-oversight-committee-releases-official-time line-of-biden-influence-peddling/

3. Beitsch, Rebecca and Emily Brooks. "Hunter Biden's Ties to Romanian Businessman Cited in FARA Questions." *The Hill*, July 2023. https://thehill.com /regulation/court-battles/4818240-hunter-biden-doj-romanian-businessman -fara/

4. Milmo, Carys. "Joe Biden Privately Regrets Dropping out of Re-Election Race." *The Guardian*, December 28, 2024. https://www.theguardian.com/us -news/2024/dec/28/joe-biden-regrets-dropping-out-re-election

5. William F. Buckley Jr. Program at Yale. "Buckley Institute Releases First National Law Student Survey." *Buckley Institute*, October 2024. https://buckley institute.com/buckley-institute-releases-first-national-law-student-survey/

6. Caron, Paul L. "Faculty Presidential Election Survey: 78% for Harris, 9% for Trump." *TaxProf Blog*, October 2024. https://taxprof.typepad.com/taxprof _blog/2024/10/faculty-presidential-election-survey-78-harris-9-trump.html

7. Hall, Alexander. "Berkeley Law Dean Caught Saying School Uses Unstated Affirmative Action." *Fox News*, October 2024. https://www.foxnews.com /media/dean-caught-saying-berkeley-law-uses-unstated-affirmative-action denysaid

8. Rosenbaum, Ron. "Campus Antisemitism Is a Symptom of Our Broken Political Dialogue." *Los Angeles Times*, October 29, 2023. https://www.latimes.com /opinion/story/2023-10-29/antisemitism-college-campus-israel-hamas-pal estine

9. Multiple authors. "Woke Mob Targets Cornell Prof Behind Legal Insurrection Blog for Critiquing Black Lives Matter." *Breitbart*, June 11, 2020. https://www .breitbart.com/tech/2020/06/11/woke-mob-targets-cornell-prof-behind-le gal-insurrection-blog-for-critiquing-black-lives-matter/

10. Multiple authors. "UVA Grad Explains How Woke Mob Tried to Ruin Her Life with Fake Charges of Threats Against BLM Protesters." *Breitbart*, May 2, 2023. https://www.breitbart.com/tech/2023/05/02/uva-grad-explains-how -woke-mob-tried-to-ruin-her-life-with-fake-charges-of-threats-against-blm -protesters/

11. Editorial Board. "A Struggle Session at Stanford Law School." *Wall Street Journal*, March 2023. https://www.wsj.com/articles/struggle-session-at-stan ford-law-school-federalist-society-kyle-duncan-circuit-court-judge-stein bach-4f8da19e

12. Multiple authors. "Georgetown Suspends Law Prof Ilya Shapiro Over Tweet Against Biden's Affirmative Action SCOTUS Nomination." *Breitbart*, February 1, 2022. https://www.breitbart.com/tech/2022/02/01/george town-suspends-law-prof-ilya-shapiro-over-tweet-against-bidens-affirma tive-action-scotus-nomination/

13. Multiple authors. "Woke, Jobless Federal Judges Say They Won't Hire Yale Law Clerks Over Anti-Free Speech Behavior." *Breitbart*, October 11, 2022. https:// www.breitbart.com/tech/2022/10/11/woke-jobless-federal-judges-say-they -wont-hire-yale-law-clerks-over-hysterical-anti-free-speech-behavior/

14. Franck, Thomas. "Trump's 'Fake News' Fight Has Helped Media Ratings and Readership." *CNBC*, April 23, 2018. https://www.cnbc.com/2018/04/23 /trumps-fake-news-fight-has-helped-media-ratings-and-readership.html

15. Fung, Brian. "Mark Zuckerberg's Meta Met with Biden Officials to Coordinate Censorship on COVID." *CNN Business*, August 27, 2024. https://www.cnn .com/2024/08/27/business/mark-zuckerberg-meta-biden-censor-covid -2021/index.html

16. Dillon, Christine. "ProPublica Donors Have History of Anti-Thomas Activity." *Daily Caller*, June 20, 2023. https://dailycaller.com/2023/06/20/propublica -donors-clarence-thomas/

17. Multiple authors. "Left-Wing Foundation Backing ProPublica Dumps Millions into Groups Targeting SCOTUS Justices Clarence Thomas and Samuel Alito." *Breitbart*, June 22, 2023. https://www.breitbart.com/poli tics/2023/06/22/left-wing-foundation-backing-propublica-dumps-millions -into-groups-targeting-scotus-justices-clarence-thomas-and-samuel-alito/

18. ProPublica Staff. "ProPublica's Most Read Stories of 2023." *ProPublica*, December 2023. https://www.propublica.org/article/propublica-most-read-sto ries-2023

19. Faturechi, Robert. "UnitedHealthcare Pushed Families Out of Autism Therapy to Cut Costs." *ProPublica*, December 2023. https://www.propublica.org /article/unitedhealthcare-insurance-autism-denials-applied-behavior-analy sis-medicaid

20. Campaign Legal Center. "CLC Seeks Referral of Justice Thomas to DOJ for Ethics Violations." *Campaign Legal Center*, August 2023. https://campaignle gal.org/press-releases/clc-seeks-referral-justice-thomas-doj-violations

21. Police Defense Coalition. "Soros Prosecutor Map." *PoliceDefense.org*. Accessed May 16, 2025. https://www.policedefense.org/sorosmap/

22. Phillips, Morgan. "Soros DAs Suffer 12 Big Defeats, Billionaire's Agenda Faces Uncertain Future." *Fox News*, November 6, 2024. https://www.foxnews.com /politics/soros-das-suffer-12-big-defeats-billionaires-agenda-faces-uncer tain-future

23. Multiple authors. "Federal Court Rules Defamation Suit Against MSNBC's Andrew Weissmann Can Proceed." *Breitbart*, November 20, 2024. https:// www.breitbart.com/politics/2024/11/20/federal-court-rules-defamation -suit-against-msnbcs-andrew-weissmann-can-proceed/

24. "Anne Montminy, Daniel Goldman." *The New York Times*, June 23, 2002. https://www.nytimes.com/2002/06/23/style/weddings-anne-montminy-dan iel-goldman.html

25. Multiple authors. "Daniel Goldman, Lead Impeachment Investigator, Claimed Steele Dossier Was 'True'." *Breitbart*, December 11, 2019. https://www.breit bart.com/politics/2019/12/11/daniel-goldman-lead-impeachment-investiga tor-claimed-steele-dossier-was-true/.

26. Johnson, Jake. "Progressives Accuse Dan Goldman of Trying to Buy Seat in Congress." *Common Dreams*, August 17, 2022. https://www.commondreams .org/news/2022/08/17/progressives-accuse-dan-goldman-trying-buy-seat -congress-new-york

27. Mallin, Alexander. "Michael Cohen 'Absolutely' Prepared to Testify Against Trump." *ABC News*, May 14, 2024. https://abcnews.go.com/Politics/mi chael-cohen-absolutely-prepared-testify-trump/story?id=97921342

28. Multiple authors. "Rep. Dan Goldman Is Client of Judge Merchan's Daughter, Says He Prepped Michael Cohen for Trump Trial." *Breitbart*, May 15,

2024. https://www.breitbart.com/2024-election/2024/05/15/rep-dan-gold man-client-judge-merchans-daughter-says-he-prepped-michael-cohen-trump-trial/

29. Multiple authors. "Democrat Lawyer Marc Elias Claims Faulty Voting Machines in New York Race." *Breitbart*, February 3, 2021. https://www.breitbart.com/2020-election/2021/02/03/democrat-lawyer-marc-elias-claims-faulty-voting-machines-in-new-york-race/

30. Epstein, Reid J. "Wisconsin Supreme Court Tosses Democratic Map, Gives Republicans a Boost." *The Wall Street Journal*, December 22, 2023. https://www.wsj.com/articles/wisconsin-congressional-maps-marc-elias-lawsuit-su preme-court-bd02c6c1

31. Office of the Texas Attorney General. "AG Paxton: Fifth Circuit Issues Sanctions Against Perkins Coie." *Texas Attorney General Newsroom*, October 2022. https://www.texasattorneygeneral.gov/news/releases/ag-paxton-fifth-circuit-issues-sanctions-against-perkins-coie

32. Ross, Ramsey. "A Lost Shortcut Might Hurt Down-Ballot Candidates, Democrats Fear." *Texas Tribune*, August 30, 2019. https://www.texastribune.org/2019/08/30/lost-texas-voters-shortcut-might-hurt-downballot-candidates-democrats/

33. Weiss, Debra Cassens. "Which BigLaw Firms Are Involved in Suits Against the Trump Administration?" *ABAJournal*, February 26, 2025. https://www.abajournal.com/news/article/which-biglaw-firms-are-involved-in-suits-against-the-trump-administration.

34. Cooke, Charles C. W. "Judge Invalidates Trump's Executive Order Against Perkins Coie Law Firm." *National Review*, October 2020. https://www.national review.com/corner/judge-invalidates-trumps-executive-order-against-per kins-coie-law-firm/

35. Editorial Board. "Why Big Law Firms Shun Conservative Clients." *The Wall Street Journal*, January 17, 2023. https://www.wsj.com/opinion/many-big-law-firms-shun-conservative-clients-politics-attorneys-6bf4db08

36. Montanaro, Domenico. "Norm Eisen Says He Drafted 10 Articles of Impeachment a Month Before Inquiry." *NPR*, July 27, 2020. https://www.npr.org/2020/07/27/895709528/norm-eisen-says-he-drafted-10-articles-of-im peachment-a-month-before-inquiry

37. Eisen, Norm. "What Trump's Conviction Means for Democracy." *Brookings Institution*, May 2024. https://www.brookings.edu/articles/what-trumps-con viction-means-for-democracy/

38. O'Neil, Tyler. "EXCLUSIVE: DOJ's Kristen Clarke Testified She Was Never Arrested; Court Records and Text Messages Indicate She Was." *The Daily Signal*, April 30, 2024. https://www.dailysignal.com/2024/04/30/exclusive-dojs-kristen-clarke-testified-she-was-never-arrested-court-records-and-text-messages-indicate-she-was/

39. Multiple authors. "EXCLUSIVE: Tom Cotton—AG Merrick Garland Must Fire Top DOJ Official Kristen Clarke; 'Lying to Congress Under Oath Is a Felony.'" *Breitbart*, July 12, 2024. https://www.breitbart.com/politics/2024/07/12/exclusive-tom-cotton-ag-merrick-garland-must-fire-top-doj-official-kris ten-clarke-lying-to-congress-under-oath-is-a-felony/

40. Multiple authors. "Merrick Garland, Kristen Clarke Silent on Campus Antisemitism." *Breitbart*, April 26, 2024. https://www.breitbart.com/pol

itics/2024/04/26/merrick-garland-kristen-clarke-silent-on-campus-antisem
itism

CHAPTER 9: THE NEW EXISTENTIAL THREAT

1. Frater, Patrick. "The White Lotus Star Carrie Coon Says Non-Binary, 'Maybe Trans' Child Cut from Show after Trump Election." *Breitbart*, March 31, 2025. https://www.breitbart.com/entertainment/2025/03/31/the-white-lotus -star-carrie-coon-says-non-binary-maybe-trans-child-cut-from-show-after -trump-election/
2. Frost, Amanda. "District Court Reform and Nationwide Injunctions." *Harvard Law Review* 137, no. 5 (March 2024). https://harvardlawreview.org /print/vol-137/district-court-reform-nationwide-injunctions/
3. DeChiara-Trainor, Emma. "How a Lone Judge Can Block a Trump Order Nationwide—and Why." *The Conversation*, April 12, 2024. https:// theconversation.com/how-a-lone-judge-can-block-a-trump-order -nationwide-and-why-from-daca-to-doge-this-judicial-check-on-presi dents-power-is-shaping-how-the-government-works-252556
4. Shear, Michael D. "Trump Backs Down, Ending Shutdown." *Politico*, January 25, 2019. https://www.politico.com/story/2019/01/25/trump-shutdown -announcement-1125529
5. Hosenball, Mark. "U.S. Judges Face Rise in Threats as Musk Blasts Them over Rulings." *Reuters*, March 5, 2025. https://www.reuters.com/world/us/judges -face-rise-threats-musk-blasts-them-over-rulings-2025-03-05/
6. Boyle, Matthew. "27 States Back Trump's Use of 'Alien Enemies Act' to Deport Tren de Aragua Gangsters." *Breitbart*, April 1, 2025. https://www.breitbart .com/immigration/2025/04/01/27-states-back-trumps-use-alien-enemies -act-deport-tren-de-aragua-gangsters/
7. Broadwater, Luke. "Trump Deportations Spark Constitutional Crisis Talk." *New York Times*, March 19, 2025. https://www.nytimes.com/2025/03/19/us /politics/trump-deportations-constitutional-crisis-impeachment.html
8. Spiering, Charlie. "Supreme Court Allows Trump Admin Deportations of Gang Members under Alien Enemies Act." *Breitbart*, April 7, 2025. https:// www.breitbart.com/immigration/2025/04/07/supreme-court-allows-trump -admin-deportations-gang-members-alien-enemies-act/
9. Spiering, Charlie. "Judge James Boasberg Threatens Contempt for Not Flying Gang Members Back to U.S." *Breitbart*, April 16, 2025. https://www .breitbart.com/politics/2025/04/16/judge-james-boasberg-threatens-to -hold-trump-officials-in-contempt-of-court-for-not-flying-gang-mem bers-back-to-u-s/
10. Associated Press. "A Timeline of the Legal Wrangling and Deportation Flights after Trump Invoked the Alien Enemies Act." *Breitbart*, April 2025. https:// www.breitbart.com/news/a-timeline-of-the-legal-wrangling-and-deporta tion-flights-after-trump-invoked-the-alien-enemies-act/
11. Gerstein, Josh. "FBI Lawyer Gets Probation in Trump-Russia Probe." *Politico*, January 29, 2021. https://www.politico.com/news/2021/01/29/fbi-lawyer -trump-russia-probe-email-463750.

12. Gerstein, Josh. "Judge Blocks Trump Immigrant Detention Plan." *Politico*, July 2, 2018. https://www.politico.com/story/2018/07/02/judge-trump-immigrant-detention-plan-692198

13. Savage, Charlie. "FBI Misused Surveillance Tool, Justice Dept. Finds." *New York Times*, April 26, 2021. https://www.nytimes.com/2021/04/26/us/politics/fbi-fisa-surveillance.html

14. Wamsley, Laurel. "Court Rules That Dakota Access Pipeline Must Be Emptied— for Now." *NPR*, July 6, 2020. https://www.npr.org/2020/07/06/887593775/court-rules-that-dakota-access-pipeline-must-be-emptied-for-now

15. Multiple Authors. "Trump Sounds Off after 'Highly Conflicted Obama-Nominated Judge' Assigned Signal Chat Lawsuit." *Fox News*, April 2025. https://www.foxnews.com/politics/trump-sounds-off-after-highly-conflicted-obama-nominated-judge-assigned-signal-chat-lawsuit-disgraceful

16. Multiple Authors. "Judge Boasberg in Crosshairs over Trump Deportation Case, Orders Preservation of Signal Messages." *Fox News*, April 2025. https://www.foxnews.com/politics/judge-boasberg-crosshairs-trump-deportation-case-orders-preservation-signal-messages

17. Breitbart News. "Schweizer: Marc Elias Is Judge Shopping to Try to Repeat Al Franken's Dubious Election for Bob Casey." *Breitbart*, November 13, 2024. https://www.breitbart.com/2024-election/2024/11/13/schweizer-marc-elias-is-judge-shopping-to-try-to-repeat-al-frankens-dubious-election-for-bob-casey/

18. KARE11 News. "Coleman Concedes Senate Race to Franken." *KARE 11*, July 1, 2009. Archived January 27, 2013. https://archive.ph/20130127063856/http://www.kare11.com/news/news_article.aspx?storyid=858569&catid=14

19. Breitbart News. "Fourth Federal Judge Blocks Trump's Birthright Citizenship Order." *Breitbart*, accessed 2025. https://www.breitbart.com/news/fourth-federal-judge-blocks-trumps-birthright-citizenship-order/

20. Julie Kelly (@julie_kelly2). "Federal Judge Blocks Trump's Order – Cites Equal Protection." *X* (formerly Twitter), April 23, 2025. https://x.com/julie_kelly2/status/1908509790285750382

21. Raasch, John Michael. "Trump Orders Millions in DEI and Foreign Aid Programs to Be Scrutinized." *Daily Mail*, March 28, 2025. https://www.dailymail.co.uk/news/article-14344255/trump-millions-dei-foreign-aid-programs-funding.html

22. Breitbart News. "Judge Who Blocked USAID Cuts Is Longtime Democrat Activist." *Breitbart*, March 19, 2025. https://www.breitbart.com/politics/2025/03/19/judge-who-blocked-usaid-cuts-is-long-time-democratactivist/

23. Archive.is. "USAID Spending Freeze Controversy." *Archive*, accessed 2025. https://archive.is/VWZMJ

24. Archive.is. "District Court Injunction." *Archive*, accessed 2025. https://archive.is/chLAZ#selection-501.0-504.0

25. Fox News. "Two Trans Inmates Ordered Back to Women's Prisons by Reagan-Appointed Judges." *Fox News*, accessed 2025. https://www.foxnews.com/politics/two-trans-inmates-ordered-back-womens-prisons-reagan-appointed-judges-injunction

26. Politico Staff. "Health Agency Webpage Removal Sparks Lawsuit." *Politico*, February 11, 2025. https://www.politico.com/news/2025/02/11/health-agency-webpage-removal-lawsuit-00203582

27. Pepes Grandma (@pepesgrandma). "Federal Judge Sides with Activists in Dogecoin Case." *X* (formerly Twitter), April 1, 2025. https://x.com/pepes grandma/status/1889686063490183231

28. CNN Politics. "Judge Amy Berman Jackson in Focus for Trump Cases." *CNN*, May 28, 2021. https://www.cnn.com/2021/05/28/politics/judge-amy-ber man-jackson/index.html

29. Marlow, Alex. "Lawfare Judges Making Unprecedented Efforts to Shut Down Trump's Agenda." *Breitbart*, February 11, 2025. https://www.breitbart.com /politics/2025/02/11/alex-marlow-lawfare-judges-making-unprecedented -efforts-to-shut-down-trumps-agenda/

30. Richardson, Katelynn. "Federal Judge John McConnell Jr. Seeks Criminal Charges Over Trump Spending Freeze." *Daily Caller*, February 10, 2025. https://dailycaller.com/2025/02/10/federal-judge-john-mcconnell-jr-trump -admin-criminal-charges-spending-freeze-dem-donor/

31. Fox News. "Federal Judge Orders Limited Dogecoin Access to Sensitive Treasury Payment System Records." *Fox News*, accessed 2025. https://www .foxnews.com/politics/federal-judge-orders-limited-doge-access-sensi tive-treasury-department-payment-system-records

32. Marlow, Alex. "Lawfare Judges Making Unprecedented Efforts to Shut Down Trump's Agenda." *Breitbart*, February 11, 2025. https://www.breitbart.com /politics/2025/02/11/alex-marlow-lawfare-judges-making-unprecedented -efforts-to-shut-down-trumps-agenda/

33. Marlow, Alex. "Lawfare Judges Making Unprecedented Efforts to Shut Down Trump's Agenda." *Breitbart*, February 11, 2025. https://www.breitbart.com /politics/2025/02/11/alex-marlow-lawfare-judges-making-unprecedented -efforts-to-shut-down-trumps-agenda/

34. Associated Press. "Federal Judge Blocks Trump Administration TPS Order for Venezuelans." *AP News*, accessed 2025. https://apnews.com /article/trump-administration-venezuelans-tps-federal-judge-d4044f1fc7cb 69985add060aeaae8731

35. Federal Election Commission. "Individual Contributions: Indira Talwani." *FEC.gov*, accessed 2025. https://www.fec.gov/data/receipts/individual-contri butions/?contributor_name=Indira+Talwani

36. U.S. Senate Judiciary Committee. "Questionnaire for Judicial Nominee Indira Talwani." *Senate.gov*, accessed 2025. https://www.judiciary.senate.gov/imo /media/doc/Talwani-Senate-Questionnaire-Final.pdf

37. Daily Caller. "Trump's Plans to Deport Foreign Radicals Temporarily Halted." March 26, 2025. https://dailycaller.com/2025/03/26/trumps-plans-to-de port-foreign-radicals-temporarily-halted/

38. Daily Caller. "Obama Judge Rules Gender Is Speech, Blocks Tennessee Law Protecting Students from Trans Teachers." June 17, 2023. https://dailycaller .com/2023/06/17/7774148-gender-freespeech-obama-judge-lgbtq/

39. Daily Caller. "Obama Judge Blocks ICE from Courthouses." June 21, 2019. https://dailycaller.com/2019/06/21/obama-judge-blocks-ice-from-court houses/

40. Wines, Michael. "Trump Administration Rule Would Limit Passport Changes for Transgender People." *New York Times*, April 18, 2025. https://www.ny times.com/2025/04/18/us/trump-passport-changes-transgender.html

41. U.S. Senate Committee on the Judiciary. "Questionnaire for Judicial Nominee Julia E. Kobick." Accessed April 2025. https://www.judiciary.senate.gov/imo/media/doc/Kobick%20SJQ%20Public%20Final1.pdf

42. Federal Election Commission. "Individual Contributions: Julia E. Kobick." Accessed April 2025. https://www.fec.gov/data/receipts/individual-contributions/?contributor_name=julia+e+kobick&contributor_name=julia+eleanor+kobick&contributor_name=julia+kobick&max_date=12%2F31%2F2026

43. Lieu, Tina. "Colorado Judge Uses Supreme Court Order to Block Trump Admin Deportations." *Newsweek*, April 2025. https://www.newsweek.com/colorado-judge-uses-supreme-court-order-block-trump-admin-deportations-2062751

44. Law Week Colorado. "Biden Nominates Charlotte Sweeney to Federal Bench as Jackson's Replacement." February 2022. https://www.lawweekcolorado.com/article/biden-nominates-charlotte-sweeney-to-federal-bench-as-jacksons-replacement/

45. Colorado Politics. "Bennet, Hickenlooper Send Recommendations to White House for Court Vacancy." May 2021. https://gazette.com/colorado_politics/bennet-hickenlooper-send-recommendations-to-white-house-for-court-vacancy/article_5bbb855a-bf11-11eb-806b-27dd91c03200.html

46. Colorado Bar Association. "CLE Faculty Profile: Charlotte Sweeney." Accessed April 2025. https://cle.cobar.org/About/Faculty-Authors/Info/CUSTOMERCD/42560.

47. Federal Election Commission. "Individual Contributions: Charlotte Sweeney." Accessed April 2025. https://www.fec.gov/data/receipts/individual-contributions/?contributor_name=Charlotte+Sweeney&contributor_state=CO

48. Colorado Community Media. "Elizabeth Schools Must Return Banned Books." March 20, 2025. https://coloradocommunitymedia.com/2025/03/20/elizabeth-schools-must-return-banned-books/

49. Karlick, Michael. "U.S. Senate Confirms Charlotte Sweeney as Colorado's First Openly Gay Federal Judge." *Colorado Politics*, May 2022. https://www.coloradopolitics.com/courts/u-s-senate-confirms-charlotte-sweeney-as-colorados-first-openly-gay-federal-judge/article_328bc2b2-dc34-11ec-9531-9f2509cd52cf.html

50. Sacchetti, Maria. "Trump's Alien Enemies Act Deportations Face Legal Roadblocks." *Washington Post*, April 22, 2025. https://www.washingtonpost.com/immigration/2025/04/22/alien-enemies-act-migrant-deportations-courts/

51. Federal Election Commission. "Individual Contributions: Alvin Hellerstein." Accessed April 2025. https://www.fec.gov/data/receipts/individual-contributions/?contributor_name=alvin+hellerstein&max_date=12%2F31%2F2026

52. ACLU. "Federal Court Orders Michael Cohen's Release to Home Confinement." July 23, 2020. https://www.aclu.org/press-releases/federal-court-orders-michael-cohens-release-home-confinement

53. Schoen, John. "Judge Rules Trump Admin Must Remove ICE Office from Rikers Island." *Newsweek*, April 2025. https://www.newsweek.com/judge-rules-trump-admin-eric-adams-rikers-island-ice-office-2064463

54. Edlesh, Dan. "LGBT Bar NY Announces Judicial Ratings for the 2018 General Election." *Medium*, October 2018. https://edlesh.medium.com/lgbt-bar-ny -announces-judicial-ratings-for-the-2018-general-election-4afbc3a82160

55. Barragán, James. "Texas, New York Face Off in Court over Migrant Busing." *Texas Tribune*, November 9, 2024. https://www.texastribune.org/2024/11/09 /texas-new-york-migrant-buses-lawsuit/

56. Ballotpedia. "Mandatory Retirement." Accessed April 2025. https://ballotpe dia.org/Mandatory_retirement

57. Ballotpedia. "Article VI, New York Constitution." Accessed May 16, 2025. https://ballotpedia.org/Article_VI,_New_York_Constitution#Section_25:~: text=A%20retired%20judge%20or%20justice%20shall%20serve%20no%20 longer%20than%20until%20the%20last%20day%20of%20December%20 in%20the%20year%20in%20which%20he%20or%20she%20reaches%20 the%20age%20of%20seventy%2Dsix.

58. Stefanik, Elise. "Election Interference." *X* (formerly Twitter), December 15, 2023. https://x.com/EliseStefanik/status/1735619828642165195?s=20.

59. Multiple Authors. "Election Interference: Elise Stefanik Files Complaint against Judge in Trump January 6 Case." Breitbart, December 15, 2023. https://www.breitbart.com/politics/2023/12/15/election-interference-elise -stefanik-files-complaint-against-judge-in-trump-january-6-case-2/

60. People Staff. "Judge Rejects Trump Plan to Strip Food Stamps from 700K Americans." People. Accessed May 16, 2025. https://people.com/human-in terest/judge-rejects-trump-plan-strip-food-stamps-700k-americans/

61. NPR Staff. "CEO over VOA Acted Unconstitutionally in Pursuing Bias Claims, U.S. Judge Rules." NPR, November 21, 2020. https://www.npr .org/2020/11/21/937467457/ceo-over-voa-acted-unconstitutionally-in-pur suing-bias-claims-u-s-judge-rules

62. Mallin, Alexander. "Judge Orders Testimony from Trump Attorney, Pierc-ing Attorney-Client Privilege." ABC News, March 15, 2023. https://abcnews .go.com/US/judge-orders-testimony-trump-attorney-piercing-attorney-cli ent/story?id=97947297

63. "Controversial Phone Call: Impeachment Calls, Trump, and the Whistleblower Timeline." ABC News. https://abcnews.go.com/Politics/controversial-phone-call -impeachment-calls-trump-whistleblower-timeline/story?id=65810201

64. WPR Staff. "Rudy Giuliani Files for Bankruptcy a Day after Judge Orders Him to Pay $146 Million." Wisconsin Public Radio, December 2023. https://www .wpr.org/news/rudy-giuliani-files-bankruptcy-day-after-judge-orders-him -pay-146-million

65. Weibel, Elizabeth. "Judge Rules DOGE, Trump Admin Gutting U.S. Institute of Peace 'Unlawful.'" *Breitbart*, May 19, 2025. https://www.breitbart.com/pol itics/2025/05/19/judge-rules-doge-trump-admin-gutting-u-s-institute-of -peace-unlawful/

66. Johnson, Gene. "Judge orders Trump administration to admit roughly 12,000 deportees." *AP*, May 5, 2025. https://apnews.com/article/trump-refugee-ad missions-suspension-ruling-aa8d219b8ad771eb6c034c45476a7ab3.

67. United States District Court, Western District of Washington at Seattle. "Com-pliance Framework." May 5, 2025. https://www.courthousenews.com/wp-con tent/uploads/2025/05/compliance-framework-refugee-admissions.pdf.

68. Richardson, Katelynn. "'Demographic Diversity': Senate Confirms Fourth Biden Judicial Nominee This Week." *Daily Caller*, March 1, 2023. https://dai lycaller.com/2023/03/01/demographic-diversity-senate-judicial-nominee/.
69. Federal Election Commission. "Individual Contributions." https://www .fec.gov/data/receipts/individual-contributions/?contributor_name =Jamal+Whitehead&contributor_occupation=Attorney.
70. United States Senate Commission on the Judiciary. "Questionnaire for Judicial Nominees." https://www.judiciary.senate.gov/imo/media/doc/White head%20SJQ%20Public%20Final.pdf.
71. Multiple Authors. "Report: FBI Arrests Judge Who Helped Illegal Migrant Dodge Deportation." *Breitbart*, April 25, 2025. https://www.breitbart.com /crime/2025/04/25/report-fbi-arrests-judge-who-helped-illegal-migrant -dodge-deportation/
72. Wines, Michael. "Wisconsin Judge Arrested in Connection with Trump Case." *New York Times*, May 5, 2025.
73. Sentner, Irie. "Columbia Student Journalist Mahmoud Khalil." *Politico*. March 13, 2025. https://www.politico.com/news/magazine/2025/03/13/co lumbia-student-journalist-mahmoud-khalil-00226729.
74. Frum, Joel B. "Left Portrays Mahmoud Khalil as Victim of Trump's Deportation Policy." *Breitbart*, March 17, 2025. https://www.breitbart.com /immigration/2025/03/17/left-portrays-mahmoud-khalil-as-victim-of -trumps-deportation-policy/
75. Frum, Joel B. "Marco Rubio Shuts Down Supporters of Hamas-Boosting Activist." *Breitbart*, March 13, 2025. https://www.breitbart.com/immigration/2025/03/13 /marco-rubio-shuts-down-supporters-of-hamas-boosting-activist/
76. Mallin, Alexander. "ICE Arrests Palestinian Activist with Green Card Attending Columbia University." *ABC News*, April 5, 2025. https://abcnews .go.com/US/ice-arrests-palestinian-activist-green-card-columbia-university /story?id=119616144
77. Federal Election Commission. "Individual Contributions: Jesse Furman." Accessed May 16, 2025. https://www.fec.gov/data/receipts/individual-contribu tions/?contributor_name=Jesse+Furman
78. U.S. Senate Committee on the Judiciary. "Questionnaire for Judicial Nominees: Jesse Furman." Accessed May 16, 2025. https://www.judiciary.senate .gov/imo/media/doc/JesseFurman-QFRs.pdf
79. Forward. "Judge Jesse Furman and Mahmoud Khalil." *Forward*, February 2, 2024. https://forward.com/news/482796/judge-jesse-furman-mah moud-khalil/
80. Forward. "Judge Jesse Furman and Mahmoud Khalil." *Forward*, February 2, 2024. https://forward.com/news/482796/judge-jesse-furman-mah moud-khalil/
81. Stack, Liam. "Brooklyn Judge Faces Scrutiny over Conditions at MDC Jail." *New York Times*, January 4, 2024. https://www.nytimes.com/2024/01/04 /nyregion/brooklyn-judge-mdc-jail.html
82. Frum, Joel B. "Judge Orders Deported Illegal Migrant, Leader of MS-13 Gang, Be Returned to U.S." *Breitbart*, April 4, 2025. https://www.breitbart.com/im migration/2025/04/04/judge-orders-deported-illegal-migrant-leader-of-ms -13-gang-be-returned-to-u-s/

83. Williams, Ben. "Moment Alleged MS-13 Gangbanger Kilmar Abrego Garcia Was Accused of Human Trafficking Revealed in New Bodycam Video." *New York Post*, May 1, 2025. https://nypost.com/2025/05/01/us-news/moment-al leged-ms-13-gangbanger-kilmar-abrego-garcia-was-accused-of-human-traf ficking-revealed-in-new-bodycam-video/

84. Frum, Joel B. "Listen to Abrego Garcia's Wife Describe Physical Assaults to Judge." *Breitbart*, May 2, 2025. https://www.breitbart.com/immigra tion/2025/05/02/listen-to-abrego-garcias-wife-describe-physical-assaults-to -judge/

85. Frum, Joel B. "Report: House Democrats Stayed in Ritzy El Salvador Hotel While Supporting Alleged Gang Member." *Breitbart*, April 29, 2025. https:// www.breitbart.com/immigration/2025/04/29/report-house-democrats -stayed-in-ritzy-el-salvador-hotel-while-supporting-alleged-gang-member/

86. American Immigration Council. "The Cost of Mass Deportation." Accessed May 16, 2025. https://www.americanimmigrationcouncil.org/research/mass -deportation#:~:text=Key%20Findings,billion%2C%20broken%20down%20 as%20

87. Pew Research Center. "What We Know About Unauthorized Immigrants Living in the U.S." *Pew Research*, July 22, 2024. https://www.pewresearch.org /short-reads/2024/07/22/what-we-know-about-unauthorized-immigrants -living-in-the-us/

88. U.S. Congressional Research Service. "Immigration Adjudication in FY2024." Accessed May 16, 2025. https://www.congress.gov/crs-product/IN124c2#:~: text=In%20FY2024%2C%20EOIR%20received%20nearly,as%20a%20de fense%20against%20removal

CHAPTER 10: THE WAY OUT

1. HCP Staff. "Meet the Activist Wife Who Networks Anti-MAGA at the White House." *Highland County Press*, accessed May 16, 2025. https://highlandcounty press.com/meet-activist-wife-who-networks-anti-maga-white-house#gsc.tab=0.

2. Winters, Natalie. "Meet the Activist Wife Behind the Anti-MAGA Nexus." *X* (formerly Twitter), March 24, 2025. https://x.com/nataliegwinters/sta tus/1904310471915610199

3. Multiple Authors. "Exclusive—'Defeat MAGA': Meet the Radical Left Net-work That Hijacked Democrats in Effort to Stop Trump at All Costs." *Breit-bart*, January 26, 2024. https://www.breitbart.com/politics/2024/01/26 /exclusive-defeat-maga-meet-the-radical-left-network-that-hijacked-demo crats-in-effort-to-stop-trump-at-all-costs/.

4. Judicial Watch. *Tom Fitton: "Trump Pardons Jan 6 Protesters—Biden's DOJ Abused Them!"*. YouTube video, 6:42. Posted March 20, 2025. https://www .youtube.com/watch?v=Aqeh5IAoSOU.

5. Trump, Donald J. "Trump Issues Sweeping Pardon of Supporters Charged in the Jan. 6, 2021, Capitol Attack." *Breitbart*, January 21, 2025. https://www .breitbart.com/news/trump-issues-sweeping-pardon-of-supporters-charged -in-the-jan-6-2021-capitol-attack/

6. "President Donald Trump Pardons over 20 Pro-Life Activists Targeted by Biden DOJ." *Breitbart*, January 23, 2025. https://www.breitbart.com/poli

tics/2025/01/23/president-donald-trump-pardons-over-20-pro-life-activists
-targeted-by-biden-doj/

7. "President Donald Trump Pardons over 20 Pro-Life Activists Targeted by Biden DOJ." *Breitbart*, January 23, 2025. https://www.breitbart.com/poli tics/2025/01/23/president-donald-trump-pardons-over-20-pro-life-activists -targeted-by-biden-doj/

8. Johnson, Benny. "Donald Trump Pardons Pro-Life Activists." *X* (formerly Twitter), March 31, 2025. https://x.com/bennyjohnson/status /1882264205988159547?s=46&t=plECD8QafDAXufA7WBT6ag

9. Gray, Zoe. "Donald Trump Orders Firing of Biden Prosecutors at DOJ." *Daily Mail*, March 31, 2025. https://www.dailymail.co.uk/news/article-14411237 /donald-trump-orders-firing-biden-prosecutors-doj.html

10. Trump, Donald J. "Fact Sheet: President Donald J. Trump Directs Suspension of Security Clearances." *The White House*, February 2025. https://www.white house.gov/fact-sheets/2025/02/fact-sheet-president-donald-j-trump-di rects-suspension-of-security-clearances-and-evaluation-of-govern ment-contracts-for-involvement-in-government-weaponization/

11. "Executive Order on Addressing Risks from Paul Weiss." *The White House*, March 2025. https://www.whitehouse.gov/presidential-actions/2025/03/ad dressing-risks-from-paul-weiss/

12. Haberman, Maggie. "Trump Moves Against Paul Weiss Law Firm." *New York Times*, March 21, 2025. https://www.nytimes.com/2025/03/21/us/politics /paul-weiss-trump.html

13. Lee, Noah. "How Harris Campaign's Big Tech Ties Could Undermine Google Antitrust Effort." *New York Post*, August 19, 2024. https://nypost .com/2024/08/19/business/how-harris-campaigns-big-tech-ties-could-un dermine-google-antitrust-breakup-effort/

14. Trump, Donald J. "Security Clearance Suspensions." *Truth Social*, March 2025. https://truthsocial.com/@realDonaldTrump/posts/114197044617921519

15. Haberman, Maggie, and Charlie Savage. "Trump Targets Paul Weiss, the Law Firm That Crossed Him." *New York Times*, March 21, 2025. https://www.ny times.com/2025/03/21/us/politics/paul-weiss-trump.html

16. Balsamo, Michael. "Trump Law Firm Tied to Mueller Probe." *Associated Press*, March 22, 2025. https://apnews.com/article/trump-law-firm-mueller-fc64fc da098b52756294c3d6a3b3d998

17. Kint, Jason. "Trump's Latest Clearance Order." *X* (formerly Twitter), March 22, 2025. https://x.com/jason_kint/status/1919198354384269682?s=46&t=plEC D8QafDAXufA7WBT6ag

18. Trump, Donald J. "Executive Order on Revoking Access to Classified Information." *The White House*, March 2025. https://www.whitehouse.gov /presidential-actions/2025/03/rescinding-security-clearances-and-access -to-classified-information-from-specified-individuals/

19. Shapiro, Ilya. "Break Up the Ninth Circuit." *Cato Institute*, April 2020. https://www .cato.org/sites/cato.org/files/2020-04/shapiro-break-up-the-ninth-circuit.pdf

20. Library of Congress. "Papers of Federal Judges: Appeals 5th, 8th, 11th Circuits." *Library of Congress*, accessed May 16, 2025. https://guides.loc.gov /papers-of-federal-judges/appeals-5th-8th-11th#:~:text=In%20October%20 1981%20the%20Fifth,with%20its%20transfer%20to%20Panama).

21. Grabien News. "Biden: 'We Have Put Together I Think the Most Extensive and Inclusive Voter Fraud Organization in the History of American Politics.' " *Grabien*, accessed May 16, 2025. https://grabien.com/story?id=519566

22. Beitsch, Rebecca. "DOJ cutting American Bar Association access to judicial nominees." *The Hill*, May 29, 2025. https://thehill.com/regulation/court-bat tles/5324916-doj-american-bar-association-judicial-nominees/

23. Miller, Stephen. "We Now Have a Surveillance State Protecting the Administrative State." *X* (formerly Twitter), March 19, 2025. https://x.com/StephenM /status/1902698650519687264

24. Vitali, Ali. "Nonprofit Groups, Democrats Sue Trump Administration over Election Executive Order." *NBC News*, June 4, 2020. https://www.nbcnews .com/politics/elections/nonprofit-groups-democrats-sue-trump-administra tion-election-executive-rcna198991

CONCLUSION

1. Johnson, Benny. "President Donald Trump Pardons 20+ Pro-Life Activists." *X* (formerly Twitter), April 13, 2025. https://x.com/bennyjohnson/sta tus/1882264205988159547?s=46&t=plECD8QafDAXufA7WBT6ag

2. Freeling, David. "We Tracked California's Lawsuits against Donald Trump. Here's Where the State Won and Lost." *The Independent*, January 26, 2025. https://www.independent.com/2025/01/26/we-tracked-californias-lawsuits -against-donald-trump-heres-where-the-state-won-and-lost/

3. Kevin Rector. "In First 100 Days, California Sued Trump Administration About Once a Week. How's It Fared?" *Los Angeles Times*, April 29, 2025. https://www.latimes.com/politics/story/2025-04-29/in-first-100-days-cali fornia-sued-trump-administration-about-once-a-week-hows-it-fared

4 Campanile, Carl. "Inside the Controversial FBI Unit Behind the Trump Raid." *New York Post*, August 18, 2022. https://nypost.com/2022/08/18/inside-the -controversial-fbi-unit-behind-the-trump-raid/

5 "Memos of special interest on Hill." *Washington Times*, November 15, 2003, https://www.washingtontimes.com/news/2003/nov/15/20031115-121140 -2918r/.

6 Mowbray, Jacqueline. "Disgraced Lawyer Kevin Clinesmith Back Practicing Law Despite Conviction for Forging Government Records." *Daily Mail*, December 19, 2021. https://www.dailymail.co.uk/news/article-10322339 /Disgrace-lawyer-Kevin-Clinesmith-practice-law-despite-conviction-forg ing-government-records.html

7 Frum, Joel B. "Meet Joe Biden's D.C. Prosecutor Who Let 56% of Arrestees Off the Hook in 2023." *Breitbart*, October 28, 2023. https://www.breitbart.com /crime/2023/10/28/meet-joe-bidens-d-c-prosecutor-who-let-56-of-arrest ees-off-the-hook-in-2023/

8 Martin, Jonathan. "Trump Delivers Fiery Post-Indictment Speech in Georgia." *NBC News*, August 15, 2023. https://www.nbcnews.com/politics/don ald-trump/trump-deliver-fiery-post-indictment-speech-georgia-rcna88561